*My Mother Before Me*

*My Mother Before Me*

*Beulah Buchanan Wilson with daughters Mary Elizabeth Wilson (center) and Ruth. (See final chapter, "Ruthless.")*

# My Mother Before Me

by Julie Kettle Gundlach

*Barricade Books, Inc.*
*Fort Lee, New Jersey*

Published by Barricade Books Inc., 1530 Palisade Avenue, Fort Lee, NJ 07024
Distributed by Publishers Group West, 4065 Hollis, Emeryville, CA 94608

Copyright © 1986, 1992 by Julie Kettle Gundlach

Printed in the United States of America.

**Library of Congress Cataloging-in-Publication Data**

Gundlach, Julie Kettle.
    My mother before me / Julie Kettle Gundlach.—Rev., expanded, and updated ed.
      p.  cm.
    Previously published: Secaucus, N.J. : L. Stuart, c1986.
    ISBN 0-942637-52-6 (pbk.) : $14.95
    1. Mothers—United States—Biography.  2. Mother and daughters–United States—Case studies.  I. Title.
HQ759.G865  1992
306.874'3'092--dc20                    91-41297
                                        CIP

To my parents,

Herman Gundlach (alive & well)
and
Barbara Jane Kettle Gundlach (1914-1983),

from whom I got my passion for everything

# Acknowledgments

First, I must thank my collaborators, the eighty women and girls I interviewed. They contributed far more than an interview; at times they must have wondered what they'd gotten into. Their families were gracious, helpful, and cooperative.

I am indebted to Gil Mende for his sensitive and skillful editorial assistance.

There are two other important collaborators—Carole Stuart of Lyle Stuart, Inc., and Sue Nirenberg. In these two women's hands the original idea was treated with the utmost respect and care. Thanks to Mario Sartori, also of Lyle Stuart, Inc., for his suggestions and encouragement.

A special thanks to all my friends and relatives for their invaluable assistance and advice, especially Herman Gundlach, Elvira and Dorathea Gundlach, Bob Woods, Anne Barnas Polzin, Mallory Gerard, Tia and Randy Padorr-Black, Toni Bernbaum, Phyllis Murphy, Jeanne Michels, Linda Penoyer, Marie Savela, Kristin Johnson, and Anna Fern Sherwood. I am grateful to those women who shared their energy and enthusiasm but whom I was unable to interview, especially, Gretchen, Martha, and Janna Gundlach; Debbie and Linda Canzoneri, and Barbara Meisner.

A million thanks to my husband, Charles Woods, for the daily front-line services performed so cheerfully: coaching, cheerleading, cooking, chauffeuring, mothering, and brothering.

As one participant in a huge group project, I am grateful for the many tasks and services performed and for the loving and serious treatment I and my idea (greatly expanded by the thoughtful input of anyone to whom it was exposed) were given by all.

# Contents

"And I wait
  overdue
    long long overdue
  for my own birth
    into a ready world."

— from "Secret," a poem by Jain Sherrard
in *Mother, Warrior, Pilgrim: A Personal
Chronicle*, copyright © 1972, American
Association for Guidance Counseling.

# Preface to the 1992 Edition

Thanks to Lyle Stuart and his new Barricade Books, I have the opportunity to provide this trade paperback edition of my 1986 book to the kind of people I have met on the road the past eight and a half years—that is, all kinds. There seems to be universal interest in the mother-daughter relationship, an interest which I have seen grow since my own was piqued upon my mother's death in 1983. In fact, I have been amazed at everyone's interest in the subject. While conducting interviews in subjects' homes, I have occasionally noticed even teenage boys of the jock kind leaning stiffly in archways, eavesdropping, and eventually creeping in to relax at our kitchen and dining room table discussions. Men, including co-hosts and anchors of TV shows, are surprised to find themselves intrigued. What surprised me more is that women and men are intrigued by my question, "What do you know about your mother's personal history?" How fascinating to consider, often for the first time, the reality that good ol' Mom is a person! One adult daughter, an engineer at a radio station, said, "It never crossed my mind." When I heard that and then kept hearing similar versions of it, it dawned on me that I could be embarking on a worthwhile journey—okay, crusade. That widespread fascination, the readiness by radical feminists and macho guys alike (who confidently deny they are sexist) to shyly concede they are perpetrators of what I call *matrabuse*, caused me to ask, what's this all about?[1] What does this say about our campaign against sexism? Women whose lives are devoted to elevating women's status, who decry their father's treatment of their mother 'as an object', discover to their horror that they have been abusing their mother in ways they would never overlook in any man's treatment of her, or of themselves or any other woman.

Why are all kinds of people of all ages so willing to concede and so eager to examine the matrabuse they perpetrate? Why are they all so interested in the overall subject of "mothers and daughters" and in the specific issue of their mother's personhood?[2] The answers to these and millions of other questions have been and continue to be the object of my quest.

After publication and promotion of *My Mother Before Me*, I was asked to give a keynote address at a mother-daughter brunch in Seattle hosted by a medical center. There was so much interest (a total of 1100 in attendance) that the hosts decided to repeat the event two weeks later. A women's center in the midwest heard about that and asked me to develop a "workshop," which I did with the help of my sister, Martha. Twice as many registered as expected. That first workshop confirmed my finding from the interviews I conducted for the book and from the stories I heard in my later travels: daughters are eager to discover their mother as a person, and mothers are eager to be discovered. After a short while, I began to call the event a "playshop," and after an English tea for participants in Dayton, I came to see it as a celebration. This "My Mother Before Me" celebration is a unique mother-daughter event. From the start it reduces and soon eliminates any apprehension mothers experience when faced with the prospect of having their personality analyzed, the quality of their mothering assessed, or the relationship with their daughter scrutinized. It lights the way to an alternative approach—that of discovering and acknowledging our mother as a person, individual, human, a woman like us. During the event, daughters are guided to put their mother before them, to cast aside the more cumbersome facets of the mother-daughter relationship for a few hours in order to have fun getting to know their mother.

At times we may be walking a fine line at the playshop when we take that first step together—learning to appreciate our mother's positive qualities, or things we like about her; it's tempting to idealize or sentimentalize her image. Yet I find that many women and girls can't get in the mood to discover their mother's personhood until they have become more aware of her strengths.

Actually, I see the whole playshop as a first step—an ice-breaker to get mothers and daughters thinking of each other as women. I don't dwell on my own relationship with my mother because the idea (taught to me by the women I interviewed) is to put the relationship aside temporarily and focus on our mother before us, on who she was as a girl and young woman before marriage and motherhood. As in any liberation movement, once she is seen as human, she can easily be seen as a subject and not as an object. I like to think of this as mainstream consciousness-raising, whereby the matrabuse can be seen in all its subtle and blatant forms. I also like to think that the personal life stories our mothers tell us are but testimony toward the larger examination of the personhood of all women.

It is exciting but also plain scary to come to suspect that a good reason for everyone's interest in "mothers and daughters" is the inchoate sense everywhere that the only hope for the world has something to do with the reunification of mother and daughter; as is frustrating clear, that won't happen overnight. Mine has been a joyful but also painful journey, partly for that reason.

My study, as far as it has gone, has shown me that one of the major obstacles to reunification of mother and daughter is that ubiquitous 'theory of separation.' There are still enough psychologists to keep it extant by having their client put it to use in their relationships, especially, the relationship with their mother. I looked into this separation theory because I was feeling disturbed during interviews for *My Mother Before Me* by the accounts of some women who had been counseled to break off from their mother, "get a divorce" from her, move far away, stop calling and writing. I added "need to separate" to my list of reasons for lack of communication between mothers and daughters; but some psychologists use it towards a daughter's struggle to 'individuate'. Unfortunately, some teach that a daughter cannot claim her self unless she tears herself away from the mother.

By now I see that a study of separation theory could take years and years; but so far I have learned, quite by accident, that the first and logical step in a woman's quest for separate selfhood is simply to discover and acknowledge her *mother's* separate self-hood. Moreover, at playshop after playshop I saw that daughters find it easy to do so. They find themselves better understood as a person simply by better understanding their *mother* as a person. In effect, "separation" is not what is required; what is required is connection.

I'm happy to have the opportunity to write this preface so that I can now pass along to the new reader the following advice from old readers. They tell me it was by reading the stories in order, cover to cover, that they were able to 'get it'; some experienced their heightened awareness in a flash of insight they called a "click." They have found that the questionnaire located in the appendix is useful in interviewing their mother and other relatives.

Also, my publisher has permitted me to add an afterword. In "Letters to My Mother in Heaven" I am now able to share some of what I've learned so far. As I wrote in my introduction to the 1986 edition (see this edition page 24), I didn't want the interviewees to have to "sit still for professional analysis." Then, when I was promoting the book, I said on a radio show that I was reluctant to analyze or judge them. The host objected; she said that analyzing is not judging. I've thought a lot about that, and I'm not yet sure it's always true. All I know is that on the heels of having spoken intimately and sometimes confidentially with mothers and daughters, it just didn't feel right to comment at all. For one thing, I'd assured everyone they could speak freely without anticipating some reaction. In fact, as I listened, I tried to clear my mind of reaction so as to truly *hear.* Later, when I transcribed the tapes, I did the same because I wanted so much to hear a clean response not wrapped up in my own notions. When I began to see that my mother had been right in her assumption that most daughters don't know their mother as a person, I then wanted to hear *why.* The second time I listened to the tapes I did, however, take some notes on the "why" for an epilogue planned for the 1986 edition, but it still didn't seem right, either to me or my publisher. I think we were in a mindset for celebrating women's, especially mothers', words.

Now various people who want to know what I think about it all and a few who urge me to 'own' my work and 'find my voice' have succeeded in convincing me to comment here. I'm still not sure it's fair to the people I interviewed, but I trust they will understand that I have already had to give commentary in speeches and in the media. I have been careful not to point to the identity of an interview volunteer, and in my heart I do not judge or blame any woman, mother or daughter, for any statement or action. One daughter said to me, "We're all turkeys on this farm." As the head of this project, I know I'm gobbling on that same farm.

I began this preface by thanking Lyle Stuart. It was his idea to get *My Mother Before Me* into trade paperback. I am grateful that both he and his wife, Carole (who first approached me in 1984 and saw the first edition to publication), 'get it'. Apparently, they also see as I do that "mothers and daughters" has become a hot topic for the '90s and because of the questions it raises will be with us for a while. I'm lucky they turned me and my revisions over to Jon Gilbert, a thorough and gentle man with good ideas.

Of those I thanked in 1986, I note the sustaining comfort and support and inspiration from my father, sisters, friends (especially, Anne Polzin, Jeanne Michels, and Kristin Johnson), and my special pal, Charles G. Woods (who also happens to be my husband). I thank my valuable new friends, especially, Kay Vennie, Don Barney, and Linda Drake. All have shared my joy and helped me brace for the pain which can come on a journey like this as one struggles to be true to oneself, to relax under public scrutiny (which has been mostly benign), to overcome years of stage fright, travel and wardrobe anxieties, fear of failure (and of success, I'm told). As I delved into what revealed itself later as two parts piñata, one part can of worms, I sometimes felt like a kid caught with her hand in the cookie jar rather than a grown woman with the right to speak her mind on an important subject. I'm grateful to all for seeing me as the latter.

My thanks to all the generous people who have taught me so much—the women and men who consented to talk with me, including interview subjects, media people, and workshop participants and hosts, mainly directors of women's health centers. Not many people have any idea how hard these centers work to get information out to women and their families.

Finally, thanks to Dr. Paula J. Caplan, who barely knows me but to whom I dedicate this edition, in honor of her unceasing effort to free mothers and daughters from this "dark web we did not spin."[5]

# Introduction

Having known the Mother,
We may proceed to know her children.
Having known the children,
We should go back and hold on to the Mother.
In so doing, you will incur no risk...

> —Lao Tzu
> from *Tao teh Ching*, translated by
> John C.H. Wu, Boston:
> Shambhala Publications, Inc.

𝑰n 1970 my parents bought a winter place in Florida. My dad still had to run his business up North, but I'd visit my mom when she was alone. In thirteen years of laughing and jawing together in that slumber party atmosphere, certain topics were, nevertheless, overlooked.

One evening January 1983, the second year of her bout with ovarian cancer, my mom began talking about her family's Sunday afternoons in the early 1920s, when her father would take the children around to visit relatives. She said she saw her father's mother "only once" and had no idea of the reason for her exclusion or even banishment.

I'd never thought about my mother's paternal grandmother, even though I have always been almost pathologically fascinated with the past—anyone's past. Suddenly, I was overcome by the realization that I did not know my mother's history.

Gazing out the west window at the setting sun, my mom silently recalled more of her childhood and was unaware of my

gaping mouth as I struggled to formulate my question, which
finally emerged as an exclamation: "You never told me that
before!" Shifting her gaze just ninety degrees, she said, "Oh?"
When I asked her why she hadn't told us stories about her past,
she looked at me and said matter-of-factly, "You never asked."

"Gee," I said, "I wonder how much *other* daughters know
about *their* mothers." I felt a surge of inspired blood in my veins
as my mother, who kept abreast of all publications, said,
"Interesting question. I suspect they know her as a mother but
not as a person. You don't care about who your mother is until
she dies—and, no, I don't think that book's been done yet."

After the sun had disappeared behind the neighboring pink
condo, my mom, weak and exhausted from the effects of
chemotherapy, headed for her bedroom. I called after her, "Next
time it's my turn to visit, you can tell your whole story on tape."
Groping her way along the hall and without turning around, she
said, "That'll be fun."

***

On April 23 I returned to Florida to relieve my sister Janna,
who planned to stay on a few days to see me. I was eager to begin
interviewing my mom, who said she hoped to live for at least
another year. But just a few days later on Mother's Day, exactly
three years ago to the day as I write this introduction, she died
before I ever had the chance to interview her.

In light of my loss, the impetus of the mother-daughter
interview project became more than a mere curiosity about other
daughters' perception and knowledge of their mothers. In my
grief I realized I had perceived my mother in relation to my own
needs, and I suffered a desperate longing for a second chance to
know her. I wanted to share my change of heart and felt that
some women—and men—might benefit from what I and other
women have experienced. I wanted to ask, "Do we pay enough
attention to our parents as individuals?"

I wanted this project to celebrate our mothers' lives as they are
being lived now and to serve as a memorial to the mothers who
have died. Understanding mothers as the fully human, complex,
whole persons they truly are can have considerable benefit in
families. Not surprisingly, many family histories yield little
information about the *women* of the family. Certainly in the past

mothers seldom talked about their own lives to their children; or, if they did, the children didn't listen. I hope my book will help dispel the needless mystery and secrecy which keep mothers and daughters apart and will instead inspire a genuine closeness.

To this end I interviewed eighty women and girls for a total of over two-hundred hours of conversation. Since I wanted to share with the reader more than just the skeletal remains of many interviews, we have included only a small selection. Although we have edited for space, these women speak in their own words. As I felt they had the right to privacy and correct grammar, they were given the opportunity to read over the rough transcript and to censor it in deference to a friend's or relative's feelings.

The mothers enjoyed the rare chance to speak for themselves. In the daughters' sometimes difficult but always valiant struggle to recall their mother's past,* some became reacquainted with her; some met her for the first time; some had always enjoyed a friendly, sisterly relationship with her. Whatever the case, together we gained more insight during our conversations. Usually, the question is, "What is my mother to me, and who am I because of her?" We asked, "Who is she?" As Mother became the subject, the extent to which she has been viewed as an object came to light—painfully, in cases like mine. I hope *My Mother Before Me* will help women to know their mothers *before* they die.

I have delighted in the wisdom of experience of women at all stages of life, from ages eight to eighty. They live in varied circumstances and settings, in cities and in the country, in all regions of the United States. Some are feminists; some say they are not. Whatever their perspective or politics, they all give clues to a better understanding of each other.

My original premise three years ago was that if there is good communication (honest and open) between a mother and daughter; if the mother is somehow able to convey the truth of her experience as a girl, woman, wife, and mother; then her daughter will have benefited and will be a stronger, more integrated person than if there had been poor communication. If

*Since the mothers have not checked their daughter's transcript, there may be biographical inaccuracies; and, of course, the daughter's perceptions may differ from her mother's.

the daughter has known her mother as a person, as a woman outside her role as mother, then she will be more likely to acknowledge and claim her own birthright on this planet—as a woman living the life of a woman, rather than acquiescing to the status quo. Women could learn so much from their mothers before them.

My only regret is that you, the reader, will not hear the voices, the regional accents, the laughter, the antique clock ticking in so many cozy kitchens, the telephone and the doorbell ringing in a busy house. Nor will you taste that special cup of coffee or tea, the family recipe, the homegrown vegetable. You will not see the artifacts and memorabilia, the raised eyebrow, the twinkling eyes, tears, and sighs that color a life and an interview. You will not meet the friends, children, pets and other family members or know the kindness and hospitality toward a stranger who carried a cheap tape recorder and at times did more talking than listening.

Perhaps, however, you can appreciate a glimpse into the three-dimensional lives shared in *My Mother Before Me*. As in reading a work of fiction, you might imagine having a cup of sassafras tea across the kitchen table from a robust and beautiful white-haired Swede, her huge tomcat lying on the window sill behind her. As she caresses an antique dress she is restoring for a museum, you are mesmerized by her melodious voice, the cat's purring, the clock's ticking.

From the beginning I was adamant about not wanting to insert my own bias, for I am participating in my own book as a daughter and not as a professional. Besides, women have been turned inside out and upside down as specimens of studies galore. I wanted these mothers and daughters to have the floor, for once without intrusion and subsequently having to sit still for professional analysis. Therefore, I have decided not to summarize any "findings"; rather, I let the women speak for themselves so that the impact for you, the reader, will approximate that which I experienced firsthand.

Well, the main task at hand is to put our mothers before us. I'm sure that, along with me, the women I interviewed would recommend that you join us. It's great fun—and a moving experience!

# *Waltz*

Mother!
Let me
meet you
again,
all over
again:

Let me
gaze straight
into those
gentle blue waters,
your own most
beautiful eyes—

I never really did.

Let me
play you
that gay music
that inspired
you so—

I never really tried.

Let me
wrap myself
around you (you'll
be the
daughter)—

I never had the nerve.

Let me
know you
this time,
the you you
were,
the you you
are—

Barbara!

J.K.G.

*My Mother Before Me*

*Barbara Jane Kettle Gundlach.*

# *My Mother Before Me*

*O*f sixteen chapters, my title story is the only one not told during an interview. It made sense to include my own mother in the book, but I wasn't able to interview my sisters. For eleven years Martha, 44, and Janna, 35, have lived far away on "The Big Island," Hawaii. Gretchen, 46, who lives in Arizona, was frantically preparing costumes for a stage production going on the evening I arrived to interview her. Besides, none of us seemed to know much about our mother's earlier life. Therefore, I had to reconstruct a story from the only sources remaining—a friend or two, a memoir of the Kettle family, my mother's scrapbook from her junior year in high school, and my father. Over the past several busy months, I have not had a chance to interview him, but he sent me mementos and shared an occasional memory over the phone.

In lieu of the kind of biographical sketch I wrote to introduce all other chapters, I offer below the "bios" my mother herself wrote for her class reunion books, followed by Janna's brief sketch.

## BARBARA JANE KETTLE GUNDLACH,
### 1914-1983

*25TH REUNION BOOK OF THE CLASS OF '35*
Barbara Jane Kettle
Mrs. Herman Gundlach
Houghton, Michigan

*Mom, sisters Martha and Gretchen, and me.*

Field: Anthropology
Occupation: Housewife
Married: April 30, 1938
Children: Gretchen Rivet, 20; Martha, 18; Julie, 13; Janna, 9
Husband's occupation: General contractor

Took a postgraduate course at Katharine Gibbs—did secretarial work for a plywood company. After a meandering tour of the U.S. and Hawaii, married and lived in Atlanta, where the two older girls were born. Spent World War II in Florida; Gunny joined us after service in Germany. Returned to Northern Michigan—Sportsmen's Paradise of fact and fiction. Swimming, sailing, water skiing, landscape painting in the summer when we live on a lake. Winter brings record snowfalls, skating, skiing (hill with a tow handy a mile away) and hunting. Indoors, although an anthropology major, I find my main interests are playing in a piano quartet and teaching French to grade-school kids—no economic gain but considerable intellectual gratification.

*45th REUNION BOOK OF THE CLASS OF '35*
Barbara Kettle Gundlach
One Las Olas Circle
Fort Lauderdale

*What have you enjoyed the most in the last five years?*
   Getting out of Upper Peninsula (Mich.) winters to Fla. and
Hawaii—no boots, no scarves, no snow.

*How are you spending your time now?*
   Feminism—NOW & WEAL activities plus creative idling—
occasional landscape jobs.

*Comments:*
   Watching four daughters and three granddaughters struggle in
a man's world has kept me in a rage for ten years.

* * *

MY MOTHER, BKG *by*

# JANNA BARBARA GUNDLACH

   Barbara Jane Kettle was born in Jamestown, New York,
February 20 of—I think—1913 [it was 1914]. I know very little of
her childhood; my overall impression of her was that she was a
quiet, intelligent, pensive child. She told me she loved to read
and was close to her father.
   She didn't express her feelings to me very much. I recall her
being irritated about people's ignorance and political beliefs,
when they caused problems or suffering for others. Social
injustice made her angry. She expressed worry and concern for
her daughters' futures and for the future of all women in society.
She made me aware of the oppression of women.
   Most important to my mother, I think, was that her daughters
be independent of men and be content with their own accomplishments. She was candid about the realities of being a wife
and mother. She warned me that falling in love is a state of
temporary insanity and that child-raising is a state of permanent
worry, that is not as easy and romantic as we are led to believe.

*Janna and Mom, 1951.*

She showed me that I had a choice whether or not to become a wife and mother, and that I didn't need a husband or a child to be happy. What I liked most was her kindness and wisdom and her concern for her daughters.

If my mother were alive, I'd ask her whether she would do things differently, if given a second lifetime; and I'd ask her what Hawaii was like in 1937. I'm sorry that as a child and teenager I never saw her as a person; that I was unable to help her when she was distressed; that I didn't spend more time with her from the time I left home in '67 until her death in '83.

The most important influence she had on me is that I learned to appreciate and love Nature. If not for her, I probably would never have seen the beauty of plants and animals. I see her in the moon, the Hawaiian sunsets, the bugs on the lettuce.

\* \* \*

# JULIE KETTLE GUNDLACH

As for my own knowledge of my mother, although I could write a book about the myriad insights gained since her death, what I actually know about her life would fill only a page or two.

## Roots

Several years before her death my mom gave us all a copy of *A Memoir of the Kettle Family*, but I didn't read it until a few days ago. In it is the obituary of Mrs. Laura Kettle Gray. My mom had written on the clipping: "I saw this grandma, my father's mother, only once. And her maiden name was *Hoyt*, tho' one would never know!" I discovered some fascinating things about my mother's family; for instance, her great-grandmother grew up in a house next door to what had been Sir Isaac Newton's home. My mother's uncle Joseph, who prepared the Kettle memoir, writes, "As a boy visiting my maternal grandfather in England, I played in the orchard, maybe under the very tree from which Newton's apple fell!"

Joseph goes on proudly to write that back in America during the Revolutionary War, his mother's great-grandmother (my mother's great-great-grandmother) was the only woman to remain behind in town when the British army was approaching. The Battle of Lexington was fought the next day, and with her daughters my great-great-great-grandmother went on to the battlefield and helped with the dead and dying.

## Mom's Memories of Home

My mom did tell me a few things about herself. She spoke of the harsh winters in Jamestown and on Lake Chautauqua, New York, and how it was her duty as firstborn to look after her two younger sisters. More than once she mentioned a particularly traumatic cold day, when—mittenless—she had to accompany her sister home from school. I say "more than once" because I remember having tried several times to discover why the incident had been so traumatic. She'd only say that in the dark and cold, she feared for her sister's safety, which was in her young hands. Her brother "Bud," to whom she was very close, was never a problem. They shared a similar—wry—sense of humor.

As a teenager she was traveling on dusty roads in the country after a date, when her car overturned and she was besieged by a gang of thugs. Somehow, crawling in the moonlight through a field of high grass, she escaped to a farmer's shack. Her father comforted her when she arrived home.

He used to wake her up in the morning by tweaking her big toe. He'd whisper, "Bobbie"—her nickname until prep school, when it became "Kets"—"time to get up." Mom described her father, Arthur, as a kind and gentle Unitarian intellectual who read to her in the attic.

Her mother, Ida Ellsworth Kettle, was quite the character and never cared what people thought. I remember her stockings, rolled at the knee, and her artist's studio above the shed on Lake Chautauqua. Ida had been Arthur's secretary at the bank. One day in the vault he embraced her and proposed. As the story goes, it was a "Pygmalion" affair; twenty years Ida's senior, Arthur sent his fiancée to finishing school.

In Mom's junior year at Radcliffe, her father, thinking he'd lost everything during the Great Depression, died suddenly of heart failure. Earlier he had dragged himself out of bed to feign excellent health over the phone to brokers and creditors. It turned out that his major investment, Gurney Corporation (which became Marlin-Rockwell, a company that produced a shock absorber for the early Fords), pulled through the Depression unscathed. The dividends from what finally became the company TRW helped support my grandmother, their four children, and even some of the grandchildren through their lives.

When I was in high school, my mother cried about her father a couple of times. Many years later, when I asked her why she had cried, she said he would love to have known that she had married my father, and that she was always sad the two never met. She wished her father had known she was "well taken care of"—an incongruity, I thought, compared to her intense desire for independence.

Mom said in her parents' eyes she could do no wrong. She was considered beautiful, smart, and perfect. Her story stopped there, but I always presumed it must have been a shock to find herself at times depressed or unhappy or unfulfilled in later years.

## Scrapbook

Such a bright, witty young woman! I remember the day my mother's 1928-9 scrapbook was unearthed for the first time in her

*Ida and Barbara Jane, 1914.*     *Barbara Jane, nurse, brother Bud, 1918.*

*Brother Bud "taking photo" of Barbara Jane (sitting on floor), her sisters Peggy and Kathryn, her father (Arthur), and her mother (Ida), ca. 1920.*

*Barbara Jane, five years old, 1919.*

*Barbara Jane,* ca. *1922.*

*Barbara Jane, about 12 years old,*
*1926.*

*Billy Bliss and Barbara*
*( "Bobbie"), 1928.*

daughters' lives. Later, my sister told me that Dad wept when he thumbed through it; he said to my mother, "I've ruined you!" It wasn't until after my mother's death that I was moved to peruse that scrapbook, which became my cherished source of information. Like my father, perhaps for the first time I saw my mother as a person.

I always told people that *both* my parents were charismatic. In fact, I would show my friends a photo to prove they were "Clark Gable and Vivien Leigh." Once, however, my father told me my mother was very shy when he met her. She had no confidence, he said. That I could not imagine. Yet it did fit with her statement, "I was taken by your father's gregariousness. He had *It.*" I remember being surprised that she didn't see herself as having It.

Now I remember that she did tell me she was shy as a girl and found it impossible to "small talk," not because she was above it, but because she "didn't know how." It was beneath her dignity to exploit people through flattery or to be manipulated by flattery. She was genuine—honest and sincere. Ironically, that is why some people found her to be intimidating. Yet she loved, accepted, and understood the very people who seemed to be exasperated by her demeanor and ideas.

Certainly, her scrapbook did not reveal a shy young woman. She was a member of the Pretenders' Dramatic Society in high school. She played the "flapper daughter" in *All the Horrors of Home,* and there is a newspaper review of their performance of *Tweedles* by Booth Tarkington:

Miss Barbara Kettle was the charming and beautiful Winsora.

In the margin she has written, "N.B.: It doesn't say anything about my great acting ability."

And there are blurbs from the society page ("Barbara Kettle just arrived, accompanied by her usual band of admirers"), oodles of match covers, party favors, bridge tallies, dance cards, invitations, and letters from suitors.

My dear Barbara:

I don't suppose you know me but that don't make much difference, it don't take long to get aquainted. You don't relize how you attracts men's attention and how much I worship you from head to foot. I have a car and will take you any place you say. You can never tell what *fate* will do.

Your love,

Fred D. 3d

P.S. I am a nice fellow and good and clean.

WESTERN UNION 2/20/29 CHAPEL HILL
BEST WISHES FOR A HAPPY BIRTHDAY STOP AND DON'T FORGET STOP
BILLY BLISS [her Jamestown boyfriend who went away to college]

WESTERN UNION 3/31/29 CHAPEL HILL
LOVE AND BEST WISHES FOR A HAPPY EASTER AND DON'T FORGET STOP
BILLY BLISS.

My father is quick to say that no one ever broke up with Barbara Jane Kettle. But, alas! like most of us, my mother had to deal with the occasional fickle lover. On the next page of her scrapbook is a letter from her boyfriend's college roommate at Chapel Hill:

Dear Bobbie,

Something has happened to Bill lately. Maybe the charms of the Southern girls have something to do with it. At the beginning of the year your snapshots adorned walls. Bill raved of you night and day, mostly at night, when I was trying to sleep. About three weeks ago, after he'd met a certain girl who seemed to attract him, he talked less of Bobbie Kettle and had more dates. The climax came today when he returned from a fast weekend spent in this young lady's company. Your pictures came down, and Bill spent the afternoon and evening wasting a lot of paper composing letters to the former object of his affection. I'm doing all I can to dissuade him from getting hooked. You are too sweet a girl, Bobbie, to have him forget you like this. Love is too beautiful and wonderful to be affected by a mere matter of eight hundred miles.

Best of luck, Bobbie.
George

## Falling In and Out of Love

On the back of a photo of Billy Bliss and "Bobbie," my mom wrote, "I had sworn not to be taken in a sentimental posture—hence my face." (She's sticking out her tongue.) And at the bottom of a note from yet another suitor saying, "Dearest, I love you, I love you, I love you, I love you, I love you—Yours, Robert Doolittle," my mom replied, "Darling: Oh, yeah?—B." Next to that is a clipping she saved, called "That Absurd Performance Called Falling in Love." I do recall my mother having told me how "crushed" she was when her first love broke up with her when he went away to college and met somebody new.

It seems that Miss Barbara Jane Kettle struggled against succumbing to romantic delusion. Yet by all reports she fell madly in love with "Gunny," my father.

I remember hearing a story about my parents' first meeting. She said she was always attracted to the intellectual types and adored Leslie Howard in *The Petrified Forest.* But at Radcliffe she was fixed up with my dad, a Harvard football captain, with whom she was "not particularly impressed"; she didn't like "jocks." Nonetheless on their first date—a blind date junior year—she had to sit on his lap, which she said was "squishy and cozy," in the rumble seat of a car. From that moment, she said, she was "a goner." My dad has always said she'd have been happier with an Ashley Montagu.

## Anna Fern

So far, the other information I've learned about my mother is from her girlhood friend, Anna Fern Sherwood from Jamestown. In response to my recent inquiry, Anna Fern sent me the following letter, which moved me to make the twelve-hour round trip to see her:

I'll be happy to tell you some things, not all I know, as that would be a book in itself. When your mother was born, I thought she was the greatest thing that ever lived, and I immediately adopted her in my mind. I used to haunt the Kettle house for a chance to wheel the baby carriage.

Barbara's birthday was the day before her father's, and they were so much alike. He was a rather reserved, dignified gentleman to meet. But when you got to know him you realized how highly educated he was, and what a marvelous sense of humor he had. He also was a keen observer of all that went on around him and was an exceptional business man. Both he and Barbara loved to read, and they used to have some great discussions together.

I was married in August 1929 just before the stock market crashed. Everyone had money and spent it. I had 22 parties and showers given for me. At a Country Club dance the night before my wedding, Barbara was the "Belle of the Ball." My cousin, quite a playboy about town, told me he thought Barbara was one of the most beautiful girls he had ever seen—and he considered himself quite knowledgeable about beautiful women.

From then on Barbara always had loads of boyfriends. She liked some, others not so well, but I don't think she was ever really in love until she met your father.

## My Dad's Input

In recent days my father has become a newly tapped source of information. For instance, he asked me whether I knew that my mom, who had her Red Cross swimming certificate, saved a man's life at Panama City Beach when my dad was stationed at Tyndall Field during World War II. It's interesting that she had told me the story of a drowning man, but never that she was the one who saved him!

Over the phone my dad has filled in some blanks for me. For instance, those creditors my grandfather talked to on the phone were conservative Republicans. Arthur Kettle, as a lone liberal Democrat in Chautauqua County, championed the working man's cause. As long as he was strong and vital, he could always ward off his enemies. Like vultures, they were always presaging his downfall. We have a photo of him from 1920 riding in a convertible with FDR, who was running for Vice President. My dad also said that FDR, as President, had approached my grandfather as a possible appointee to the Supreme Court. And according to a clipping in the family memoir, Arthur had also turned down an invitation to run for Mayor of Jamestown. It's incredible to me that my mother and I didn't talk more about her illustrious father.

My dad has also sent me some intimacies—letters and poems my mother wrote—saved for many years in his bedroom dresser:

February 16, 1929

Dear Mother,

Well, consider yourself lucky. I have finally found a second to write to you. I have been rather busy lately with music lessons, Spanish lessons, pledge meetings, editoring, and a French play squeezed in somewhere. Thanks loads for the darling jewelry. I wore it to a banquet that night with my black velvet. You really have no idea how positively stunning, my dear! Also thanks for the maple sugar candy. Bud and I hogged it all. I bought two new records, much to Dad's disgust. Also a good-looking necklace, which took what money I had on hand. Maybe I can worm some back allowances out of him. No progress in Victrola, radio, or new house.

A newspaper article on the death of her father says that at one time before the Depression he was a multi-millionaire. He was not an ostentatious person, sometimes to the exasperation of his family, as he was afraid the children might be kidnapped if his wealth were apparent.

The letter to her mother concludes:

A minister stayed to supper with us tonight. Here's hoping he doesn't stay and talk all night. I've got a heavy date with Bob Doolittle. Don't forget to let Billy know you're in vicinity. He'll show you a hot time. One wow of one sure keen time.

Farewell, etc.
Barbara

My dad just called tonight to tell me that at the fiftieth reunion of the Class of '35, Barbara's old friend Ros from prep school and Radcliffe, said, "Barbara was the smartest girl in our class," to which another classmate replied, "I don't remember seeing her name on the Magna Cum Laude list." Ros said, "But she could have been." The classmate replied, "Oh? Then why wasn't she?" "She fell in love!" Ros impatiently exclaimed. My dad said that when he and my mom were at Harvard together, they would pay the milkman 25 cents to ride the milk wagon around Cambridge before my dad would deliver my mom to her dormitory—"at the crack of dawn."

Among the mementos my dad just sent me were two letters my mom wrote before leaving on the ship for Hawaii. We children had always heard the story of how Mom got only as far as Honolulu on her trip around the world, when she decided to return to my dad in the States; so it was great fun reading these letters.

Nov. 2, 1937
Mission Beach, California

Dearest Gunny,

Your question (am I dating?) practically brings tears to our eyes because no matter how one scorns the race of men, they are awfully handy for getting places, and how are we to find such handy articles—! We are cold-blooded sight-seers and have encountered no debaucheries since we left the Ellsworth clan (Mother's relatives), which was strictly *en famille*. I feel like an old family woman, or something, now. I wouldn't know what to do with a "date." Kid stuff, frothy, unimportant—guess I'm too serious about you.

All my love,
Barbara

October 30, 1937

Darling—

I am getting very tired of not having you with me, Gunny. Even when I've got my mind off the thought that it won't be "soon" that we'll be together, I keep wishing and wishing that you could answer all my thoughts—haven't got over the habit of making remarks to you when you're not around. So there is really not even fun for the moment except out of sheer stubbornness! It is my turn to read a mystery story, so to close, with much love,

Barbara

## Her Gifts to Me

Otherwise, I know my mother only by her influence—far too extensive to go into here. She taught me a love for so many

*Ida and Barbara Jane, 1937.*

*Barbara Jane at Radcliffe,* ca. *1931.*

*Mom in Honolulu, 1936.*

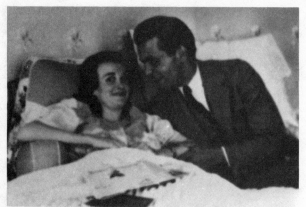

*Mom and Dad after birth of first child, 1939.*

*Mom and me, 1947.*

*Mom, her daughter Martha, and granddaughter Michelle, 1972.*

things—to mention a few: Gershwin, Sinatra, and "Lucy Ricardo"; foreign languages, the study of "Man," which later expanded into a passion for feminism; music, which she played on piano, especially classical and jazz; comedy and drama (she loved Sid Caesar, Ernie Kovacs, George Sands, Alec Guiness, Cary Grant, Bette Davis, Diana Riggs); dance—ballet, modern, ballroom (she used to madly fox trot around the living room, teasing my dad about being a lousy dancer); modern art and architecture; the tantalizing mix of skepticism and romance, science and mysticism; the beauties and forces of Nature and the greater Cosmos.

Last, but not least, as I describe in the introduction, she inspired this book. She herself was always going to write. With my help, she had turned the third bedroom into an office, and she kept enormous clipping files—Watergate, the Supreme Court, the Equal Rights Amendment, the Nixon Administration (later supplanted by the Reagan Administration), "First for Women" (the first female high school football player, the first woman in space, the first woman to visit the Yale Club). After our mother died, my sister and I had to dismantle her bedroom and office. It was a poignant moment when we removed and read, one by one, each yellowed clipping tacked to her large corkboard, which was reserved for items marked "Immediate Attention."

I also came across a bluebook English exam dated 1933, her sophomore year at Radcliffe. Actually, there are two books full of beautiful, flowing fountain pensmanship on "Lyric Poetry of the 17th century." Later as a "housewife" and for no particular reason other than her own enlightenment, she wrote a paper on "The Suite Form" and also on "Spanish and Portuguese Music." I remember her telling me that she would go into a "trance" when she wrote exams and papers and that later on she couldn't believe she'd known all that material. The same thing has always happened to me.

One of the things my mom and I did together at our "slumber parties" was to come up with topics for articles or ideas for books. When I was nine, I wrote a novella, which she typed and submitted to a publisher. She'd always encouraged me to write; in fact, just today I ran across a letter she wrote me when I was ten and away at Girl Scout camp. Any grown child will understand why I kept that letter for thirty years:

> "We just love your letters—you are a very neat and clever child!"

## Ahead of Her Time

Barbara Kettle Gundlach, born on the cusp of the Victorian and the "flapper" era, was a modern woman. It was not easy for an unconventional person to live as a wife and mother in the fifties and early sixties, and even later, in a small town. Although she always said that the people were friendly and that she had a lot of fun, nevertheless, it seemed that hardly anyone there understood her, a fact which to this day makes me sad and sometimes resentful. Gentle, unassuming, unaffected, she was not the forceful or aggressive kind of person who might leap to her own defense. I think people mistakenly believed that she was cool and invulnerable. Like her father the virtually lone liberal in a bastion of conservvatism, she was the butt of a lot of ribbing.

In later years, she found allies in the National Organization for Women, the local chapter of which she helped to found; and the women in her consciousness-raising group, of course, came to know her well. From conversations with them, Sam Oliver, the minister conducting her memorial service, was able to glean the kind of life she faced without succumbing to artifice. To quote part of his eulogy of her:

> She was an able, even brilliant woman, one whose competence covered a broad range of interests: music, art, literature, religion, social ethics, philosophy—so much more; and it was not just an interest but a knowledge of these things, an understanding of them, that gave her the ability to speak with some authority.
>
> Unlike many who are given the gift of great intellectual capacity, Barbara didn't advertise it. Indeed, there were times when she preferred not to show it at all. She had the unique ability to affirm and lift up those around her, to inspire them, to move them, to liberate them, to give them a vision. Some have said that in many things she was ahead of her time, that the things she was thinking about and the causes that commanded her

attention were sometimes issues that most of us were not ready to address—at least, not yet.

I think it is important to say that many people did not know Barbara well. There was a private, personal, contemplative part of her life which she shared only with her family and good friends. It was not an easy kind of thing to maintain, but she was able to do so, sometimes at the risk of being misunderstood. It was this private part of life where her husband and her children and her close friends were able to know her as the woman she was, and it is there that the deepest, most significant memories are lodged— memories of the love, the laughter, the sharing, those moments of deep meaning.

When my mother died, our family friend Joan Monberg sent us all a copy of a letter Joan received upon her mother's death. It was from my mother:

> Our hearts know we must outlive our parents,
> but our minds are forever tied, somehow.
> There are so many regrets and anger and love
> unexpressed; but, finally, only dear memories.

*Mom (front left) with some of her NOW group.*

*Elsie Wentela, 1984.*

# *"Sisu"*

**E**LSIE, 64, was the youngest of five daughters born to a hardworking Finnish immigrant couple. Within a year after her mother died, Elsie's father married a widow with five sons. Now a widow herself, Elsie had ten children, two of whom died as babies. A retired postal worker, she has applied to the Peace Corps because she would like to work with children in Central or South America. Elsie's daughter Kris, 35, is a very active feminist in her local NOW chapter, which she helped found. She sympathizes greatly with the struggles of mothers, and I think she considers it her duty to do the work of *dozens* of people because, although she is married, she has no children. Following Kris's and Elsie's stories are excerpts from Elsie's daughter Mary Lou's paper based on her own interview of Elsie. These "Maid Stories" were presented at the local Suomi (means "Finland") College, where Mary Lou was a student. She has just received her nurse's cap.

## KRISTINE WENTELA VAN ABEL

One day I looked at my mother and was startled to realize she was getting old. I happened to be sitting in the living room when she walked past carrying a load of laundry. There was nothing particularly ominous about the day. Sunshine was pouring in through the windows, but Mother looked tired. Suddenly I was afraid.

For the first time, I realized my mother was another very mortal human being. At that point, I grew up a little and, in so doing, grew away from my mother. I began to understand in an obscure way what a burden it had been for her to give birth to ten children, survive the death of two of them, and raise the remaining eight.

My mother was a pretty girl and is an attractive woman. She was born to an immigrant Finnish couple almost sixty-three years ago, the youngest of five daughters. Mother idolized her parents and always missed her own mother, who died of tuberculosis when my mother was only five. She has only recently mentioned that traumatic experience. When her mother was taken to a sanitarium for TB, she was brought to her aunt's. Children weren't told about death back then. As the car taking her mother to the sanitarium drove down the driveway, she saw her mother for the last time. Watching the car go by, she wondered why she was being left behind.

Within a year, her father remarried a widow with five sons, and she became the "baby" of twelve children. The rest of mother's childhood sounds like the first part of the Cinderella story—conflict and jealousy among the large group of stepsisters and stepbrothers, antagonized by parental favoritism. Frequent moves, provoked, perhaps, by charges of Communism against her father, as well as the Great Depression, complicated her adolescence.

Mother, who speaks proudly of her intellectual ability, spent a year with relatives in a western state. She did well in school and was promoted ahead of her classmates. She's always had a fierce pride in her Finnish heritage, too. In 1981 Mother, who still speaks fluently in "old style" Finnish, made a trip to Finland to see the homeland and renew family ties.

I don't know where she finished high school, but she spent a year at college in either Ann Arbor or Ypsilanti. During or after that she worked as a telephone operator.

I don't know how my parents met, but they lived in the same area and were married in May 1941. My oldest brother was born in November 1942. As World War II escalated, my parents traveled from one army base to another down South, having to deal with food and gasoline rationing.

## A Difficult Life

Once the war was over, they returned to Father's home in Nisula, where they had nine children and managed to scratch out a living. Mother's life was again a difficult one. Her mother-in-law, with whom she did not get along, lived next door.

For almost forty years, Mother has lived in the same place. She has gone through the births and deaths of children and grandchildren; buried her father, stepmother, husband, mother-in-law, two sisters, as well as other friends and relatives. She has suffered the agonies and shared the delights of her eight surviving children's lives, watched the world change, and tried to adapt as best as she can.

## ELSIE TAMMELA WENTELA

My oldest daughter has been urging me to write things down: some kind of record, so it won't be lost.

My parents and grandparents could have told us so much. My grandmother came to America as a child. My mother was born here, but my father was an immigrant. How different their lives were from ours! My father had a very hard life. A quiet person, he hardly spoke to us about anything. My grandmother said she would tell me the story of her life, but I had small children and was expecting, so I just didn't find the time before she died that year.

And my father didn't know how to talk to daughters. He once remarked that he would have been a more successful parent to sons. I remember him as gentle, soft-spoken, and kind.

After my mother died, my father remarried; and I think he tried not to favor his real children over his stepchildren. As a result, we left each other alone. He didn't know how much we loved him because he didn't give us a chance. He treated my stepmother and her children very well, but there were personal problems among the stepchildren, and then my sister became ill. I don't like to speak ill of my father because he had more heartache than one man should have. Yet I did have mixed feelings towards him.

My mother died when I was only five years old. She had tuberculosis—and too many children in too short a time: five girls in five years. I was number five. I must have been a big pain to my mother. They probably wished they hadn't had me because they had had enough. But I'm still glad they let me come: no matter how bad life has been at times, I've always been glad I was born.

We were "Depression-bred." Those were hard times, but since we lived out in the country there was always enough to eat. It was just the bleakness of life. Looking back, I see it as terribly grim, though at the time I didn't. No electricity, no modern anything. But the Finnish people (I lived in a mostly Finnish town) were self-sufficient and hardworking. I didn't realize that anyone was suffering, but now I see that they were. Nobody talked about it; I guess that's because everybody was in the same boat and didn't know anything different.

My father always had a car, but we walked, and in the winter we carried a lantern. There were homemade skating rinks all over. We could attend programs put on in connection with the public schools, and we had a community club that put on plays at the Town Hall. We thought that was great.

In the 1930's the WPA came into being, and they brought in people who gave piano lessons to the residents for ten cents a lesson. My father didn't even think of telling us to go take lessons, even though he himself was a talented musician. I've held that against him all my life. Did he expect us to go up to him and say, "Why don't you let us have piano lessons?" We knew there was no money—no use asking. Yet I think he might have thought about whether any of his kids had talent, since everyone in the family in the old country had been musicians.

I went to Finland and met them all. I made the point that my father had left the old country with the idea that his family would have a better chance in life than they would in Europe, but it seemed to me that by far they have progressed more over there. Perhaps it would have been different if he hadn't lost his first wife and then remarried—if he had not had so much heartache. Relatives and others who knew my mother and remember how my parents worked together that they were a loving and happy couple. I was glad to hear that.

My father remarried very quickly. He was concerned, I think, about raising four young girls. My sister died of brain fever when she was only six years old, just a year before my mother died. That was an awful blow to my father, too, because he loved her as much as my mother did. So we had two deaths in the family in one year. As we four girls grew a little older and became increasingly disgusted with conditions, we used to say, "Shoot, he didn't have to get married to take care of us. We could have managed ourselves."

## The Immigrant Work Ethic

Children of immigrants had that work ethic thrown at them day and night. We didn't have to do *extra* work on Sundays, just the usual: dishes, beds, and so forth. And *maybe* on Saturday afternoon, we'd stop. But Monday through Saturday there were always jobs. Our stepmother was also an immigrant who always had to work very hard. She didn't have education, but she was talented in practical ways. If you sat down during the day, you should do something with your hands—sew or crochet. She couldn't stand to see anyone just sitting and reading, except in the evening. She brought that attitude over from the old country. We resented her and tried to sneak away to the woods or the river, claiming we couldn't hear her calling.

In the summer, there were garden chores: weeding, gardening, berry-picking. And the bugs! There weren't as many chores in the winter, that's true; but then we froze without central heating. Now I'm used to the cold. When I get up in the mornings, my kitchen is fifty to fifty-five degrees, but I never have colds and am never sick.

I really have suffered. We have a Finnish word "kituaamista," meaning really dragged-out suffering. So I experienced "kituaamista" as a child, and I always say that's why I am so healthy. I really should not be healthy, when you think that I was exposed to TB in the house. I did find out years later in Detroit that my lungs were badly scarred.

## Strength of Character

My sister had TB, and they didn't expect her to live. She fooled them through her own stubbornness and willpower. She just lay there and said, "I will not die, I will not." There is a case of "kituuamista" and also of "sisu," which is "guts." This long, drawn out suffering has to do with relentless abuse in order to increase strength of character. I don't think it has a religious basis.

Among immigrant groups, the religious are very religious. My father was a member of a temperance union, so I never saw even a bottle of beer until I left home. I wouldn't have believed when my children were small that someday I would enjoy a drink with them. My husband didn't drink at all. He didn't criticize anyone who did, but he wouldn't have let me drink—or smoke. Although there are some Finnish matriarchs, usually the head of the household is the man. They let their wives work, though. That's one thing they don't oppose. Fortunately, my father and husband weren't like that.

My father was already educated before he came to this country. His brothers and sisters were born and educated in St. Petersburg, right in the shadow of the palace, during the time of the czar. I've always dreamed of going there, just across the water from Helsinki. I'd like to see the buildings where my father and his family went to school. They were well educated, and I think that was why he was so nice to women. He had a way with people—different from the ordinary.

## A Gentleman—and Nearly an Officer

My husband was truly a gentleman, though he had only nine years of school. His father was killed by a train when my husband was only eleven, so he had to work hard all his life. He was a handsome man—very strong, very smart. He was sent to OCS (Officer Candidate School) along with the Yale and Harvard graduates. He didn't complete it because the math, he said, was just too hard, but it was good to be singled out like that. He asked to be sent back to his old unit, and when he was overseas, he was made a lieutenant and received a Bronze Star. If he had a good education, there's no telling what he might have achieved. I think back on how smart the children were who went to school with me. They went out into the world and, even without much education, made a lot of themselves. There's no limit to what they could have done if they had been formally educated— Finnish girls, in particular.

My father never asked his daughters if we wanted to go to college. He wouldn't help us; we had to do it on our own. I went one year to Wayne University in Detroit. I didn't flunk out. I finished the freshman year but had no desire to go back. It was so different because I also had to work at a job. I felt inferior. It seemed all the other students were so bright. They were talented in music and sports, and I had nothing. I felt that I couldn't even get up and recite in class the way they did because I had come from a small town. I tell my children if I hadn't had that inferiority complex or been so shy, I could have licked the pants off all my classmates. There were times I knew the answers, but I wouldn't speak up.

I had spent eight grades in a one-room schoolhouse, except for the year at E.L. Wright School in Hancock, Michigan. From there I went to Horace Mann School in Oklahoma and stayed there with my stepsister. She had a baby and was lonesome, so she and her husband wanted someone from home for company for her.

## Honors List

They put me through school that year, a lab school on the college campus. It was good, but I was so shy. I was only twelve years old when I entered ninth grade, and there I was taking Latin and mathematics. I was one of three freshman on the state honors list. I wasn't afraid to speak up in Latin, English, or mathematics because I loved those classes. History and civics, however, had huge classes with some seniors in them, and I sat way in the back.

The year at Wayne University did me an awful lot of good. I lived with a bunch of girls in a house sponsored by the Board of Education for worthy students of low income. We had so much fun, and they all accepted me as I was. They treated me well, and because I could speak another language, they thought that was fun. That was where I overcame a lot of my backwardness. Then the boys began to notice me, and, of course, you do get over some of your shyness after you marry.

I laugh and joke with my kids now, although I didn't when they were young. I feel bad because I think that's what I should have done. I took things too seriously. I thought that work came first and that *everything* had to get done, so I was short with them. Of course, I had had ten children within a short time. If I had a weakness of the lungs like my mother, I probably would have died.

Lots of people I know thrive on hard work and say they would not have it any other way. They could not *be* if they weren't working. They don't know how to enjoy leisure time even to watch a sport. I think that's terrible. I always wanted my kids to have leisure time. I often felt sorry for them while they were growing up because we weren't well off. But I was always so proud of them. My husband was a hard worker, and he believed strongly in the work ethic, too. "The more you work, the better."

## Feelings of Inadequacy

He never in all our married life hired outside workers. He knew how to do everything himself: electrical work, plumbing, masonry, mechanical work on the tractors, everything. I felt lucky and in awe of him. I thought if he had known how little I knew, he wouldn't have married me. If I had been as versatile as many of my neighbors, I could have saved him a lot of work. All I did was take care of the kids and keep house. He didn't complain, though, because he probably figured I had all I could handle.

I also used to think, "A man with all his brains—why doesn't he try something different? He could be more than a laborer." As an officer in the Army, he could have stayed in the reserves. I didn't want him to re-enlist when the war ended. I wanted him home. At the mine, they made him a foreman after he'd only been there a while, because he was so capable. He had a long way to travel and two shifts, so we tried to keep the house quiet with four little ones underfoot. And two of my children died while he was working at that mine.

## The Deaths of Children

Shirley was sixteen months and Lisa was fourteen months. They died, one after the other. Shirley had a bout with polio, which took her in just three days. That was the first death I really suffered over since my dad had died of multiple sclerosis. (We had more than our share of serious disease in my family: cancer, multiple sclerosis, polio, tuberculosis, rheumatic fever, brain fever.) Lisa and five other children in our area died of an intestinal infection. I had grieved when my father died, but when Shirley died that had to be the worst. My husband took time off from work only from her death until the funeral. It was bleak, the weather was cold. I went down to 103 pounds; I couldn't eat; I wanted to die. I think if I hadn't had other children, I probably would have killed myself, but I couldn't go around crying in front of them. My oldest one said, "Mama, you never smile." So we weathered that one, and when Lisa died, I was expecting. As bad as it was, we at least had the hope of another life coming. It was a girl, too. She was really welcome and took away so much of that grief. That first year we all *hovered* over her. She was so good because she got all the attention.

My husband and I didn't discuss how much we missed those children or how sad we were. I know he felt bad because he was a really good father for the little ones, very close to the babies, all of them. It had to have hurt him, but a man takes it differently because he has to go to work and can't be crying and carrying on. It got to the point that we could again mention their names: "That was Shirley..." or "That was when Lisa..."

I found out that people don't want you to talk about your sorrows. I was really run down physically and had to go to the doctor for some shots. My doctor said, "When you feel bad, come on in and talk to me. Don't go to the neighbors; they don't want to hear it." Also I found out that a person who has not had sorrow doesn't know what to say to someone who is suffering. They just want to forget it: "It was meant to be," or "She's better off." I think anyone who has suffered to the same degree knows what to do, what to say. As my Shirley was dying, poor little thing, we didn't even know it. They were trying to reach us, but we didn't have a telephone. As far as we knew, she was getting better. The doctor had wanted the hospital to run some tests. I'm glad I didn't know one of them was to have been a lumbar puncture, as I would have been frightened. They didn't have time to do one, anyway, before she died. I think about how frightened she must have been, and I wasn't there. In those days, they didn't want parents in the hospital. If it happened today, they couldn't pull me away from my child. I would have held her until she died. Both of them, for that matter.

The second one was tied down with tubes in her. The doctor said she either had spinal meningitis or polio. I asked, "Will there be brain damage?" He said, "Well, there's still hope." All I could think was if she would just live, I wouldn't care what I had to do for her the rest of my life; that's the *only* way I felt. Someone had come up to me and said, "Better she dies." I feel about my own self that I would rather not survive as a vegetable, but when it comes to my children, I would care for them all of my life.

## Good Children

As for having children, if you asked me at the time it was happening, I probably would have said, "Oh, Lord! deliver me from this." But once they were born, we were so happy with them. I had ten healthy babies, and none of them was a crybaby. I nursed the first ones but not the later ones because I just didn't have the time. The only time I was up with them at night was when they were sick, and that wasn't often. Even the two that died had never really been sick before in their lives.

My late sister once remarked that it was unusual for a woman to have ten *healthy* babies, especially the last one, since I was forty-one when he was born. John, my tenth, was really more Kristine's baby because she helped me so much with him. Kristine is my fourth, and I used to say, "Well, I owe her many years of babysitting pay."

I heard an Evangelical preacher a couple of years ago who made me feel a lot better when he said, "Nowadays, when people do wrong as adults, they are excused with the remark that they were like that because their parents made them that way, and if their parents had not done this or done that, those kids would have done such-and-such."

Well, that's partly true. There were cases where I could have told you the kids were going to end up in a lot of trouble because the parents treated them so ill. But the preacher went on to say, "My parents weren't perfect, either. They made all kinds of mistakes, but I don't blame them. I'm a parent and do many things that are wrong; but I don't want my kids to blame me for everything." I was glad he said that because I had begun to think, as I got older and remembered things from the past, "Oh, I shouldn't have done that. I shouldn't have been mad, shouldn't have slapped them or been unreasonable." I can't undo all that, which makes me feel bad. Of everything in my life, the very worst thought is having been cross with my kids when they were little, because I can still see their little baby faces. They'd look surprised or puzzled about something I said in anger.

My third child, a touch precocious, was almost five years old when Kristine was born, so he had a chance to be the baby longer than the others. But when Kristine was born, he had to quit being the baby. That was the year that I started being more cross, demanding more and more, and not paying attention to him. I know he felt badly; so once, I did tell him, "There were times when I didn't even know where you were. How could I have been so thoughtless?" He was a little kid and would go to visit his friends, and I didn't know where he was. If some mother did that nowadays, I'd say, "You ought to be in jail for being so careless!" But in those days there wasn't that much danger. He assured that everything had been all right: "I was having a good time." But, I can just picture him now: he had ill fitting shoes; his feet were sore; there were bears along the road. He was so good-natured, and I was so cross.

There are times when I think that the luckiest people in the world are those who never had children and never had any regrets because of what they themselves lacked: presence of mind, knowing what to do, knowing how to handle it all. If I had it all to do over again, I would be perfect.

I had a very hard time saying I was sorry, even to my children. When I lashed out at them, I never apologized. Now that I have grown up I can say it. We all grow up too late.

I didn't ever say I was sorry to my husband, and he never did until later years, just before he died.

He had an innate refinement. Although our house was far from elegant, *he* had elegance. He spent money he shouldn't have, buying me flowers or an expensive piece of jewelry (which I hardly ever had a chance to wear, anyway).

That last year, not long before he died, he said, "If I had it to do all over again, I'd probably do it the same way. I'd just try to make you happier." I wonder if he had a premonition and felt he'd better say it before he died.

## A *Look at the Past*

Looking at my whole past, I realize I did so many things wrong. I wonder if everyone feels that way. My regrets are mostly about relationships with the people I love the most—and hurt the most. Other regrets: what I could have done with my life or could have learned to do; but those don't bother me so much. Personal relationships bother me most because they are so important—how we treat loved ones, or even neighbors. There are people who are still alive that I might have hurt but with

*Elsie as a teenager.*

*Elsie holding Kris at one year. Mary Lou is at left.*

*At Mary Lou's capping ceremony, 1985. (Front) Mary Lou and Elsie. (Back) Mary Lou's husband Wayne, and daughters Lisa and Jennifer.*

*Kris with her husband.*

whom I can still go about making amends, but I feel badly that I can't do that for those who are already gone.

I did hold another thing against my father. My sister Edith was very, very smart but couldn't go beyond sixth grade. I don't know if it was nervousness or what, but she used to have terrible headaches. My father didn't know that Edith needed something special. She went through a hell of a life, and he could have done something for her.

## Shipwreck

Earlier, I mentioned that my grandmother had a world of interesting things to tell me. I *have* heard a few things from my aunt. She is only seven years older than I because my mother was the oldest child in her family. My aunt tells the story of my grandparents settling in the Misery Bay area and then moving to Agate Beach. There was a shipwreck on Lake Superior, and everyone got off the ship and stayed there at my grandparents' cabin. When they left, they told my grandfather he could go and take whatever he wanted from that wreck. I don't know if they got anything off it or not; but in part of that ship that was left above water, there was a perfect area—a nice, smooth floor. The young people started rowing out there on moonlit nights to dance on the smooth floor of that ship—that is, until people who thought it was a sin went and burned it. There would have been so many stories like that if someone had just listened to my grandmother.

I don't think I told Kristine many things. At the time she left home, I was still busy with five young ones. When Kristine finished high school and started college, I was still very occupied because I worked for fifteen years as a postmaster, starting when my youngest began school; so my days were quite full. It was only last year that I started telling my own children about the past and about my life.

## Morality

I've enjoyed these youngest children's growing-up years very much because I'm more flexible. They tell me things that happened that I think are a riot, whereas if they had told me the same things years ago, I would have been shocked. My youngest daughter was a motorcycle person, but she's a good girl—good *woman*: she's twenty-five. I wouldn't have allowed my older boys to do the things my youngest boy does. It's a matter of changing times. You can't fight it; you have to join in. My basic values are still the same, though. I'm just not so rigid. Their mistakes are nothing compared to what mine have been.

I grew up in a terribly moral climate. There was no swearing, no dirty books, no drinking. As I said earlier, I never saw a bottle of beer until I left home. My stepbrother-in-law drank some in front of me and I was so shocked. I thought, "My father wouldn't have let me come here had he known I was going to see beer in the house." It was very intolerant, and I was like that with my oldest children. I thought it was the only way to be.

I really don't know how Kristine got to be a feminist. It's a puzzle to me. I don't disapprove; I think it's really good. When I read books about the ways in which women were put down; and when I see how they are in Europe; and when I think of the women who settled here—they never grew up. They died. Men had young wives because of this. (I had a great aunt who had nineteen children, but she was healthy. I probably got my good health from her.) So I'm very proud of Kristine and delighted that she feels the way she does.

I do wish for a job for me somewhere involving children—an orphanage, a school, a hospital. Last year when I knew I was going to retire, I applied for a job with the Peace Corps, but they don't want me because I don't have a degree. I have a foster child in Guatemala. At least he gets a decent lunch out of the money I send. You can send only money, and I would rather send things.

## A *Precious Memory*

My mother must have loved me because she saved my life. We were all at a picnic—just mothers and children and some young singles who gathered at the river bank. I remember a shady, sandy area where we ate lunch that day.

It isn't just that I was told. I actually remember that episode at the river. All of a sudden, an enraged bull came out of the woods, and there was no place to go. Everybody, including my sisters, scattered in a panic. Each mother grabbed the closest kid, and my mother and I were trapped. She was trapped between the water and the bull, and because everybody else had fled, the bull singled her out. You must realize her lungs were already bad, because that was just a year or so before she died. She grabbed me, kicked off her shoes, jumped into the river, and swam across, putting one arm around me and swimming with the other arm. Luckily, she was a good swimmer, having grown up on the shores of Lake Superior. My head would go under water, and my childish mind would tell me, "I'm going to drown, I'm going to drown." She hung on to me, and said—there was a log sticking out from somewhere under the water—"Elsie, if you can't climb on to that log, we'll drown." So I helped myself because she was exhausted. We lay on that log until my father and my older sister came to look for us. They came the long way around to get us from the other side of the river and had to walk across a terribly high and dangerous railroad bridge. My father carried me home on his shoulders, and my mother walked beside him. That is the most precious memory of my mother, especially her holding on to me in the water. I told my kids that story just this year.

I don't know if my children are going to have any memories of me. I've never done anything heroic. Having more than one child is the bravest thing I've done. You know what you're facing after you've had one child and keep on having them.

My first two children were born during World War II when my husband was in the service. He didn't go overseas right away because he was in training camp. He *did* go overseas while I was pregnant with my second child, and I didn't even know where he was when she was born. That was during the bad fighting, too.

When my first child was born, I agreed with the woman in my room who had also had her first: no more babies. She said, "I'm going to put up an electric fence around my bed." She went on to have six and I ten. It isn't that I don't believe in birth control; I was just too dumb. If it had been easier, I would have used something. I certainly didn't need that many children, but now I'm happy they were born, and I think they are, too.

A mother never quits worrying. And now I have to worry

about my grandchildren. Just the other day I told my friend, "You're one of the luckiest people in the world because you never had children." What brought it up was that my oldest daughter is going through divorce. When she was over the other night, her eyes were so sad that I could hardly stand it. So I said to my friend, "I feel all the pain they feel. You never had any? Be glad.

## MARY LOU WENTELA NIEMI

Elsie attended eight different schools as her father changed jobs and moved several times. She was bright, skipping two grades and graduating with honors. Graduation meant adulthood and independence, and Elsie knew she was expected to look for a job and most likely to leave home as well. Her father was then working at the old-age assistance office in Houghton. Through contacts in that area, he learned of a position available as a maid in a home on the elegant College Avenue. Two of her sisters were already maids in Detroit, so this wasn't disturbing to Elsie, although she admits to having been very nervous, not knowing anything, not having worked for "outsiders" before.

The house was owned by Mrs. G., a wealthy eighty-year-old widow with five grown children. She had inherited money from her brother, the "Copper King" of Calumet, a mining center in the Upper Peninsula. She lived alone and employed a cook, a chauffeur, and a laundress. Elsie became the "second maid," the older servant Josephine then being considered the "first maid." The chauffeur and the laundress didn't live in the home, so Elsie and the "first maid" shared the huge, third-floor bedroom.

The employees were all Finnish, and although they *could* speak English, they spoke Finnish with each other. This allowed them to "...get their kicks by making jokes about the family behind their backs."

Elsie's employer was a socially prominent member of the upper class Irish-Catholic community, and besides entertaining guests many times a week, her children and their families were there all summer long and had to be treated the same way. "They were something like aristocracy," as Elsie described the situation. Elsie's duties were cleaning the house and serving meals and afternoon tea. Coming from a strait-laced, unsophisticated immigrant family, she was unprepared for some of their social habits. "I remember serving the Monsignor who came to see Mrs. G. when she wasn't able to go to church for Communion. He was a very dignified priest, very happy to come to see Mrs. G., who gave a lot of money to the Church. My first encounter with him was when Mrs. G. rang the bell for me. 'Bring the Monsignor some beer,' she said. I had never in my life even *seen* a bottle of beer, so I almost fainted when she said that. When I brought the beer up on a tray, the Monsignor said, 'Bless you, child.' I got used to that and all the other things I saw that went on in the family the rest of that summer."

## A Six-Day Week

Elsie worked six days per week, with Sunday and Thursday afternoon off, for sixteen dollars per month. She didn't consider the work back-breaking, but it was "fussy," and there were long hours with no breaks in the afternoon at all. Dinner was never before seven o'clock. Having been hired to clean and serve meals, she found that she was also expected to babysit quite often for the four- and five-year-old visiting granddaughters in the evening, which, Elsie said, "wasn't part of the original deal...no extra pay, no tips.

"And then the two little girls' parents—he was Mrs. G.'s son and an attorney living in Chicago—wanted me to go back to Chicago in the fall to live with them. In return for babysitting, they would pay my way through business college. I was thinking of going, but I changed my mind after spending more time with those children because they were too hard to handle."

To a young girl who had lost her mother early in life and then had been a stepsister in such a large family, the cook Josephine's companionship, training and solicitude were comforting. "She was so efficient and competent, and she taught me everything that I had to do; and when there was a lot to do, she'd help me."

## Plenty of Milk

Also, Mrs. G.'s interest seemed "grandmotherly." And one *nice* thing about working for Mrs. G. was that she didn't skimp on food. "We could eat as much of everything as we wanted and could buy on her bill anything we wanted if she didn't have stuff we liked. In my case she had told the cook to be sure to order plenty of milk because she figured, since I was a young girl, I would like milk. She never griped about food; she always told us to eat. That was unusual in houses where there were maids because in most places the maids practically starved. I found that out when I went to Detroit to work. At my first job there, I thought to myself, 'Now's a good time to lose weight,' because I had gained weight at Mrs. G.'s. Mrs. G. was generous with our food, but she could have been *more* generous with our salary."

Elsie considered the fifty cents per day wages plus room and board rather meager for the nine months she worked at Mrs. G.'s. "But, all in all, I don't regret that time because I was able to see how different people lived."

In those years, as soon as a young adult could get a job, he or she would have to send money home to support the rest of the family. Elsie's father was able to support his family well enough so his daughters didn't have to do that. "The first thing I bought with my pay, when I had my first big sixteen dollars, was a pretty dress for my stepmother. It cost about four dollars. It looked so nice on her—just her size. I know that my dad must have been pleased to think I would buy Mother a dress with my first earnings.

## A *Slave's Habit*

The Finnish domestic workers in Houghton and Hancock had commonly been neighbors or relatives or school friends in their hometowns, and in order to socialize, they would meet in town on their free time. "Things were so cheap then that we could go to a movie for just ten cents. We never ate a meal out, only an ice cream sundae. We walked everywhere we wanted to go and didn't buy clothes, so we were able to afford our recreation.

"Not having to purchase work clothes was a big savings. It was customary for the employers to provide the dresses, aprons and little white caps for our heads. We used to call our uniforms 'orjan puku,' which means 'slave's habit,' and many girls did not like to wear those. When there was formal entertaining, we really had to be spiffed up in our organdy aprons with ruffles."

Within that wealthy social circle there seemed to be some spirit of competition—perhaps on the part of the domestics as well as the employers—as far as showing off the home goes. Mrs. G.'s eightieth birthday party lasted from breakfast until late at night. "Everyone said it was a big success. Guests and relatives always did say that at Mrs. G.'s place you always had the best food because she had such a good cook, and the house always looked nice because her help worked so well. It really was in perfect shape all the time. We were conscientious because we were *Finnish*."

The frustrations of long days, no overtime pay or tips, menial work, and inconsiderate employers and guests would have been more difficult if the women hadn't had the luxury of speaking Finnish in the kitchen. "We could say anything we wanted. Josephine was really even-tempered and easy to get along with. She never showed anger, even if she was completely disgusted with them; she'd just put on her poker face and say, 'Yes, Mrs. G. Yes, Mrs. G.'"

Good domestics were sought by acquaintances, neighbors, and relatives. "When Mrs. G.'s son was trying to lure me to come work for him, he asked what I was being paid, and with a very straight face, he said, 'Well, we'll give you more.' It was so funny how people would like to have hired Josephine away, and since she received only sixty dollars per month, I think anyone would have paid her more—because she was such an excellent cook. Then Mrs. G. died and Josephine no longer had a job with them, and Mrs. G. had not left her a single thing, not a penny. If she had known that she would be left nothing for all her faithful service! Maids and cooks in all other homes had a day off during the week and Sunday afternoon, but not Josephine; she never complained. She got nothing for all that.

I had the feeling that we must never be idle, and one day I decided to scrub the maids' stairway, right from the basement up to the third floor. By the time I got to the second floor landing, all of a sudden the door opened, and Mrs. G. was standing there. Gruffly she said, 'You don't have to kill yourself.' When I told Josephine, she said, 'Well, she never told *me* all the years I've worked here that *I* didn't have to kill myself."

In March 1939, Elsie went to Detroit to be her sister Edith's replacement as a maid and "mother's helper" for a family with four young children. She worked there for about four months, when Edith returned. They were "nice" people, but that is where she almost starved.

## Maid's Day Off

"On 'Maid's Day Off' we'd always met under Kern's clock or at Hudson's, and then we would go to eat in a *restaurant*. I was always happy to do that because I was hungry. We'd go window shopping or visit somebody or go to a movie or a dance, mostly at the YMCA downtown. It's a wonder nothing ever happened to me because I would go home alone. I'd get off the bus and usually run home because I was afraid someone would be hiding in the shrubbery along the way. It's terrible, the chances we took. In 1934 a girl from Calumet who worked as a maid in Detroit was murdered on her way home; but I didn't know that at the time because I was in Oklahoma that year. I found out just last year when I was reading 'Fifty Years Ago Today' in the local paper."

Elsie's second maid job in Detroit was short-lived. "Oh, that was terrible. My employers were so arrogant, and although they had just one baby that I wasn't expected to take care of, I had all the rest of the house to take care of. It wouldn't have been so hard if I had realized that I could cut corners and not do everything so thoroughly. I had to wash all the baby's clothes and diapers by hand. One day I was in the basement washing the diapers (I had to wash them every day), and she called me upstairs *just* to fluff the sofa pillows. I decided then and there she wasn't the type of employer I wanted."

From July to September 1939 Elsie worked for a Finnish lady with one pre-school child. Then she enrolled full-time at Wayne State University. She had received a National Youth Administration tuition grant and borrowed twenty dollars per month from an uncle to live on during the school year. She returned to the Upper Peninsula in May 1940, living both at home and with a married stepbrother, for a short time helping with their two toddlers. She returned to Detroit but couldn't afford to go to college and didn't really want to. She did work for the next six months, rooming at a boarding house for two dollars per week. A sister in Ann Arbor got her a telephone operator's job, which was a welcome change and a nice increase in wages—six dollars to thirteen dollars per week. She married Uno Wentela in May 1941 and didn't do any outside "domestic work" until 1984, when she had the opportunity to be at Mrs. G.'s old house again on College Avenue.

## Back Again

Jennie M., Elsie's great-great aunt by marriage, purchased the house in 1949. She recently asked Elsie to be a part-time companion for her. Elsie agreed, so after forty-five years she is again working at the house where she once worked as a maid.

## The Smell of the Rich

In describing her reaction to returning to the house, she said, "Yes, when I worked there, there was that certain smell in the kitchen—just ours—because that was *our* place to be, that's where we always were if we weren't working in other parts of the house. Every time I'd go through that swinging door into the dining room and then into the living room, that *rich* smell would hit my nostrils. It was the smell of elegance, something that wasn't in my living room; it was a good smell, like the mixture of everything rich.

"I guess I associated that smell with wealth, and when I worked in those rooms, I always felt as though I was part of an elegance. Yet when I returned in 1984, I didn't notice that smell at all when I *visited* Mrs. M., but the very first time I went to stay, as I left the kitchen and got halfway through the dining room, that smell hit me in the face again.

"I could only think that it isn't the smell of the people; it has to be in the walls and in the rich Oriental rugs (the one in the dining room is the very same rug of 1938 and doesn't show any wear), in anything which is so very expensive that the smell remains. I've never noticed that smell—almost like flowers, not like a funeral home but close to it—anywhere else.

"But it was funny when I was back to visit Jennie in the house where I had been a servant. Now I sat in that elegant living room as a guest and was waited on."

*Kate Buddeke Kanaley and Adele Kanaley Christensen.*

# *Peacework*

dele Kanaley Miller Christensen,* 72, herself a peace-worker, is the mother of the current Director of the Peace Corps, Loret Miller Ruppe, 49. The third child in a large family, Loret lost her father (Fred Miller of the Miller Brewery) and her brother Freddie in a private plane crash in 1954. Loret lives in Bethesda, Maryland, with her husband Phil, a former brewer and congressman from Michigan. They have five daughters, one of whom is in the Peace Corps in Nepal. I also interviewed Adele's younger sister "Speeder" (Loret's aunt, Kate Speed Kanaley), who is single and lives, at least part of the year, at the very tip of Michigan's Upper Peninsula. Speeder's thoughts on their mother (Loret's grandmother, Kate Hamilton Buddeke Kanaley, deceased) are interwoven with Adele's later on in the chapter. This tale of five generations of stoical women illustrates the transmission from mother to mother to mother of a major family value, which in this family—reminiscent of the Kennedys—has been the personal development of strength and integrity for the sake of service to others.

## ADELE KANALEY MILLER
## CHRISTENSEN

My mother was raised in an era when balancing social life with taking care of children was considered important. We were raised by nurses, and we always had a cook, a laundress, and a yard man. On the nurse's day off Mother cut our nails, shampooed our

*Mrs. Christensen, having since married her third husband, is now Mrs. O'Shaughnessy.

hair, and arranged various activities for us. We had a Danish
nurse who was very athletic-minded. I can still see that volleyball net. None of us liked volleyball, and whenever the nurse
wanted to start playing, we'd all disappear. We lived on a block
where there were many playmates: three girls in the house next
door, two girls beyond that, and another girl across the street.

Mother wore her hair in a pompadour, and I can still see her,
in an evening dress and coat, coming down the stairs to go out
with my father. She was always gentle and quiet. She had a
fantastic memory, was well-read, and knew the "Rubaiyat" by
heart. She believed in discipline and afternoon naps. The
neighborhood children didn't have to take naps, and we'd lean
out the window talking to them until we were found out, and
then we were supposed to go back to bed and rest.

## Summertime

Mother liked to ride horseback, and I truly do not remember
the horseback riding, except in Kodak pictures, and there are
pictures of me in my old three-cornered hat and puttees.

In those days everyone went someplace in the summertime.
The men stayed at their club, and the wives took all the children
and the nursemaids to a resort.

We didn't swim much in Chicago. Lake Michigan was always
very cold and, even in those days, quite dirty, so we went to the
South Shore Country Club to swim every once in a while—
which brings to mind one of Mother's favorite stories: She was
brought to Chicago in her teens, and they stayed on the south
side at the Chicago Beach Hotel. One time when we were
moving, she came across her old diaries, and we started reading
them. She wrote, "I fooled all of them. They thought I was
swimming, but I had one hand on the bottom all the time." I can
just see her in the water with her hand on the bottom. We had
only read the first page when she snatched the diary from us.
She was so annoyed that we were laughing at her entries that she
burned it. We were just sick. Now that's gone forever.

I think my mother would have liked above all else for her
children to graciously get along with everyone. She was cour-
teous and saw good points in everyone and, as far as I know, had
no enemies.

I wouldn't even want to imagine life with a different mother. I accept what I have, what I am, and what has been given.

At the present stage of my life there is not much that I'd want to change. However, in the past there were probably many things I *might* have changed: I *could* have been nicer, I *could* have been kinder, I *could* have been more considerate. But that's over and done with. I can try to be more considerate now, but in retrospect I probably would not have done any differently. I can't say I ever looked with any kind of judgment at my mother or ever assessed her influence. She loved her children and grand-children, and she had a close relationship with the ones who remained in the Chicago area. We all remember her with the greatest love and devotion, and my friends adored her. Every time she came up to Wisconsin from Chicago, my friends gave luncheons and bridge in her honor. Soon they would be back to say, "When's your mother coming back?" Most of their mothers had died, whereas my mother lived to be ninety-two.

## Charity

Mother's favorite charity was anything for the blind. She was so thankful for her wonderful eyesight that there wasn't an appeal that came through the mail which she didn't honor. One result of that was that my sister Audrey, who lives in Winnetka, has done a great deal with the Hadley School for the Blind in her area.

My mother's influence was undoubtedly a factor in my peacemaking activities. She insisted on three years of Catholic schooling, so I went to the Sacred Heart Convent in Lake Forest, which is now known as Barat College. When I was a junior, a woman named Dorothy Day spoke at Barat. She was to be a prevailing influence all through my life.

I was born at Mercy Hospital on the South Side of Chicago. Probably my earliest memory was of making life miserable for the nurses who took care of us. I was born, then my sister Audrey came two years later, my brother Byron nine years later, and my other sister Kate eleven years later; and that was the whole family so there weren't *that* many of us. We had to kneel down next to the bed and get "what Paddy gave the drum," as our Irish nurse used to say.

I don't remember too much about elementary school, just Miss Betsy in first grade, whom everybody adored. The teacher I remember well was Miss Jowdry who really made me think. She was ahead of her time; she was out of the textbook and into clippings from *The New York Times* and she brought us up to date on the international questions of that day—'28-'29. Through Miss Jowdry I realized there was more to a historical perspective than one learned from a textbook. I more or less relied on newspapers, since we didn't have television.

The greatest thing I got out of elementary school is poetry, which I can still recite quite accurately, as well as aphorisms and mottoes. When my children were young, I read to them a lot. That may also be an offshoot of my mother because she read to *us* a lot. I hadn't thought of that but I'm sure that's what happened to me: my mother read to us, then I read to my children, and they have read to theirs. All of them are interested in books.

When I was a little girl, we used to make paperdoll clothes, houses, and furniture. There was a series of books called *Jimmy Dale and the Phantom Clue.* We'd go through magazines and cut out people for the characters in the books. In those days there was the handsome Arrow Collar Man. That would be Jimmy Dale. We had a big sandbox and made castles with moats and sand cakes that we'd sell in our "bakery." We also used to enjoy climbing on a neighbor's garage roof. She'd have her chauffeur hose us off, and our parents never knew why we were coming home so wet! We always played jump rope and "Tap the Ice Box" (one our favorite games), "Run, Sheepy, Run," jacks—a whole plethora of games. I was pogo-stick champion of the block and held that record forever. Nobody else wanted to be such an idiot, going up and down three thousand times.

## Ah, the Boys

I always had quite a few boyfriends. Quite a few special ones. In fact, I still meet people who say to me, "The Kanaley sisters? Oh, we still remember them!"

After the two years of school out East, I got married. Let's see, how did it all happen? After I met Fred, he called me and said, "I'd like to come down to Winnetka and visit you." I was crazy about somebody else, but my mother said, "You have to go out with Fred." I said, "Mother, I can't!" She said, "You're going out with him." I called the current love of my life and said, "I can't go out this weekend." Fred and I went to the country club my mother and father belonged to. In those days there was the cut-in, the big stag line, and if you danced fifteen steps with one boy you felt you were *stuck* for the rest of the night. Well, I didn't know anybody there. That was a horrible experience—to dance forever with one person. The next time, Fred and I went to a place that *I* knew; it was an Evanston Women's Club dance. Then I went away to boarding school in Philadelphia, and I guess he wrote me and said he'd come down and take me out Christmas time. I said "I *think* I can fit you in." Those were the days.

Fred was quite a bit older than I, and so were all his friends, so he took me to all these nightclubs. I was shocked. Girls came up runways and danced on the tables—and in those days I didn't drink. I went back to school, and he wrote from Milwaukee to ask me to meet him in New York. My school believed in chaperones, but I managed to ditch mine. My mother and father had friends there, and they said I could stay at their apartment overnight.

## Heartbreaker

The former great love of my life? I saw him until Fred and I were engaged. I think he sent some nasty, anonymous letters, and there were a couple of other fellows, too, who, I guess, thought I was going to marry them.

I'll never forget Fred's proposal. It was in the moonlight, at Leo Reisman's Casino in New York, overlooking Central Park, and he said, "Will you marry me?" and before I had a chance to say yes, he said, "I'll take you to Honolulu on our honeymoon." Now, how do you turn down an offer like that? We got married in 1931 and stayed married for twenty-four years until he was killed in 1954.

Fred and I entertained a lot at home. That's kind of a German characteristic. We belonged to many country clubs, but we did a lot of family entertaining, as well. My husband came from a fairly large family, and, actually, we were closer to his family than to mine.

I never consciously imposed my thinking on my girls, and now they are past the point of learning, except by my own example. Unfortunately, my children were in the same position as I. I had servants to take care of them, so then I was probably not with them as much as I might have been. Still, they seem to have survived nicely, and I think we all have a good relationship. I try to keep the conversation in pleasant channels. If I do have critical thoughts, I keep them to myself. I feel they're all at an age to make their own decisions. In the case of the grand-children, their way of life is so foreign to the way that I was brought up that in my deepest feelings I do not approve of many of the things they do or the way they live. It's not my place to spurn or berate them. They'll work things out for themselves.

\*   \*   \*

*When Adele visited her sister Kate ("Speeder") Kanaley at Eagle Harbor, Michigan, they reminisced together about their mother Kate. The following story is told in both voices.*

Our mother, Kate Buddeke Kanaley, was a wonderful woman, who never played favorites. She was never one to carry tales and only had praise for anyone she had visited. To her, cheerfulness was truly a philosophy of life. She believed in seeing people; otherwise, one might become stagnant. However, she also taught us that one must learn to be alone successfully. As for loneliness, a friend once complained to her that no one ever called. Mother said, "Well, the cure for that is: Pick up the phone and call someone."

Mother would allow only one minute per child for a "health report." She didn't believe in resting. "You will rest a long time after you're dead," she'd say. We also learned there could be no tattling. She who tattles will be punished.

Mother was an early riser. Every morning, even in her nineties, she would make toast and watch the news on television. Then she would take a cab around the block to the Drake Hotel [in Chicago], tip the driver handsomely, and order wine with lunch. She told us about walking in the Windy City to do some banking one day. The wind was so ferocious that she found herself holding onto a bush for dear life. A policeman rescued her and helped her into a patrol car. Mother said, "I'm glad I hadn't been drinking that day. I would have been detected in the squad car."

Mother, because of her remarkable memory, always had the appropriate remark. Once turning down an opportunity for an after-dinner drink, she quoted the end of the "Rubaiyat":

> And when Thyself with shining Foot shall pass
> Among the Guests Star-scatter'd on the Grass
>     And in Thy joyous Errand reach the Spot
> Where I made one—turn down an empty Glass!

## Travels with Papa

In her travels with Papa, she went off on her own from time to time. Once in either White Sulfur or Hot Springs, Virginia, the two of them passed by a group of three to whom Mother was drawn. They were looking for a fourth for a game of bridge. Papa didn't play, but he told Mother to go ahead. She was accustomed to play for a quarter of a cent, and these people advised her they would play for a "quarter." At the end of the game, having won, she was handed a whopping eighty-five dollars and only then discovered they had played, not for a quarter of a cent, but for a quarter of a dollar. She said, "It's a good thing I didn't lose. Papa would have had my head!"

From 1960 to 1981 she lived as a widow and traveled all over. History and art were her fortes. Once at a museum she told a group the entire history of a royal family depicted in a painting. When she was eighty-one, she accompanied Adele on a bus tour in Austria and held the attention of a considerably large coterie, going on and on with facts as she unwittingly offended the tour director, who simply could not compete with Mother's vast knowledge.

## Willpower and Stamina

The key to our mother's health, happiness and cheerfulness was *willpower* and incredible stamina. Our sister Audrey phoned her one day and found Mother to be slurring her words—her speech virtually unintelligible. She was in the midst of writing letters, and, as it turned out, she had had a stroke. Yet when Byron [Adele and Speeder's brother] arrived to check on her and, subsequently, to take her to the doctor, Mother insisted on completing her letter writing. Then, outside in the arcade and still slurring her speech, she disappeared momentarily. Byron discovered her undaunted, determined to mail her letters in the mailbox.

On another occasion Mother's doctor felt she was unfit for the trip she planned to Winnetka. She had barely been able to sign her name properly. For his approval, she absolutely *willed* herself to prove her capabilities by signing her name just as beautifully as ever.

Mother never complained. For instance, when Speeder was eight and had polio, Mother had to take her and Byron, who also had polio, for therapy sessions four times a week. That was a big responsibility. Mother would never let them lose a shred of personal confidence. She expected them to partake in all of the activities of a normal child. "Go ride your bike," she would say. And she never discouraged them from skating on the asphalt "Snake Hill" with the other children.

Mother was a fine, cultured lady. Her mother had been a lovely, genteel Southern belle who then taught her daughter the fine art of being a lady. Mother was proud of her formal garden in Winnetka. She indulged in yelling at the Italian gardener. They both talked boisterously and used their hands profusely during their communications.

Mother had two years of college at Barat at Lake Forest. Her graduating class of nine girls wore laurel wreaths and white dresses. When the Bishop of Chicago bestowed the diplomas, no family members were permitted to participate in the cere-monies. Of her school days Mother remembered a day in chemistry class when she added one too many ingredients to a potion and blew up the nun's habit.

Mother's father was a doctor. Perhaps, that was the key to her good health and stalwart attitude. Through force of will, Mother decided after a hip operation that she would walk without a cane and not limp. Likewise, it was once found that she had been suffering from a gallstone. The doctors warned us that it would be normal for her to "hallucinate" after the operation. Yet when members of the family visited her, they discovered her to be carrying on with her characteristic cheerfulness: "Isn't that the best looking hat Carrie was wearing?" she said brightly. She was entirely lucid—and entirely not living up to the doctor's expectations.

## The Iroquois Theater Fire

We were all told a story from Mother's childhood which illustrates her character from an early age. Mother, a survivor of the Iroquois Theater fire in Chicago, was attending the theater with several girlfriends as part of a birthday party. Mother remembers seeing an overhead spotlight fall to the floor, just as a performer came out over the audience in her swing pushed from onstage. A fire was started from the spotlight's sparks, and Mother saw the fire begin to spread. The theater had just been painted, and side exits could not be opened because they had been painted shut. From the balcony level, people shoved each other out the exit doors and fell to their death because the fire escapes had not yet been installed. Mother remembers climbing backwards in the rows over the seats, somehow escaping the theater. She remembers becoming angry at a fellow who was throwing her against a fence outside. "Why is he manhandling me?" she cried inside. It turned out that the back of her coat had been on fire, and the man was trying to help extinguish it. Mother then ran to a drugstore and asked to use the phone to call her mother. The druggist told her she couldn't do that. She said, "But I must let my mother know what has happened and to come pick me up." The druggist said, "No, I mean you can't call her because the side of your face is all burned off."

Mother's mother met her in a buggy and took her home to her father, the doctor. Mother would tell us how awful it was for her father having to plaster tape all over her face and then to rip off the tape so the top layer of Mother's skin would not grow back before the lower layer. Grandfather had discovered the scars would not form as long as the top layer of skin was not permitted to grow before the lower layer. In this way, Mother never developed scars. It was very painful for Grandfather to be forced in that respect to cause his daughter so much agony.

## *The Day of Her Death*

Every day Mother attended mass at 12:10 at DePaul University Chapel, ate lunch and played bridge. On a Friday the Thirteenth, she got up, made toast, returned to bed, and at age ninety-two died. The night before, she had been able to have her favorite lasagne. Her desk had been cleared and everything taken care of.

Here is the last letter written the Saturday before her death that Speeder received from Mother.

March 7, 1981

Dear Speeder,

Loved your letter and glad you are having a Holiday getting out to Eagle Harbor. Have been busy here, Saturday lunch at the Pump Room with Geri and Kathy. Sunday brunch at the Drake with Helena. Byron called me when I got home that Edna Graham died at 4 AM that morning. She had been in the hospital in Houston, Texas, for a month, had had cancer for ten years, so it was not unexpected. Byron picked me up on Wednesday, and Geri, Byron and I went to the Wake in Wilmette. Thursday the funeral at Sts. Faith, Hope and Charity. We went to the Mass and Cemetery All Saints, Christine and Kathy with us. Then we were invited to a buffet luncheon at their home in Kenilworth by Bill Graham. All the family were there, and I had a visit with all. Sis [Agnes] and her husband from Pittsburgh. After lunch Geri and Byron brought me home. Friday was the First Friday, and Helena with me to Mass and afterward to Women's Athletic Club for lunch, so today I am resting. Tomorrow the twins pick me up and we go to Mass and to lunch. Wednesday a permanent wave and will take it easy the rest of the week unless something turns up.

With love,

Mother

# LORET MILLER RUPPE

I presume Mother was born in 1912 in Chicago though I don't know for sure. My mother was the oldest in her family, followed by her sister Audrey, brother Bryon, and sister Kate everyone calls "Speeder."

My mother loved and respected and appreciated her mother, Kate, who lived to be in her nineties.

As a young girl, Mom, an active child who liked to get into mischief, attended a military school and marched around in uniform. One time she banged a girl over the head with a cast she had on her arm. Then she hid in the attic and wouldn't come when she was called. Mom, who seemed to be popular, enjoyed telling stories about her boyfriends and their snappy cars.

I've always thought of Mom as very bright; she was Valedictorian of her class. When it came time to work on her speech, she was "out of it" because there had been so many parties. She laughed and said that some "bright young man" wrote her speech for her. But I don't believe that.

## A Whirlwind Affair

When Mom and Dad met after Dad's graduation from college, he fell very much in love with her, and they embarked on a whirlwind affair. So that Dad could ask Mom to marry him, he had to borrow money for a ring from his uncle and get a jeweller to open up his shop. Even though the families had known one another for quite some time, Mom talks about being in awe of Dad, who was a little older. They married in 1931, and I was the third child.

I took my relationship with my mother for granted. Our family was split up geographically much of the time. Mom used to go down to Florida in the winter taking the younger children along. Clara, Freddie and I would stay in Milwaukee with Dad. We always went to camp in the summer, and the rest of the year we were in school. When we were with Mom, I didn't pay much attention to my relationship with her, and she didn't have much time because the other kids were small. In a large family, you'd go with the flow. We grew up sensing that Mom was closest to our older brother Fred, who died in the plane crash with Dad. Mom and Fred had a very special relationship, probably because there were so many girls in the family.

I recall a time when Freddie, Clara and I were engaged in some big fight for about an hour, and Mom would call up every once in a while: "Stop arguing!" Finally, she absolutely lost her temper and charged in with a hairbrush. Poor Freddie was the closest one in sight, and she started beating on him with the brush. All of a sudden, she gasped, looked down at her finger, and walked out of the room. Well, it turned out she had broken her finger. For some reason, we thought it was awfully humorous.

Since we grew up with cooks and maids and nannies most of the time, I didn't learn much about marriage and motherhood. As a small child, I was given a little cookbook and encouraged to bake, but there wasn't much advice on the challenges of being a wife and mother. I didn't expect advice on the subject. Except for when my brother Carl was born when I was twelve, I was too young to remember Mom with any babies. We children were close in age, and nursemaids were there to take care of the babies. I don't remember being particularly close to Mom, but I always admired her for her hard work and accomplishments.

It was only as I got older that I realized the pressures Mom and Dad had been under.

Perhaps I wasn't very observant as a child, but I don't remember my parents ever fighting. Growing up in a Catholic atmosphere, you never consider the possibility. It was just Mom getting upset from the pressures she had with all those kids!

Mother was once quoted in an article as having said something like, "All children are little animals until they're twelve years old." Thinking we had all been insulted, we said, "Oh, how can she say that?" Actually, from the way we generally behaved, we didn't think it was very far from the truth. We were just embarrassed.

Whenever we were sick, Mom came through. After a bath, we came back to our room and the bed would be changed. We were sick a great deal because all the contagious childhood diseases were still so prevalent in those days—chicken pox, measles, mumps, German measles.

We were a religious family and we kids were raised strongly in the Faith by both Mom and Dad. Mom had to do all the real work because Dad was gone a lot. I don't know how she ever got us all straight for church; in those days we all had to wear hats and gloves. Oh! to get everybody synchronized and out to the car on time. Dad insisted on that.

## *Reaching Out*

What I remember most about Mom is that she was always involved in various groups as well as the church. She was interested in sharing and having good relationships with the neighbors, and she'd go visit whoever was sick.

Mom has influenced the lives of a great number of people. She has reached out to others, no matter what social group they were in, especially the sick, shut-ins, people whose quality of life she could try to improve. Now that she's so active in peace work and in trying to direct our country's leaders towards more peaceful means—peace through development, outreach to Russia, people-to-people programs with Russia—she's contributing quite a bit. I like her unflappable optimism, her positive approach to life. Sometimes she doesn't see that other people don't have her feeling and compassion, but I like her willingness to be committed and involved.

As Catholics, we were raised to offer everything up and were not prone to talk about our own feelings. Certainly, Mom was always rather frank about her opinions and beliefs in politics and religion. She liked to talk about that, and I'd say the most important thing to Mom was living up to her potential as a person, especially in a spiritual sense, as well as to see her children becoming involved in social action. She wanted us to be well-educated, loving, reaching out to help others, and to have strong families.

Our family was not politically involved. Dad drove a car for Thomas Dewey one time. Given a couple more years, Dad might have seen politics as an avenue, but as a relatively young man, he was preoccupied with business and civic involvement. He was forty-nine years old when he died—my age now. Fred, my brother, was just twenty.

## *A Religious Upbringing*

Well, that was something when Dad and Freddy died. Mom was like a rock. The funeral people couldn't believe it—this "pillar of strength," they said. A lot of that came from growing up Catholic. We were all brought up believing that everyone is

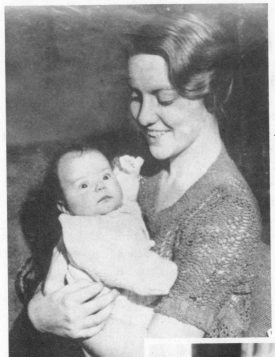

*Adele Kanaley Miller
and baby Loret.*

*Kate Buddeke Kanaley
(Loret's grandmother).*

*Loret Miller Ruppe, Director, Peace Corps. (Courtesy of* Detroit News*)*

*Mrs. Kanaley and daughters (from left) "Speeder" Kanaley, Adele Christensen, and Audrey Nalser.*

going to die, that people die as a result of accidents, and that the dead are definitely going on to a better life in heaven.

I personally feel that my religious upbringing helped me. I have good feelings about it, whereas some of my sisters feel that it hurt them, that it trapped them into certain actions that they probably wouldn't have otherwise taken. They tend to question things that I've accepted, maybe because I'm too lazy. I've always been a little afraid to rock the boat, and then, I haven't had much time, either.

Anyway Mom is something. After Dad and Fred died, she took all of us to Rome. Clara had married, so that left six of us. Mom rented an apartment, and we all went—for a year. In the fifties that was quite something.

## Heart to Heart

Now that I've matured, I'd like to hear Mom's life story and to have more heart-to-heart talks. Our experience with our oldest daughter being in therapy has helped me understand the importance of getting below the surface, the need to discuss feelings and not just our activities. When I got married, I had virtually no idea about anything. Even though I was close to my dad, we talked about relationships only in very general terms because I was quite heavy and not dating; and, of course, he died when I was only eighteen. In school we got lots of "No sex." *Everything* was a sin. Although I do think Mom could have explained a few more things, I don't know that I would have listened, anyway.

And then—not that I wanted it that way—I did the same thing with my own daughters, which is odd because I did think they should learn so much more than I had. With our five kids being so close together, so much of the time and energy was spent just taking care of them. It seemed that whenever I made the effort, the children weren't particularly receptive: *"Oh, Mom. I already know that."* A mother goes through all the different stages with her daughters, and although limits must be set, *always* the goal should be friendship.

I always felt good about my life and what I was doing. Whether that was right or wrong, I don't know; but I wasn't going to tamper with it because I figured, if you're on track, you might as well stay on track. That I attribute to Mom and the way she raised us. What's amazing is just the other night I was telling her that, and for the first time she began telling me about all her past indecisiveness and lack of confidence. She said that it had been so incredible to her that Dad wanted to marry her. I was so surprised. She always seemed so in control, so sure and steady. But I guess I didn't really know her.

I don't recall Mom ever particularly discussing her girlhood aspirations, except that she always wanted to be popular and have every dance on her dance card filled. Dreams of success? We all lived in such a spiritual world that we didn't measure success by conventional standards. It was more important to be a good Catholic, to love your neighbor.

My mother won the Charleston contest on New Year's Eve 1936; I was born January third!

As a young girl, I tended to make friends rather easily. Mom and Dad always insisted that we had jobs in the summer. I often think that my job with Peace Corps, as well as whatever volunteer work I've done—including working with Phil in the campaigns [for congressman and senator]—has been as a result of my parents' influence, especially, my mother's. Although Dad was kind of famous for his civic involvement and his years at Notre Dame, we were never aware of all that he was doing. Since Mom was at home, we could really see what *she* was doing—and she always talked about social consciousness. We grew up in the days of segregation and were raised to insist all people were equal and that the System was not right.

I remember when we first heard the segregation decree being overturned by the Supreme Court. I don't expect we knew much about what it really meant; having grown up in Wisconsin, we'd had no contact with Black Americans. Still, I remember how happy we were about that Court decision.

Mom always seemed so smart to me. She could recite poetry beautifully and was so good about reading to us, even though she didn't have much time.

I loved sports, which were my hobbies, actually—riding, tennis, swimming. We're an active family; lots and lots of activities are going on all the time. We lived on a lake, so we waterskied and swam, went to camp, and learned many skills.

I was overweight—really fat—during most of my growing up and teenage years. Mom tried to get us to slim down (a losing battle), and her mother, thank goodness, used to have me come down by train to Chicago for two weeks on "the Mayo diet." Gosh, she'd take twenty pounds off me and proudly send me back to Mom and Dad. I'd be determined never to eat too much ever again in my entire life. Grandma would come up to visit a month later, only to find me five pounds heavier than where I'd started. I was miserable being fat, *hated* being fat.

Luckily, Grandma would try again, helping me see it could be done. Each time I berated myself I got a little stronger, which helped me to succeed.

I met Phil through a cousin of mine who had gone to school with him, and he invited me to spend a vacation weekend at a beautiful retreat that my dad built out in the lakes and forests of northern Michigan. Mom talked me into agreeing to meet "this nice young man." The night before, I said, "Oh, I don't want to go. I just don't have the time." I was going to be leaving for Europe within a week, and I hadn't packed or anything. Mom was smart. She said, "Well, you're right. It's too late to call, but I can go out and tell them that you can't come." I thought it was so crummy to chicken out like that. I ended up going, and I met Philip up there. We had an absolutely marvelous weekend. He had the best sense of humor, and I laughed at everything. I went off to Europe, but he wrote, and then Mom was smart again and invited him down for my sister's wedding in August. Before we knew it, we had set a date to be married at the end of November.

When Phil ran for Congress, I did have help. As a matter of fact, I enjoyed campaigning because, as I used to tell people, it was a lot easier going to banquets than it was doing dishes and laundry. I took to campaigning with great gusto. That Kennedy public service mystique and my own upbringing in a similar atmosphere inspired me, and later, I felt that for Phil to really represent the district, his wife should be involved.

## The Key

I hoped that my daughters would learn to have a loving heart and try to give of themselves as much as possible. I've really found that's a true key to happiness. I hoped that they would look for friends and companions with good values who really love them and that they would be involved in meaningful work that taps their special talents.

I have regrets about almost everything because I always see that there's so much more I could have done. Having been content as a self-possessed, independent person, *now* I wish I'd had a more sharing, communicative earlier life with my own mother because then I would have been far better able to meet some of my daughters' needs. Because of the fast tempo of our life and the sense of duty to represent "the people" and so on, I failed to help my daughters through their times of stress. I found that watching television reduces free time and is a barrier to communication, as was having the children so close together. My biggest regret, I'd say, would be that the children didn't have as active a family life with their cousins and aunts as I had growing up. For me, family life was very supportive and helpful.

I used to think that my being at home automatically counted as time with the children, which is not necessarily true. I'd be on the phone a great deal or preoccupied cooking or planning. There is, of course, a tremendous amount of work involved with five children and a large house and a husband who has to spend most of his time in his work. You really do have to be sure there's quality time. I say, if you must be gone a great deal, you must continually explain to your children why that has to be. Children simply don't understand why you have to be gone or what you're doing, and you should never assume they understand.

Another regret I have is that since I thought my husband's role in Congress was so important, I allowed him to fall into work habits that kept him away from home. We rarely sat down to a meal together with the children. I was really doing *him* a disservice because those years go by so quickly, and all of a sudden the children are gone. He missed out on a lot of steady, day-to-day or even weekly communication with the children.

My advice to anyone is spend as much time as possible with those you love.

*Becky's mother.*

*Becky at the same age.*

# *Radical Changes*

**B**ecky Duncan,* 40, lives in Sonoma county, California, with her husband Angus, two daughters, and a son. Becky, who sees her radical feminism as a natural progression from the thirties liberalism of her mother, works at a woman's health collective she co-founded in the seventies. She has created the kind of relationship with her children she dreams of having with her own mother. Lily, at 14, expresses gratitude for the candor and care in her mother's communication, which permits a more equal relationship between mother and daughter and grants Lily a more realistic view of the world than a young girl might otherwise have.

## BECKY DUNCAN

My mother was born in Kansas City, Missouri in 1918, but she grew up in Jefferson City. Her mother went to the University of Missouri, which was very unusual in her generation and also in her class. She met my grandfather there, and like most women in those days, went on to become a teacher.

My mother was close with her two younger brothers, who were very close in age and were twin-like. She must have felt left out of that partnership. I don't have a lot of stories about Mom when she was really little, but she did talk about being delirious several times during illnesses in the pre-antibiotic days. I was always amazed that she could have been alive so long ago that people got delirious. To me that's something out of a novel. Once

*Names changed to protect Becky's mother's privacy.

I asked her if, as a child, she had met Abraham Lincoln. Since he was in Illinois and she was in Missouri, I imagined they were quite near neighbors.

## A *Family of Readers*

Mom was always a totally addicted reader. That has gone in direct line from oldest daughter to oldest daughter through the generations. She studied violin and piano and has always been able to play for singalongs. She was very bright in school, skipping at least one grade, if not more. Then she got a scholarship East to Bryn Mawr.

I almost forgot: Mom was a very enthusiastic Girl Scout. I recently found out Girl Scouts in the thirties was still a fairly radical feminist organization. It was founded as an organization whose purpose was for girls to get comfortable with the outside and with being on their own and self-sufficient. I'd always thought of it as a training ground for housewives.

I have a fair number of stories and impressions of my mother as a teenager. If you wanted to go roller skating, you went with the boy who was fun to roller skate with. They tended to do things in groups and didn't "go steady." Mostly what she's talked about is her gang, and she's been in touch her whole life with every single one of them who hasn't died.

## Foreign *Service*

My father joined the Foreign Service in 1957, and when we were living in the Far East, these old friends would come either on holidays or business trips. In would come this guy and his wife, and it would be some old beau of Mom's. But I never heard about her being madly in love with anyone. I spent my whole adolescence being madly in love with one person after another.

I don't remember exactly how my parents met. Both of them out of college moved to Washington just before the United States got involved in the Second World War. They were on a double date but not with each other, and they liked each other better than their dates. They hung out together for a long time, and Dad asked her to marry him. She really liked him but just couldn't see settling down or committing herself to only one person.

She tells the story about how she was on her way home from work one day. Just as she was about to step into a bus, she said to herself, "Well, what if you never see him again?" Her heart dropped to the bottom of her boots, and she realized, "Oh, *that's* how I feel about him. I guess I do want to marry him."

There was a certain amount of brouhaha because Daddy was Jewish and Mom was Presbyterian. There was never any serious objection on either side, just cold feet. I tried to unearth the feelings in the family and was told rather sternly to remember that, after all, at the time Hitler was exterminating anyone who had fifteen minutes worth of Jewish blood, and, of course, my non-Jewish grandparents didn't want their grandchildren to be exterminated if Hitler made it across the ocean. My parents got married in a Presbyterian church. Sometimes it makes me mad that I was deprived of a lot of my Jewish heritage.

Later, my parents got involved in founding a Unitarian Church where mother taught a class in comparative religion. I became fascinated with the subject and still am. Now it's anthropology and religion mixed together with the origins of sexism and racism and all our other evils.

## One-Way Street

My mother loved her mother. As our relationship has gone up and down, I've tried to find out more about theirs. I don't remember her ever saying anything negative about her mother, which, I daresay, increases my feeling of guilt when I say negative things about my mother.

When I was ten my grandmother died. I don't remember a lot about it, except that my mom was down on her knees next to me, hugging me and crying. That made a big impression because I'm not sure if I'd ever seen her cry before. She was always very physically affectionate; we all have our hands all over each other. But as for her own vulnerability, I don't get that kind of thing from her.

A major source of contention between my mother and me is that I strongly believe that my relationship with the children can only be strengthened by being open and that they see me as a real person who's got, not just bad days and good days, but a lack of confidence and a vulnerability. My mother has never shared those things with me, as I have with her. As a toddler I had a terrible fit of croup. She took me into the bathroom and let the room steam up, and as soon as I stopped crouping, I swiveled around in her lap and said, "Don't worry, Mommy, I'm all right."

In later years she didn't exploit that sympathy. Confiding has always been a one-way street: she's been free to ask and I to answer. If she and Daddy ever had any fights, they were held in secret. I don't know if she thought that I wouldn't sympathize or that she just didn't want to be vulnerable. She does think that there are only certain things children should know. Her need to appear perfect creates a gulf, so that we've never managed to develop an adult relationship. There have been periods in her life when she had a confidante. In Thailand there was a wonderful radical, loudmouthed, crazy woman that everybody in the diplomatic community hated, but mother just loved her. At Bryn Mawr there were only two other women in physics, and they were good friends. I would have to guess about any negative feelings Mom had about being the scholarship kid in a school of basically rich people. But she always told us that we were as good as anybody.

## Careers

I think of my mother as being a very powerful mistress of her destiny. Actually, she was following my father around the world, having babies every two years, doing a fair amount of official entertaining, living out in the country and ferrying us children to and from lessons and Little League.

I knew that my mother had been a physicist and had worked, but it seemed to make perfect sense that she didn't do that anymore. I always assumed when we kids left the nest, she would get back into her field or something related to it. Just recently it came out that she wanted to go to medical school.

When my sister wanted to go to vet school about ten years ago, mother was massively enthusiastic. From all the way over in the Far East she wrote to colleges to get catalogs sent to my sister. According to what she told my sister, my grandfather had refused to put out any more money for her education; he had two more sons to put through college. I don't know how much Mom wanted to go or how hard she pushed Gramps.

Instead, she got an M.A. in physics at Minnesota, went to Washington to work in the naval ordinance lab during the war, and met my father. She never went back to work outside the home for pay until 1967 or so. They were in the States for about two years and about halfway through that time she went back to work but didn't work for too long because then they got transferred out again. So much for her career in physics.

I wasn't brought up expecting to have a career, whereas my mother did grow up expecting to have a career. I saw this as very different. I expected to go to college, to work, and then to stop working, marry and have children. When my children got older, I expected to go back to work. I put virtually no energy into figuring what that work would be. I just expected I would get trained in college for a job, but I didn't foresee a career—archaeologist or businesswoman or doctor or mathematician or even an academic. I was talented and capable; obviously, I would be able to get some kind of moderately interesting, moderately well-paying job, just to tide me over until I started having kids. I was going to be really good at what my mom was really good at—being a mom.

## Spider Webs

I don't think my mother had really focused on how feminism had been part of her growing up and then kind of got whooshed away. For instance, her mother was a suffragist and a member of the Women's Christian Temperance Union, which I looked at with great contempt in my youth. It wasn't until ten years ago that I found out what a militant feminist organization the WCTU was.

I don't know what is wrong between my mother and me. Certainly, feminism—in its most radical form (plus a lot of other "isms")—is the scapegoat for our recent separation. My mother considers herself "a feminist, so what's all the fuss about?" But she had heard all these things before. What she forgets is that I hadn't. When I was in women's studies at Sonoma State, she suspected we were there to complain about our mothers. The truth is I was telling everyone what a wonderful mother I had. If you measure her on any standard feminist scale, she comes out with a score four times that of your average mother.

During those hysterical days when I was ranting and raving about sexism, she would say, "Your anger is so unattractive. I wouldn't mind, if only you weren't so unhappy." True, I was angrier than hell, but I was also happier than ever.

In the past my parents were so progressive, and that really influenced me as a child. It's hard to reconcile with how conservative they sound sometimes now. Angus was on his way to be the president of some corporation. When we dropped out, everybody got all upset. My mother and father were Depression generation children. I think my mother figured I was safely tucked into a certain kind of life—my beautiful wedding, my perfect husband, my three nice children. She feels uncomfortable that she's not as radical and wonders if I look down on her for that.

I used to love it when she came to visit. Then things were idyllic between us. I have a friend in Berkeley who said, "I've never met a grown woman before you who really, really, liked her mother." Lots of people have said that to me in one way or another. Now I'm on the verge of telling her that I dread her criticism and that we need to do something drastic. Actually, it is a two-way thing: I care too much whether she approves or not. I'm probably laying too much of a trip on her. Yet I tend to see it in terms of her trying to control me. I, too, want my children to be what I want them to be. Since it's something we work out with our friends and colleagues, we should be able to do that with the people who happen to be our relatives.

One of my mother's old friends visited a couple of weeks ago, and I ruefully apologized to her about the spider webs and dustballs in the house. Then a little while later, when we looked at the overgrown vegetable garden, I again apologized. This friend said, "Oh, there are just so many more important things to do, aren't there? How you do all the things you do, I'll never know. It's not surprising you didn't get to the vegetable garden this spring." I could live for twenty years on just one comment like that from my mother.

I read an essay on giving "strokes" to people. How par-
simonious we are about something that should be given freely all
the time! It made me think of things I should be sure to say more
often because people can't read my mind. I wish Mom could
read it, and that it would have the same effect on her that it did
on me because I do think she has a very high opinion of me. At
some level she thinks I'm terrific.

I guess she would never agree with this, but I feel that she
doesn't respect me, even at this advanced age, for just being the
person I am.

I wish I could say more about what my mother was *feeling*.
Obviously, I paint a picture of her as I see and saw her, but I
guess it reflects how little I paid attention or how little she
shared with me.

## Stages

I've been thinking so much about my mother, myself, and my
children. This was sparked a lot by reading old letters that I
wrote to my parents between 1973 and 1977 and a wonderful
book called *Between Ourselves: Letters Between Mothers and
Daughters.*

I see my life in thirteen-year stretches. There was a break in
consciousness when we moved to Thailand in 1958 when I was
twelve. I spent the next few years having a big rebellion with my
parents. Before that, I thought my mother was pretty much
perfect—full of life and laughter, making everything more
elaborate, more fun, and more creative.

I really idolized my mother again during my twenties. I guess
I've been a feminist my whole life and have always insisted that
women were as smart as men and could do anything that men
could do. But I also accepted the wife and mother stuff and
didn't notice that so many of my heroes and role models were
men and so few of them women—though in school it was always
Penelope I was writing about rather than Odysseus, or the
women in a Thai village rather than "the people" or the cows. I
pretty much did what my mother thought I should do: after Bryn
Mawr, where I did well, I worked and had a big wedding right
after graduation. Then I started having kids and wasn't able to
defy or to risk estrangement from Mom because that's when it's

*Lily, Becky and grandmother.*

*Becky Duncan.*

really important to be close. Part of me feels she misled me into expecting motherhood to be idyllic. Maybe it was easier for her than for me. As she said, she's more phlegmatic than I. She doesn't have my streak of perfectionism about the house or the need to have the children all shiny and dinner exquisite—even just four days after childbirth. It recently dawned on me, too, that my mom had help most of the time.

I was always so proud of my mother and bragged to my friends that I had a mother who stood on her head and ate brown rice and for whom sex was not a no-no subject. She was grossed out about going steady, and one time when we were playing "Spin the Bottle," she was upset to find me having a big, passionate kiss. Yet I never got the message that sex was sinful or dirty, just that it was extremely private.

It was hard to be a typical American teenager in Bangkok, but I did my best. We'd go to the movies a lot because we could sit in the back and neck. There were curfew rules, but they were totally reasonable.

When I was leaving Thailand to live for a year in the States with my grandfather, my father said that I was a warm and friendly person who should use my head or I would get carried away. He wasn't telling me not to be sexual, which is all that any other adult was saying to any other adolescent at that time. He was saying, "Don't forget to take care of yourself." I was certainly impressed with so progressive a message. Just before my senior year in college, Angus, whom I'd met in Laos, arrived to go to business school in the United States. My mother said to me casually, "Well, don't jump into bed with him the first night, dear." I bragged that I had a mom who was not telling me, "Wait until you're married," but just "Wait twenty-four hours." I certainly believe that sex is not something to be hidden away, and I'm really open with my kids, but I find the topic of sexuality harder than any other.

There was another period that was really exciting for me in my relationship with my mom. When we were getting the clinic together and the third bank loan that we'd arranged fell through just before opening, my parents lent us money.

My mother supported the whole clinic project, not just with the loan, but with incredible interest. There was a warming bond between us. In some way I was fulfilling my mother's lost dream of being a doctor. Also, she has supported Planned Parenthood for the last fifty years and has been a staunch pro-choice person her whole life.

It felt so good to be on the same side of something. I opened up to my mother more during that period and really liked it, but in general things have not improved as I had expected. Part of me wishes she would take me in her arms and tell me she loves me just the way I am and always will and that she'll help me and I can help her. Another part of me doesn't want that at all. I don't know what to make of that, other than not wanting to get hurt again. Part of it is pride: I know that a reconciliation requires both of us admitting we're wrong; or maybe she honestly thinks she's never been wrong. I just know I couldn't feel this hurt if I didn't love her so much.

## Spheres of Influence

My life would have been very different with another woman as my mother, and I've been conscious of that my whole life: my mother was different, my family was different, and I was different. I've reacted to that with a mixture of pride and shame, defensiveness, arrogance—none of which my mother would approve. She wanted us to be healthy, loose, well-rounded, liberal-minded people; to be like her—hospitable, smart, generous, relaxed (slightly sardonic definitions I imagine her using).

It is my parents who made it possible for me to make the choices I have made in my life. Despite how weak I've felt, I've spoken out, I've stood up for things—sometimes in clumsy and naive and arrogant ways, but that impulse to justice came from my parents. I didn't do things when and how people expected, but I knew I could not settle for a comfortable life in a world that was not comfortable for most of the people living in it. I'm proud of that, and I do credit my parents with it. I wish that my mother would take pride in the things that my siblings and I feel are good about us and which she finds politically or personally repulsive.

In my early childhood my mother was the dominant influence, the center of our world, more than Daddy was. It's true in most other families and directly relates to hours spent with the children. I credit my mother—and father (particularly, considering he's a man)—with creating the warmth and closeness of our family, so that I'm still close—in war and in love—to my siblings. They're my favorite people in the world to interact with.

This is something else I got from her: she's gregarious but doesn't consider solitude a burden and uses her time alone for many projects. She hasn't only sewed clothes for us and curtains for all of her houses and all of her children's houses but has also worked in many different media. She needlepointed a big, beautiful design of all the houses Angus and I have lived in— with the children and pets and cars and gardens and significant events appropriate to each house. We also have paintings of hers—acrylics, watercolor, Chinese scrolls. In Taiwan, she took Chinese painting lessons, and she learned to pot.

During my childhood, if I wanted something, her reaction was always, "Well, let's figure out how to make it." I grew up thinking we were poorer than we actually were because we never bought anything. Recycling was part of good country people's frugality. Gramps's navy wool pinstripe pants became a skirt for Mom when she went to college, and it was changed around again when *I* went.

My mother has also influenced the lives of other people. As a diplomatic wife she met a trillion people, from all the servants in her household who came to her with their stories and confidences, to kings and prime ministers. There were journalists passing through, and the wives of young diplomatic people thought she was just wonderful. She must have reassured them and helped them get through culture shock and the shock of being a young married woman isolated from her support group.

I admired her totally egalitarian delivery. She would talk to a prince and a redneck with the same tone of voice about the same esoteric subject, totally relaxed, equally respectful of and confident with either one.

There was an incident which really impressed me. My brother's whole baseball team came over for their end-of-season picnic at our house. I found my mother talking about the temples of Angkor Wat with these two beer-bellied Marine-type men, who were entranced with her. Listening, I remembered I had once heard her talking about Angkor Wat to the King of Laos. Surely, I learned from her there's nothing inferior about a woman's mind.

My mother would still say that her children's happiness was always most important to her. Absolutely no doubt about that. She did give up all the rest of her selves to become a wife and mother, and becoming a diplomatic wife took over where being the mother of small children was about to start tapering off. I could say my children's happiness does not define my success or failure, but it is one of the major factors. In secret I take great pride and credit for how wonderful my kids are.

Today my mother lives in Boston with her husband of the last forty years. Mom goes through periods of intense entertaining connected with my father's work as a professor. They invite students just as much as professors, and the students love them. When my dad isn't teaching, they live in Washington and Maryland.

What my mother mostly does is travel. They still have millions of friends all around the world, and every time they go anywhere for pleasure or business they call on friends—as many as they can. When she turned sixty-five years old, she became eligible for a senior citizen's pass to travel all year long within the United States for something like a thousand dollars. She can take her grandchildren along at greatly reduced rates, so she now comes out here, stays for a while, takes a grandchild back to Boston, where he or she stays for the traditional summer visit, and then my mother gets on a plane and brings the grandchild out here at the end of the visit. It's cheaper for her to do that than for the kids to fly back and forth.

It made me sad, when in the early days of our feminist fights Mom finally said that she was too old to change, that she didn't want to know a lot of this stuff. I guess part of the reason I don't want to make friends with her again is feeling angry that such an incredibly talented, powerful, competent, skilled, creative, beautiful woman might waste her life in her older years.

Yet I know it's a great accomplishment to have brought up five kids, who, I confess, are all very interesting and worthwhile people even though we're not what we were brought up, socially speaking, to be. My mother was a really good mother to little kids. She was warm and interested and giving; teaching, but not stifling. She was always quite aggrieved and shocked—and I'm the same way—when her kids didn't feel confident.

I learned a lot about mothering in terms of general atmosphere and in terms of specific tricks of the trade and priorities that have gone into whatever good mothering I get credit for. A lot of that credit belongs, in turn, to her and, from the way she talks, to her mother. I wish I knew what kind of a mother my grandmother's mother was.

I don't know what my mother's hopes or fears or dreams are for now. It's as if she's checked out and is retiring, but I may be wrong. Maybe she'll get all involved in something new again. I guess that's what I hope for her.

## LILY DUNCAN

I'm embarrassed: I know where my grandmother was born, but I'm not sure where my mother was born. She lived in Maryland for a long time and then moved, first to Italy, when she was still small. We have a scroll of the family history, so I know a little about my mother's childhood.

There is one story about her learning songs in playschool and taking over the piano at home because the family were singing wrong: "No, no!" she said, and directed them all.

In another story from the scroll, they visited Venice, and when they came down in the morning, their hotel was flooded.

My mom told me about going to school in Thailand. All I remember is that the school was small. I know some stuff from looking through her junior high school scrapbook. She was so unlike herself now and so unlike me. Apropos of something I was going through, she said that she was different from the other kids but was always trying to fit in. In her scrapbook from school are programs from graduation and many pictures of her friends. She was a member of a stupid little group. They had code names for each other like Angel and Cupid and Devil. From her scrapbook she seems like all the girls I never want to be like.

When I recently had my fourteenth birthday, she told me that when *she* was fourteen, she got into sex and drinking and just being totally teenagerish and revolting. A horrible year.

Let's see... Then they were in Italy. They were always fairly

*Becky and her mother,
1947.*

*Lily and her
grandmother, 1972.*

*Lily and her mother.*

rich because of my grandpa's job as ambassador to Thailand and to Taiwan, so they always had the best of things. I'm not sure why he was in Italy, though. Then I guess they came back to the States for a little while before they went to Thailand. I suppose that's where she went to elementary school. When she came back to the States to stay with her grandparents, she went to this prissy school where all the girls were upper class and looking down their noses at her. She didn't like that at all. I guess she thought it was boring and everyone was snobbish.

From all the pictures it seems she was all girlie-girlie, into clothes and painting her fingernails. She's told me stories about her sister Mary, who was a pain and with whom she shared a bedroom, and about complaining to her mother about her sister. She said that unlike us, she and her siblings never fought.

I think she was a bookworm like me and her mother. Other than that I can't really think of any particular interest that she has had except for art work.

## The Clinic Collective

Politics is her main interest now—women's issues, the anti-nuclear movement, and feminism a lot. I suppose her kids are most important to her. I mean, that's what she worries about and also what she can get the most ulcers from. The women's clinic collective is also something that she's very involved in, but I think she's kind of pulled out because of all the things that have been going on with that—which I won't go into. She had more enthusiasm awhile ago.

She met my dad in Laos, when she was in high school and my dad was working for Shell. The story is that my aunt wanted to go to these Scottish country dancing lessons, and my grandma said that my mom had to take her because she couldn't go alone. That's where she met my dad. My aunt holds herself responsible for it all. But it wasn't love at first sight; my mom doesn't believe in love at first sight. I'm sure they didn't immediately decide they would marry: she was only sixteen years old, and he was six years older. They were separated when she went to college and got a degree in anthropology.

I don't think she had any major aspirations. At least, she never talked about having any. I don't think she really planned on getting involved in anthropology. She was a different person back then.

## *Goals*

You'd have to know my school—it's a private school and it's radical. We were having a Prom Queen contest, just as a joke. I was playing the part up, and one of the questions was "What are your goals?" I said, "To be a housewife and a good mother." To me it seems that's all that a lot of people think of, still today.

I don't think my mom planned on getting married. I mean, I don't know what she planned on doing. I know that she wishes she hadn't gotten married and is even contemplating a divorce— *not* to leave my dad, whom she loves, but only because she opposes marriage as an institution. Otherwise, I'm not aware that she had ever regretted any of her decisions.

Her worries involve her kids, mostly. My brother is super into sports, and Sally insists on doing the opposite of whatever my mom might prefer. Sally loves Barbie dolls, Cabbage Patch dolls, pop music and Madonna, and fluorescent clothing; and she says she just can't help herself. Some things my mom and I discuss, but I eavesdrop all the time, too. It's okay with her, but that makes it hard to say how much she's told me directly. Some mothers quickly change the subject as soon as their kids walk in.

I have been so glad that I have an honest and frank mother. I've never been afraid or embarrassed to discuss anything with her. Knowing my parents don't like ballet at all and, in fact, disapprove of it, I was a little timid about asking for point shoes. Otherwise, I can't imagine wanting to do anything my mother would disapprove. I have thought, god! what could I do that would be totally different—marry a lawyer? somebody like Richard Nixon? Marriage is something I don't believe in, either, but not something she's told me to avoid. She's been fairly explicit with us about how she works twice as hard as anybody else in the house, how she doesn't get any respect. Still, I think I'd like to have kids. Whatever I do, I hope I end up being a performer of some kind because I love being on the stage.

What I like most about my mom is her strength, her willpower, her beliefs—the same things I like about my grandmother. To my mom I attribute my own strength and willpower, and to both parents, eloquence and language and a certain amount of intelligence. My parents are both very intelligent people, and I think they've handed that down to all three of their children. Oh, and awareness of the world! You know, a lot of adults think parents have to hide things from their children and not let them know. My parents have never tried to hide anything at all from me; they've tried to let me know everything that there is to know. I know some people think that talking frankly can be a burden on a child, but I've looked at it this way. The world that we are in today is a burden, period, and there is no way of getting away from it. In a way we can say it is a burden on children; but they have to face it someday, and there's no point in not facing it because that's not going to make life any better.

You can't fight against anything if you don't know what you're up against. If you don't know what's actually going on, then in a way you're lying to yourself, you're out of it, you're under a shadow. It's unreasonable to build a life like that.

If you keep things from your kids, it's unfair to them because it doesn't let them do anything for themselves. Even though the truth can be a burden, there's no way for it not to be. In fact, it would be a burden *not* being told because kids always hear things, anyway; parents can't hide anything, really. I mean, a young kid always kind of knows what's going on, and it just seems unreasonable to lie.

Now I'd like to ask my mom, I suppose, what she wanted to be when she grew up, her goals in life. I never would have thought about that before. I don't know what she wanted to do or what she regrets. My mother is not exactly the typical mother, and I know I'm lucky: all I have to do is ask.

*Elizabeth S. Hernandez, 24, and Lydia Esther Hernandez, 9 months, 1946.*

# *"Desarrollo"*

*E*lizabeth, 63, was born and raised in a traditional south Texas Chicano family (near Corpus Christi), but her life veered off the groove because her father and her husband were not so strongly "macho." Unlike other married girls, Elizabeth left the extended home circle to move away with her husband when he joined the Air Force. Hers is a tale of resolve and resourcefulness and dedication to her children. Her daughter, Lydia, 40, is the divorced mother of 11-year-old Elisa. An extremely articulate, attractive, and "together" woman, Lydia counsels clients in a lovely restored house near Colorado College in Colorado Springs.

## LYDIA CONTRARAS HERNÁNDEZ

My mother's name is Elizabeth Salinas Contraras, and one of the family jokes is that Salinas is "salt," and Contraras is "contrary." The women in my mother's family are notorious for being a little salty and a little contrary.

My mother was the baby of the family, and that was a source of some conflict for me, a firstborn; while my mother had a special relationship with her mother, my mother and I were frequently at odds. I wanted more attention and didn't get it, even though rural South Texas families indulge their children.

In the fifties and even before the War, young Chicano men either stayed in their community, frequently getting into trouble, or they made a life for themselves by going into the military. That's what made sense for my father, who joined the Air Force.

I never realized how strong my mother is until I began to think about our life together. With my father being in the military, it was not easy for her, having to move so much and trying to partake of the major society. Because she's the baby of the family, she's been a shy person, even among her five sisters. Even now she speaks English with a Spanish accent and lacks assertiveness from having grown up in a society where one's minority status also means a different kind of political status. Nevertheless, I'm proud that she's found a strong sense of family loyalty and is a leader in other ways, such as dealing with the system on behalf of her older sisters.

In the church she now attends, she's an Elder, even though frequently only men are Elders. She was instrumental in setting up a daycare center and the "Care and Share Food Closet" sponsored by the church. I inherited her propensity for nurturing and putting others first.

Usually, when we visit, we have at least one major shoot-out. I have a slightly different perspective, as I am more acculturated than she is, so that, one: the form in which I care about what other people think or how other people perceive me is a little different from her form (although still, I have a good dose of that); second: in terms of what people think, then, she and I differ on the question of what you should do out of obligation and social courtesy. My culture is very solicitous—and very gracious at the same time. I don't want to lose that.

There are other times, for instance, in situations with men, when it does not feel okay. Certainly, in my culture men and boy-children always come first. As a therapist for Chicana women, I have often seen that theme surface. My mother was content to be in the house with Grandmother helping with womanly things. The older girls, my aunts now in their seventies, enjoyed riding horses, wearing coveralls, and doing "men's work." Once married, they had to give that up.

## Home to Texas

One of the things that I've enjoyed doing in the last few years is going home to Texas and making a point of listening to the women. As family historian I have even set a date to videotape and record my oldest aunt, who's terribly funny and articulate, and who really calls things straight.

Last summer my mother, daughter, several aunts, and I traveled to our family graves. Seeing the sisters together was really wonderful. Everything was Spanish. My daughter was just fascinated. She's been studying Spanish for a full year with an individual tutor but, of course, couldn't begin to catch it all: "What are they saying, Mother, what are they saying?" She's at the perfect age for eavesdropping, when a child loves to find things out about the older generation.

## Matriarchy

Chicano families are frequently matriarchal, although the woman lets the man appear to be boss. When the chips were down, I saw that my mother had the power. She might disagree with that. When my father died at forty-one, it was a tremendous shock to her. Here she was, a widow at thirty-seven with three children, she didn't drive, and her only potential source of income was to work as a sales clerk. She had to spend some time sorting through how to manage as a single parent and how not to be controlled by her family. By the end of the school year she had decided what to do.

To young clients I sometimes tell this story about separation. When I was fourteen, I had started having just the beginning of dates—boys riding me home from school—and it really concerned my mother. She decided to send me away to a Presbyterian boarding school in South Texas. After a year of my being away, she came to work at my school and enrolled my sister and brother. She deliberately chose a church-related school because she needed the structure of people with positive values around her and because she wanted us not to be "wild" (that might be her word for it) and to have religious values. Certainly I wasn't aware enough to realize that it was probably because of my emerging sexuality, but I did see it in terms of my personality, since I had always been strong-willed.

## The Story Unfolds

My school had international students from Mexico, Central and South America, Puerto Rico; and there were many Cuban

*Lydia's parents as teenagers.*

*Lydia, mother Elizabeth, and sister Elisabeth, 1949,*
*South Dakota.*

*Great aunt Julia, Lydia with daughter Elisa (center) and Elizabeth Hernandez, 1979.*

*Sister Elisabeth and Lydia (right), 1983.*

refugees. As a result of that connection, I was a foreign exchange student to Mexico the summer of my fifteenth and sixteenth year. In terms of my own personal identity and, in Spanish, "desarrollo," it was a truly wonderful experience.

"Desarrollo" is one of my favorite Spanish words and I often use it in therapy. It has a meaning similar to "development," but I especially love "desarrollo" because it means, literally, "to unroll," unfolding like a flower, or as in "the story unfolds."

The whole boarding school period was another part of my mother's life. She became the head dorm mother and had a comfortable apartment in the dorm, as well as an old farmhouse on the campus. The arrangement was really a very good one for her, as she had protection and shelter from the outside world and had found an environment that she felt was good for her children. My mom launched us reasonably well and was not overly attached to us. We've all done relatively well emotionally and, certainly, professionally. My sister, a lobbyist on personal retainer to a coalition of five major corporations in Arizona, has been fighting big dragons for four or five years. After about five years of being quite rebellious and belonging to militant Chicano groups and doing drugs, my brother now seems to be following in my father's footsteps and is even in the Air Force.

## *Father's Input*

I've been in therapy on and off since I was twenty-one, and a major issue for me was my father's death. However, the most important thing I've learned was how much I'm like my mother. I always thought I needed to work on my father; instead, it's always my mother I talk about, which is nice.

I've certainly thought about my father's input. Even though my family is six or more generations in south Texas, like many immigrant families, they put education first. It's quite possible I would have gone to boarding school even if my father had lived. However, from a poorer Catholic family, he was less materialistic and ambitious than my mother, whose family were Presbyterian—unusual in Chicano life. My father clearly gave my mother the lead. In fact, he converted to marry her.

The school experience my mother provided for my benefit greatly expanded my mind and personality. I, in turn, want my daughter to be able to go to Mexico by the time she's fifteen. I would like to see her travel and spend a year abroad, both in high school and in college.

Next, my mother sent me to an expensive Presbyterian college called Trinity University in San Antonio—quite a culture shock for me. Certainly, it was her value that I go to college; that was already "pre-ordained," if you will—a Presbyterian concept.

At times I was embarrassed about my mother's accent and that she wasn't very educated. I felt a little uncomfortable about my background. Once I got out of college, I began to put things in perspective, and in my first therapy experience, I saw how strong and admirable my mother was. As I became more comfortable with myself, I liked that she has an accent.

## *"Sentimiento"*

I'm reminded of the book *The Hunger of Memory* by Ricardo Rodriguez, in which he writes about his acculturation in terms of language and language development; about the softness and "sentimiento" in Spanish, as compared to the harshness of English; how eventually he became a Rhodes Scholar and lost touch with Spanish.

My acculturation process has to do with education and comparing myself to people in the major society, and to the extent that acculturation is becoming different from your main group, college was probably a critical and crucial time for me.

I was also programmed to marry, and my first year at college I married my college sweetheart, whom only a year ago I divorced. I was one of the first people in my family to marry outside of my group, but my mother was very accepting of him because he was a Presbyterian.

## *What About Sex?*

I'd like to tell my daughter, Elisa, who's eleven, about the male-female relationship. One time she wanted to take a whole package of gum to some little boy, and I said, "Why don't you give him just one stick?" I want her—and me—to learn how to conduct ourselves in a positive way with men without taking away from our own self and development.

Things about sexuality are the hardest to tell. She's asked me if I'm gay, if I'm going to become gay—which I can respond to. But there are questions yet; for example, that I have had an abortion. I became pregnant during a very difficult time in my marriage. It was a definite crisis and probably an omen of the marriage ending. Elisa has so much wanted a sibling (although I'm quite convinced that she wouldn't like it as much as she thinks). I don't know if sixteen will be the right time to tell her, or as she gets into sexual activity, but I certainly don't want to wait until she is, say, twenty-one.

My mother doesn't know about the abortion, either. The hardest thing about my divorce was telling her because I knew how disappointed she'd be. I really think that if I told her about the abortion, she would understand. Yet there is the whole value of sacrificing everything for children and putting them first. I certainly have that value: my whole role as the mother of Elisa is very important. I wish I could discuss the abortion with my mother and daughter.

Now I really want to ask my mother about how she has taken care of her sexual needs. Does she have them? I mean, what I'm trying to find out is whether she masturbates. I was in college the first time I asked her about birth control. I said to her, "We kids are two and a half years apart; you and Dad did a good job of spacing us. How did you do it?" I thought about how it was a pretty personal question and she might not want to answer it.

## *"Aunt" Terry*

My daughter and I have a very good mutual friend, Terry. She cannot have children and has always taken a special interest in her friends' children. Since I've been separated and divorced, Terry has been a second parent, picking up Elisa at the daycare center, taking care of her when I was out of town overnight; they have a very close and fun relationship, which I have encouraged. Elisa talks about even more interesting things with her "Aunt Terry" because she's not her mother. ("Oh, Mom, you're so embarrassing.")

We talk enough, though, and she's curious enough. She plays this game with me: "What secret have you never told me?" She's like a Watergate investigator, my daughter! She does things to trick me into telling her some secret. It's important that young women have other women they can talk to. That's certainly the role I play as therapist.

There are some things I won't do because I'm her mother. I have a sense of having to set some sort of limits, and/or that Elisa is embarrassed and needs to set some sort of limits with me. That's part of the separation and individuation process. I don't feel hurt by that; she *has* to say, "Oh, Mother!" Still, she does perceive me as being more candid than most parents.

## The Clear Red Stone

Elisa started menstruating at ten and a half. I waited for a full moon, and the Sunday before I sent her off to visit her father, we had a ceremony for her. We all sat in a circle, and one of my friends played "Scarlet Ribbons" on the piano. Another friend made Elisa a lavender flower brooch to which were attached five scarlet ribbons, each a different shade, symbolizing the five women in my women's group. Even the food was red—strawberries and cherries and punch. Everyone then shared menstruation stories and readings they found significant. We read from a wonderful book called *The Clear Red Stone.* Elisa has since read it to her friends. The clear red stone is the first drop of menstrual blood. To acknowledge the beginning of menstruation, her father gave her a garnet ring.

## Spiritual Ethics

Two things have been most important to my mother; first, her involvement in the Presbyterian church, her spirituality. I see that in her; I saw that in my grandmother. One of my strong images of my grandmother is reading the Bible at the kitchen table early in the morning. If you asked her, that's what my mother would say is most important in her life; second, her children and her extended family.

She wanted me to be religious and spiritually oriented. She does say sometimes, "You might feel better if you'd go to church." I do have a strong sense of morality and ethics, which relates to one of the other things I want to eventually share with my daughter. In terms of what I lived up to and did not live up to, the subject of extramarital affairs is an important one. My actions were not always compatible with my beliefs. In my past sexual expression when I was married, I didn't have to face that too much: either I was faithful, or I was unfaithful, and I knew that I was not correct. Suddenly, as a single person, I've had to struggle with what I think is correct in my sexual expression.

Elisa teases me about whom I'll invite over when she's not home. It's my house, but how I conduct myself when she's at home is still an issue for me. It might be embarrassing for her; and I have to resolve the need of acknowledging my sexuality. Certainly the sexual needs of a single person exist, but one of the nice things about being married is being able to have sex within the context of a positive, meaningful relationship.

I'm like my mother, in that a sense of family is really important to me. We both value family connectedness, caring, and loyalty. Despite my acculturation and my distance from Texas, I still have my extended family. Like a conquering heroine, I'm greeted with total acceptance and interest. People want to see me, and special things are done for me.

## Family of Choice

However, in my day-to-day life is what Betty Friedan calls the "family of choice," including my women's group, Aunt Terry, and another friend. Together we observe certain rituals and traditions. When something significant happens to Elisa, such as getting her first bra, we go to a particular restaurant owned by people who have known Elisa since she was a baby. To me it's important to share that connectedness with my daughter and to pass our family's values down to her.

# ELIZABETH SALINAS CONTRARAS

God gave me the most wonderful, strong mother—and a woman of prayer. If there was something she wanted to do, she asked the Lord. Then if she had any problems, she would have faith. She showed me how to pray. Several times my prayers were answered, so I knew there was a God that my mother had known. From then on I didn't hesitate.

To me that is the most wonderful treasure she could have given to me because when I lost my husband in 1959, I knew who to go to with my problems. I was sad, yes, to lose my husband; yet I knew how to keep on going. I had three children to care for. Lydia was about thirteen. Elisabeth was eleven, and David was nine.

In our family there have been three or four generations of Presbyterians, including my mother, her mother, me, and my children. I was able to send them to a private Presbyterian Pan-American school that a friend of my mother's recommended. I went to work at this school in order to be with them. Through the school they got scholarships and I was able to send all three through college. I told them I would give them each four years and after that they'd be on their own. Now Lydia and Elisabeth have their Master's degree, and David graduated from college and then enlisted in the service. I give all the credit to the Good Lord and my mother, whose gift—that faith in God—I hope I have given to my children. I know they believe in God, but sometimes when children are young they stray away.

For me religion is number one. God is my source for everything—my job and everything that brought. Believe me, I had that experience of communication and oneness with God. In return I will serve. When I promise something, I try my best to do it; and I expect the same in return.

## A Way of Praying

When I pray, I just talk the way I'm talking to you or the way I would ask my mother or father for something when I was little. When my husband died, I took it up even more. I would wake up in the middle of the night and think, "What am I going to do with these children?"

Then I asked God to give me the courage and show me the way to provide for them. I wanted to send them to school and to college so they would be able to take care of themselves because I won't be here forever.

## Josefa

My mother Josefa was born in Brown's Valley in South Texas. My grandfather said the boys could go off to school, but the girls would have a tutor at home to teach the basics. That definitely was a double standard. In my time the girls did go off to school.

My mother was raised by her grandma. I've heard of other mothers doing that and sending daughters elsewhere to help out in other families. For instance, my mother raised my niece until my sister remarried, and then she took my niece—because that was the custom then, not because she wanted it.

On weekends the grandmother would take my mother home so she could visit her mother and play with her sisters. The sisters *envied* Josefa because she stayed with the grandma, and they had fun playing tricks on her. In playing "Hide and Go Seek" they would never come out, and she would be looking for them forever.

My mother and I would sit down and just talk. She told us about her boyfriends—their names and what they looked like—but they didn't go on dates in those days. They had to ask permission, even though they would be right there in the house. That was the beginning of my parents' courtship. My daddy was a good dancer, but the grandparents wouldn't let my mother go to dances. Then they got married, and that was it. They started having a family and had to save some money and work and take care of the family. There were nine of us.

My mother's grandma taught her to sew so she became a professional seamstress. She could look at a picture and make a dress, and she made all my pretty clothes. After my daddy passed away—when he was only fifty-one—that's how she earned her living. She'd stay up until one or two o'clock in the morning sewing for people who wanted their dresses for a certain day. I felt badly about that. After I started working, I told her, "I don't want you to stay up late just to buy the groceries or pay the utilities."

## Prayer Partners

She always talked about her worries with me because we were prayer partners. If we had problems at home like needing money to make a payment, she'd say, "Well, let's see how we can manage." She'd go to me instead of to my older sisters, two of whom were married. There were only three of us at home. We were very close.

My mother was so brave! When my brother was killed in a car accident, I was afraid she'd be sick because she had heart problems, and I had the minister tell her. She took it very well. As she said, we have to accept things as they come and make the best of it.

She never did express fears of any kind. When I lost my husband, I told her about worrying in the middle of the night, and she would say, "Just go ahead and pray; teach your children the right thing." She reminded me that, although children often get side-tracked, there is a promise in the Bible that they will come back.

Of all my sisters I was the only one who did not stay there right next to my parents. I don't know what made me different. When I got married and my husband went in the service, I followed him wherever he was sent. I learned to think for myself and care for my children. My children also are independent. My Lydia is in Colorado, my Elisabeth is in Arizona, and my son is in Florida.

I didn't want my daughters to think they had to stay with me. I had already taught them right and wrong; they had to follow their own conscience. I wanted for them whatever they wanted for themselves.

Even when I was married, I'd go home once a year and stay for a month. So I was always able to share with my mother whatever I needed to. As friends, we would tell each other our troubles. She showed me how to keep house, how to cook; and I loved her so much that I wanted to be exactly like her. In fact, she'd say I was going to be exactly like her, especially my health, because she was always so healthy and was eighty-three when she passed away. I've worked all my life; now at sixty-three, I still work eight hours a day, so my mother's words did come true.

## Reticence

Women didn't talk about themselves in my mother's day. I think it's better to be open. When I was about to be married, she told me what I should do. Even after I was married, she would still give me helpful advice on what I should do with the children. For instance, her grandmother had taught her things about herbs and teas for different ailments.

Of course, in our culture, you must be submissive to your husband. When he comes home, you're supposed to have the dinner ready and the children bathed and clean. Those were some of the basics to be a good wife, and my mother did teach me that.

When Daddy would sit down with us at the table, all the food would have to be nice and warm. She'd be cooking the tortillas—Daddy liked them hot—and he would feed us, but my mother would still be at the stove. After I got a little older, I said, "Mama, I don't want you to be standing up while we're sitting down. You fix the tortillas, and we'll just wrap 'em up, and they'll stay warm. If Daddy wants, then I'll get up and warm up one or two." I used to do that for her, and I would also fix his chocolate the way he liked.

## The Best Piece of Meat

When *I* got married, it was different. My husband always served me first and gave me the best piece of meat. He took such good care of me; but then I had to stay behind when he had to go away. He was the most wonderful man in the world. That's why I never got married again; I'll never find another one like him. We were in love all the time. Although we were together only ten years, it seemed like two or three years. After he died, I went out with couples, but I never dated. I didn't mind not having a man around because I was so busy raising the children, and at that school I felt I was working twenty-four hours. I had contact with all different kinds of people of all ages. It was one big family.

Back then one man did propose to me. He was a good friend of the family, and he had all the qualities I prayed for. But I couldn't love him. When he proposed, I said I had promised myself I wouldn't leave Pan Am until David finished school. He said, "Now, that's enough for your children. Think about us!" That turned me off. I said, "If you're ready to get married, go ahead, but I haven't accomplished my goal yet."

Lydia, my daughter, said, "You have to get out in the world. Do you expect God will drop somebody at the door?" I said, "Well, if it takes that, I'll just wait."

## Daughters

I talk with Lydia most because Elisabeth gets upset and nervous so I don't tell her any problems or my deepest feelings. I love and trust her, but I don't want her to get hurt.

I've told some stories about my childhood, when we lived out in the country and my daddy was a farmer. We'd ride horses and go on hayrides. It was a lot of fun to get up on top of the hay and slide down.

When I was thirteen, my daddy quit working and we moved to the city, where he had to be much stricter. We girls didn't give him much trouble, but the boys did—because he had a double standard: the boys could drink and go to dances, but we couldn't. At least, he was more liberal with me because he liked my fiancé and actually let us go out without a chaperone. But I was angry at first about my daddy's double standard. Then my mother said, "It's for your own good. Your daddy knows what he's talking about." Later, my husband said that the only reason he married me was that I wasn't wild like some other girls. Then I appreciated my daddy: I may have ended up with a husband who left me after a couple of years or who was not faithful. Families like my daddy's had such high standards that they would not tolerate divorce.

I wanted my children to accept people as they are; and I believe they have. Lydia is always helping somebody, and my son, just like my husband, is friendly and willing to do almost anything to help people. I always wanted my children to be like my husband—compassionate and sensitive without expecting anything in return. To him, nobody was a stranger.

## A Regret

Lydia wants me to move to Colorado. That's still a big question mark. For two years I think I'll stay where I am because I want to work until I'm sixty-five to get more Social Security. I might as well work as long as I'm healthy. Yet I would like to move because right now Elisa, my granddaughter, will need someone to be there when she comes home from school. And by watching me she may learn a thing or two.

I'd like to have a good talk with Lydia because I feel guilty that we haven't been close. We used to talk on the phone and write, but still....I want to communicate better and iron things out. I want to know what's in her little mind. She seems to be doing pretty well, but she works long hours. If I were in her job, I would get so involved that I would feel that it's me who's hurting all over instead of only the case client. Well, Lydia likes to help people and I guess that's why she took that job.

## Prejudice

I lived by certain goals and standards and always taught my children that all people are equal. We all are human beings. The color of our skin didn't make any difference because we were all made by God. For myself I never felt I was discriminated against. I've always had good friends of all nationalities and religions. But when you're in different places and out of your group, some will discriminate against you because of your skin color or nationality. I remember when they had one fountain for the blacks and one for the whites. That I couldn't see.

Right after I got married in 1944, my husband was stationed in Louisiana. There was a sign that the blacks had to go to the back of the bus while the whites sat in front. One time it was cold and rainy, and these two girls of color (they had blue eyes and, mixed with French, I think, were lighter than I am) had to stay behind because there weren't enough empty seats in the back. The bus driver was about to let me in. I told the girls I felt so bad, and they said, "We don't blame *you*." I said, "I want you girls to know that I love you as much as my own daughters." They were lovely girls; why wouldn't the driver let them ride? I guess he had his orders. I never had such treatment from anybody. That's what makes you feel bad.

# The Money Tree

*H*ere is a glimpse into the life of a small town northern girl who didn't feel the full effect of racial bigotry until she worked in Washington, D. C., during World War II. Her daughter "Mike" marvels at her mother's charm without seeing that she herself has obviously inherited it. Recently retired, Hazel lives with her architect husband in Barrington, Illinois. Mike is a bank officer in Los Angeles.

## HAZEL MORTON BLAIR

I was born in Haverstraw, New York, but my first memory is of another small town in upstate New York—Bushnellville—up towards the Catskills. My parents were there to run a boarding-house for the laborers who were building the Ashokan Reservoir. I can picture the house and barn, a cow and some pigs. There was no running water, and we had an outhouse.

One thing stands out. I was standing on a big trough at the side of the house, where my brother and I liked to drink the nice cold water coming out of the pipe. Well, I fell in! I must have been about four years old; and I have a memory of turning around and around in the water because it was churning. Now, every time I've tried, over the years, to learn how to swim, I can't.

When we moved to Kingston on the Hudson, almost directly across from Hyde Park, we used to go to the Dutchess County Fair, where I remember seeing Mrs. Roosevelt (she had a blue gauze dress on and wore a band around her hair) but not the

*127*

*Hazel's mother.*

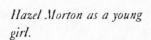

*Hazel Morton as a young girl.*

President himself. I did see him at the ferry. Their son, John, who was the youngest, rode in the horse show. My younger brother Les rode in the pony show and won the Silver Cup.

## No Horror Stories

The day my older brother died, it was during an exam period in school, and since I had never missed a test or anything, the first thought that went through my mind was, "Oh, now I can't go to school. I can't take that test!" Imagine—worried that I wouldn't pass. I do know that I passed because I skipped a grade. Mom and Dad always read their newspapers, listened to the news on the radio, and impressed upon us the importance of education. It didn't come too hard for me because I liked school a lot.

Growing up in a small town was....Well, what can I say? Except, being black where there were not too many black people, and my family were Democrats in the Republican Ulster County. Most of the black people were blue collar; so I guess there was some kind of tacit prejudice that you weren't quite aware of. I was always aware of being black, but, of course, then it was "colored." Nobody would ever talk about that, and there weren't any horror stories. Black people lived in scattered little enclaves around town. I would assume that if they had money, they could have lived in the wealthy part of town. Now, maybe that isn't true; that's an assumption I made.

We had to do everything better. A lot of people—black people—still grow up with that feeling. You didn't use the term "to be accepted"; I know my parents didn't. The only way you could get ahead was to really bust your buns. I remember my mother saying, "If you are a dishwasher, you have to be the best dishwasher there." Nevertheless, I lack ambition. I'm content with small things. Yes, I could have been more than I am. I was always on the Honor Roll, and my parents were proud of that because neither of them finished high school. Daddy didn't even finish grammar school. He raised dogs for families in the area, and managed a small farm, so we were never hungry during the Depression. He was never too proud to do anything, so we never had to go on relief. He worked on the WPA, digging or street sweeping or whatever people did on the WPA in a small town, but he preferred working for himself. For a long time he used to taxi people back and forth. They called it "hacking" in those days.

Mom worked for a while as a cook for dinner parties. I would go with her sometimes and help serve. I remember working at one dinner party, when a lawyer came up to me and said, "Hazel, it's too bad because you're a smart girl, and if you weren't colored, I could have you in my office to read law." I had wanted to be a lawyer, but since I was "colored," he wouldn't have me. When you're black, people think you don't have feelings; anything can be said to you. I felt, yes, it is too bad I'm colored. There goes an opportunity.

## Low on the Totem Pole

Now, as I grow older, I become angry when I think about it. At the time, even though I was bright, I didn't realize it. Before the civil rights movement, we tended to go along, and while we didn't think of ourselves as second-class citizens, we didn't think too much about rising above our station in life. Another thing: if you live in the city, you have a lot of role models, whereas in a small town you don't. I knew that I couldn't be a lawyer, anyway, because we didn't have money enough for law school; so I set my sights lower. That's why I say I'm not ambitious. There are people who come from meaner backgrounds than mine who have made it because they're willing to sacrifice and work hard. I say, I just didn't have the toughness. Mike might say I would make a good politician because she would also say I'm so wishy-washy. Politicians can see both sides, and they promote the side that's more advantageous at the moment.

After high school, I went to business school and got a job on the National Youth Administration. I was the first black to ever work for the Department of Unemployment Insurance in Kingston. Everybody knew I was working there: "Hazel Morton, working in an office!" When a family friend's checks came through, he would tell Mom and Dad it was because of me. Of course, I had nothing to do with it; I was low on the totem pole. Yet people have always trusted me. They tell me all their business that I don't even want to hear. I don't know why.

Later I took a Federal exam for stenographer and was called to go to Washington. The day I arrived, it was pouring rain. There were black taxis and there were white taxis. I thought, oh, my God, I'm in the South. There was nothing like that in Kingston—not being permitted to eat in certain places, and so on. Somebody told me I should stand "over there." Then I noticed everybody was black "over there," you know.

I went to work for the War Department, as it was called then. I remember the day war was declared. There were people coming into Washington to work by the droves, thousands a day. I was put in a pool because, believe it or not, they hadn't been hiring black people as anything but messengers. I found out later they had college graduates working as messengers—and elevator operators—because they were black.

I'd never heard Southern accents before. Some people looked down on you because you were black! I never had that kind of feeling in a small town. It was really blatant, and I just couldn't understand it.

The black fellows in the pool were assigned as file clerks. They refused the jobs. They said they didn't come as file clerks; they had passed the typist exam, and that's what they wanted to be. Well! That caused a big stink. Finally, they were given assignments as typists. Still, we girls didn't get any assignments at all.

There was a pool supervisor who was a real "cracker"—a red-faced one with an accent you could cut with a knife. I went up to her and said, "We've been here a long time and should be assigned someplace." Well, she said, she didn't have the authority to do that. One of us said, "Well, surely somebody does. Why don't you speak to your superior and see about our being assigned?" She stomped out of the room and came back with her boss, who said that he'd heard that we were dissatisfied. The supervisor said, "I've done everything I could to make you happy." I said, "We came down here to work, and you don't have anything to do with our being happy." Oh! Her face got redder than ever. We were the troublemakers, and we got assignments—the next day.

My first assignment was in an office with counters. To enter the office, people would open a door and go to a counter. The door opened inward. We were seated so that when people came in the door, they wouldn't see us.

Eventually, I went to the office of Robert Weaver (who later became the first black cabinet member), stayed there almost a year, and became a senior secretary. My progress was the result, not of ambition, but of being a good worker.

Once I was assigned to a white man with a thick southern accent. He never called me "Miss Morton," just "Ma'am." I think southerners didn't like to call black people by Miss or Mr., and that was his way of getting around it.

Finally, I got assigned to a man who decided to quit the government because he had a job as executive director of a race relations group in Chicago. He asked me if I wanted to go, and I said yes.

## Ted and Mike and Butch

In the meantime, I met Ted. He was in uniform at the time because he had been in the service. We started going around together, and then I told him I was going to Chicago. I had always wanted to go there, ever since I studied economic geography as a kid. It sounded like such a bustling town. I flew in at night in '44. Oh, I was thrilled! When I woke up the next morning, I was disillusioned: it was a drab November day. I thought, gee, I wonder if I made the right move.

When I got to the Loop, I didn't have any more misgivings. I met a lot of people, and the work proved to be interesting, concerning itself with the plight of minorities.

In the meantime, Ted followed me here, and we got married on the Fourth of July 1946.

I worked until the end of July the following year because Mike was due in the first part of September. One night at the movies, the ladies' room matron said, "Child," (she was a black woman), "what are you doing down here? You've got no business coming to the movies." I said, "Oh, I have lots of time. I'm not going to have my baby until the first week in September." She said, "You're having that baby sooner than that." I laughed it off, but that night I was twisting and turning.

I'd told Ted I didn't want to be alone. He'd called the Palmer House to say he wasn't coming to work. Even though he belonged to a union, they fired him on the spot. Here we were with a baby and no job.

The next morning Mike was born. A woman in the next room had been screaming at the top of her lungs, and when she stopped, I thought she'd died. I asked the nurse, "What happened to that woman?" She said, "She had a baby." When they showed me Mike, I thought, "Oh, my, I've got to do this all over again because I bet Ted wants a boy." It turned out, he didn't. They kept bugging me for the name of the baby. Finally, I said, "Well, her name is Leslie." When I told Ted, he hit the ceiling because he thought I named her after my brother, whose name is Lester. Her middle name is my maiden name. Ted didn't like it, so we decided she would have a nickname. He said, "Let's call her Bumps." I said, "She might not like that, being a girl. Suppose she has acne or something." So he said, "OK, we'll call her Mike." He always called *me* Butch!

## First Step

Mike took her first step on Election Day in '48—but before then she'd been talking for a long time. I'd pretend I was asleep to see if Ted would get up—because I'd get so tired; and one night I heard her say, "Daddy, change me! I'm soakin' wet!"

When she was five, we enrolled her in lab school, an adjunct of the University of Chicago, where I was working. I don't think Mike took full advantage of lab school because there was a period as she got older when she became quite rebellious.

She and I liked to go down to the public library to hear the storyteller and to Goodman Theater for the children's programs. I bet she doesn't remember that.

There are things I would do differently. You never get the second chance, though. For instance, Mike didn't want to take piano lessons, and Ted said, "Well, if she doesn't want to, she doesn't have to." Now she'd be happy if she'd had piano lessons. Even in lab school they said she had an "affinity" for music. Ted felt that you needed to learn only those things related to making a living. I didn't have the power to override him. I didn't even have the feeling that I should. I guess I was afraid that if I opposed him, he might leave. As Mike says, "You never want to rock the boat." *Everybody* said, "You can't be without a man," which is not true, but I didn't know that then. If I had it to do over again, I'd say, "You do it."

Ted was a good provider. Yet his attitude had its effect on Mike's not being independent earlier in life. He wouldn't let her help out or even babysit for our neighbors. People always want to give their kids more if they come from a deprived background. That's the trouble with the world today. I can see that somewhat because black men are the most deprived people in the United States, but I don't approve of it because I think it's wrong. I don't understand his not reasoning it out: "Her parents are not always going to be here; she'll have to take charge of her own life. Why not prepare her?" Making a living and providing for his family was uppermost in Ted's mind. He thought the rest would take care of itself.

## The Dark Period

I've never said anything to Mike about Ted. Whatever bad attitude she has about her father, I didn't want it to come from me. Whenever she said anything about him, I'd say, "You know how your father is." She'd say, "You always say, 'You know how your father is.'" Ted was charming, the light of everybody's life in his family. They would excuse everything by saying, "Oh, well, you know how Theodore is."

Looking back, I think Ted had a way of undermining my confidence in myself. I had once felt I had competence in some areas, but soon I felt I had none in any area. Still, he was a good man, as men went in those days. He didn't run around, he didn't gamble, he never came home drunk, he always brought his paycheck home. Women I worked with had husbands who did all those things.

All this came to an end when Ted asked for a divorce. He said I wasn't an asset because I was afraid to do everything. After nineteen years of marriage, I agreed to the divorce.

Just before the divorce, I got a call from Mike, who by now was in college. She was crying, and she told me she'd failed. I went down to get her.

It wasn't that she couldn't do the work. In the first place, at sixteen, she was a little young to go away; she was getting out from under her father's tight hold on her. He was permissive in some respects but not as far as boys were concerned. Nobody was good enough.

Well, Mike's leaving college was the last straw. Her father just blew his stack. When she came back home, he seemed to wash his hands of her. It was a case of conditional love: 'If you don't do the right thing, I won't love you.' I didn't go along with that and tried to help her, but she wouldn't accept my help. Her self-esteem was low.

When she was eighteen, Ted left. From then on, she and I had a strained relationship. She wouldn't confide in me, and I didn't know what to do about her. I just had to think it would right itself. It didn't.

Meeting and marrying Dennis has been one of the great things in my life. He was the kind of person I'd envisioned I could be happy with; but I couldn't conjure him up.

Mike seemed to be happy that I had somebody to see—and then to marry. After Dennis moved in, Mike had a change of heart. Here was another man of the house. Again, she and I weren't communicating at all.

## Healing

Then it developed that she had cancer. That was when we started getting closer because she had a sense that she would die and never recover from the operation. During the convalescence, we came to talk even more about her feelings of losing so much with the hysterectomy, and she would break down and cry.

After the operation, Mike got a job and saved up enough money to get her own apartment. I would stay overnight with her. We'd have dinner, go shopping, and talk well into the evening. We enjoyed being with each other, as we did when she was little.

With her being away we're able to say things on the phone that we couldn't say face to face—not because we were afraid, but because we never had the opportunity. When we were together, there was always somebody else around or we were always going someplace. On the phone, we have each other's undivided attention.

In the meantime, there's an area that is still uncharted. For instance, I've never known her true feelings about her father—or about me. I have thought, I'll have to write about Mom and Daddy, where they were born, where they grew up, and other things Mike doesn't know because we didn't talk about it.

My mother never had much time for talking; she was too busy

with the kids. It was not something I expected, but now that I'm getting older, I wish for it. I've never been privy to Mike's thoughts, and she's never been privy to mine. I don't know if she's ever wanted to be, and that may be it: we've never given each other any indication of mutual interest. If she sees something about me in this book, she might open up.

What I wanted for Mike more than anything was for her to be happy, to have some goal, something that would make her feel true to herself, that would fulfill her reason for being. There was a long period when Mike didn't want to do anything. To me, that's the worst thing in the world.

I could never think of myself as a role model because I felt that I was a failure as a mother. There was so much inside her which I didn't do anything to nurture. It seemed that everything I did was wrong, especially, when other people's daughters were doing this and that: "And what is your daughter doing?" I never blamed her; I blamed myself for not having a real goal for her.

I do want Mike to know that one of the proudest moments of my life was when she earned her Bachelor's degree on her own (without my help or prodding). Another was her acceptance of her cancer and her determination to go on with her life.

Now I feel *wonderful* about her, and I'm so sure that she's going to make a success of it. I don't think she'll be the bank president, but I know her new position as a bank officer is just the beginning of her taking advantage of her capabilities. Now, although I don't know him very well (I just talk with him over the phone), I think Danny is a good thing in Mike's life. He seems to want her to do something with her life and is not jealous and seems to be happy for her. He provides a bit of stability and seems to care for her. That to me is the most important thing.

## LESLIE MORTON ("MIKE") WEST

When my mother was born I don't know. The earliest story I have from her is that my grandfather bred dogs on the Holcomb estate in, I think, Albany.

Mom has usually just talked about isolated incidents and small items. One is that there was a bulldog named Ned who would let people in the house but never out! Another is that she

*Hazel Blair.*

*"Mike" West.*

*Baby "Mike."*

*"Mike" and "Butch."*

is unimpressed by cars, doesn't know a Cadillac from a Chevy, remembers that Mrs. Holcomb gave Mr. Holcomb a steel gray 1936 phaeton for his birthday. The thing that made it a phaeton was the convertible top. That was the only time my mother ever commented on a car; she said it was just beautiful.

I'm really not sure what their life was like there. I recall that Mr. Holcomb always had to drive Mom to school because she was always late. To me that's funny because my mother, who's always up early, said she was always oversleeping in the morning.

Mom's oldest brother Edward died at eleven or twelve. As the oldest of four for most of the time, she had to take on certain duties in the house and was responsible for the younger children. One day Uncle Les fell asleep on the running board, apparently on the side of the car away from the front of the house. They looked for him everywhere. That was considered to be Mom's fault, and she got a spanking.

That's about all I can really remember about my mom because we never talked about her youth. I never asked. You don't say, "Mom, tell me about yourself." Yet I don't feel as though I have no idea of her childhood. You tend to find things out indirectly.

She was about six years old when the stock market crashed. The Depression had something to do with my mother's obsession with food and with always having "enough." But she also said they never went hungry. Again, you don't ask your mom, "Tell me about yourself."

## Climate of the Times

There may be a few things Mother may feel she would have done if she had had more confidence or if the climate were different in the country. She and I have differences of opinion, for instance, as far as her career goes; I think she "stifled" herself.

If she had any regrets, one might be that she concerned herself too much with other people's business. Now that she's retired she will say, "I should have told that boss to stuff it." A couple years ago the boss was working her nerves, and Mother told her so. I was really surprised. She said, "I just told her, 'Fire me, if you want to,'" or something equally bizarre. Maybe she wishes she had stood up for herself a little more. We've had discussions about the work ethic. My thing is, hey, you don't owe the corporation. My mother had to be totally broken down before she could take off from work.

I do know how Mom and Daddy met, but I can't remember if it was in Washington or Chicago. I remember saying, "You mean you let Daddy pick you up?" They were married in... Well, now I don't know that either, come to think of it. I assumed they were married in Chicago.

I never asked her if she fell madly in love. My father isn't the kind of personality who, if you didn't show any interest, would make a real big effort to pursue you. For all I know, she may have been wild. She did think he was pretty cute. My mom's pretty cute, too, just like now, so I can see why Daddy tried to move in. I have no idea how long it was after they met that they got married. Daddy wasn't overseas, so it must have been after the War.

## First-Class Citizens

For eight years I enjoyed being the only grandchild on my mother's side and the only niece of about four aunts and uncles, all of whom married late and whose children are much younger than I. I spent a lot of time in Kingston with my mother's parents and her brothers and sister. That gave me a sense, a general picture, along with the tidbits from Mom, of her family and past. Grandma was a handsome woman. She died when I was five. I don't remember her ever standing up: she had leg ulcers and was in a wheelchair. I loved Kingston. There were huge sunflowers behind the garage, and they had a funky little house with colored glass embedded in the stucco. We greedily mined those "jewels," until soon, up to a certain level, there were none left.

Both of my parents were dedicated to education, and they gave me a background that was definitely to my advantage and unique for a black kid. My parents were not rich; they made a lot of sacrifices to send me to a private school. It was not evident by my grades that it was a good investment. At my school there were exceptional people: exceptionally bright, exceptionally eccentric, exceptionally everything. It may have been an artificial setting, but I'm grateful to my parents for providing, not only the academic influence, but also the exposure to people of diverse backgrounds. It gave me ease and poise so that I would never feel like a second-class citizen.

My mother also gave me my facility in English. I always wished that she had pursued a career where she could put her *amazing* knowledge of the English language (and other abilities) to use. In my whole life I think I have asked my mother two words that she didn't know. When I was working downtown at Prentice-Hall, my boss was impressed with my ability in English. It got to be a game of "Stump the Stenographer." As I was transcribing a dictation tape, I came upon this sentence: "We are not an eleemosynary institution." By this time, in every office where I'd worked, we'd make quarter bets and call my mom for the answer, which she always had. "She'll never know 'ele-emosynary.'" She did! Now, why would she know that? She'll tell you, "Well, I read..." Now she's doing crossword puzzles, so she's *really* good.

Mom had an amazing amount of energy. Only since I've grown up have I begun to appreciate her. She worked all the time, always doing office work, plus she was involved with me. We'd go to the library, which had all kinds of special events, and to the Goodman Theatre, which had shows for kids.

I never remember there not being dinner on the table. When she got off work, Mom would spend a lot of time cooking because my dad was not one to help out in the kitchen or with housework. I have since told her, "I appreciate how hard it must have been for you to come home and cook every night."

## Taking a Stand

My mother has never complained about anything. She's the kind of person who either feels okay, or she's displeased. I have to fall out and turn blue, but Mother will just say, "I'm not going to have that, and I'm very annoyed with you," and you cool out immediately. The other day I myself said that to someone who thought that was so funny because it's archaic. You're supposed to say you're "pissed off." My mom is refined. I've been going a long time, and the only time I ever heard my mother swear was in a joke. Even then, everybody said, "Ooo, I can't believe she said that!"

Some people seem to have power but no control. Mom has

control. She gives the impression of being easygoing and going along with the program. Yet one time my father wanted my mother to quit work. In his family—a big family—he was "the man" early on. His father had died when he was only eight, the older brother had died, and then the other brother had a stroke and was physically incapacitated; so my father was domineering and used to having his way with women.

My mother stood firm on the issue of her working. I can just hear her saying, "Now, Ted, I'm not going to quit work." My father always spoke in the Royal We. My mother never had to; she had the ability to draw the line. I've tried it, and it never works. *I* get a big, "So what?" Obviously, I don't have the whole picture.

My mother never had that feeling of being totally dependent or of having to suppress her feelings or of denying herself as a human being. Not being a homemaker saved my mother from a lot; she had some autonomy. Most of her regrets concern me. She would say there are some things she wishes she had done differently in rearing me, certain matters in which my father had the last say. He didn't want me to know anything unpleasant. He didn't want me to see anybody drunk or ragged or poor or starving. Period.

Mom was more realistic. She wanted me to be complete, to see all sides. She didn't want me to suffer from seeing any of it, but she wanted me to be aware. My father wanted to pretend all sides weren't there. His position prevailed. I had a one-sided view for a long time, as was evident when a girl asked me where I was from. I said, "America!" My father's desire to insulate me meant that it took me a long time to develop a sense of responsibility.

One Christmas I was opening my presents, and when I looked up at the tree, I saw a ten-dollar bill—and another, and another! That money tree was fabulous. It was my father's idea, not Mom's.

## A Mother's Fear

When I had chicken pox, Mom didn't take off work. But when I had cancer, Mom took off work. I think parents plan on dying before their children, and Mom feared that this cancer was going to take my life. I don't think she is afraid of too many things, but I could see fear in her face when the doctor said I would have to have a hysterectomy.

Now that I think about it, I'm sure there were many things my mother was afraid of—thousands of things. As in the case of her regrets, a lot of her fears and anxieties involved me. Since I moved to L.A., where, she's heard, everyone's coking their brains out, she's had fears of my becoming a cokehead and things like that. She still wonders if I eat my veggies, if I'm flossing— Mothers have to have a hands-on thing. They have to see how you look, whether anything's been amputated or fallen off. I'm sure she was devastated when she found out I had polio when I was five.

Five years ago, there might have been things I wished I could ask her or tell her, but by now I've developed an ability to tell my parents how I feel. When you're a child, you use them for all you can. You have to be an adult to understand all the day to day pain and sacrifice that go with parenthood. I don't have any children, and I don't think I would be as good or as dedicated a mother as Mom.

It would interest me to know more about my mother, if it weren't an artificial situation, if I could spend two years with her on a desert island and things would come out naturally. Yet I am happy that I am able to see my mother as a person, and I don't feel as though she is a stranger. Something my parents always did (and this was a real binding force) was to play all kinds of music, much of which was from their teenage years. A certain tune would precipitate a discussion: "Oh, remember when we used to go there?" Those fragments paint a picture of what it was like.

## Syndromes

I'd taken a lot of obstinacy from my father's character and I went through what I call a "pseudo-rebellion," whereby you want to hang out and do your own thing, but you don't want to leave home or pay your own bills. My mother said, "We gotta get her in to see somebody right away." My problem was my father because there was nothing truly objectionable in Mom. One day the therapist asked, "Do you think you can change your father?" I said, "Well, no—not really." That's when I realized that parents are human beings. Parents think they have to be perfect, and they get caught up in that whole syndrome.

My mother is one of those people who measure their happiness by their children's happiness. Now that I'm settled in L.A., happy and achieving something, *she* can be happy, and she has tried to accept me as an adult.

Unfortunately, however, *I'm* most important to my mother. Unfortunately, because I'm mortal. The worst part about having cancer for me (and my worst fear) is the possibility that I would die before my mom. I don't think she would ever be able to enjoy life again. That's my biggest thing.

With our family there isn't too much concern about white-black. Mom has Dennis, I have Danny. I think with my father there might have been a little concern, but my mother is more pragmatic: "Do you like him? Does he like you?" Mom's biggie is having someone who will nurture and not abandon you.

## Good Vibes or "The Way"

If I hadn't had Hazel for my mother, I *know* my personality would be different. I wouldn't be as amiable. I feel a certain ease with people that my mother taught me, a willingness to go with the flow.

I wouldn't have a joy of life if I didn't have my particular ma. That's the way to sum it up because I'm glad to be alive. I would have been less willing to explore. Lately, she's been taking helicopter rides and things. I can't believe my mother—in a helicopter over Niagara Falls! Dennis wanted to hangglide, but Mother wouldn't let him. She said, "I'm not gonna have that."

Another way to sum my mother up is to say that I have never met anyone who didn't genuinely like her. She would have been, not a good sales person—because my mother has a lot of integrity—but a good politician. She is a sincere and lovely person. She probably wouldn't think so, but I do. She gives off good vibes. That's something I had to learn from her.

I remember going through a period having a negative attitude. It was not so much the political climate of the sixties or my social philosophy; it was just a case of teenage hormones—that whiny period. My mother is one of those people who wake up every morning and say, "Good Morning!" They're Mr. Sunshine, and you hate them. I'd say, "What's so good about it?" and my mom would say, "Why don't you just try to turn around your attitude?" I don't think it happened immediately but, as the years went by, I saw that if I just started out the day with "Good Morning," it would go a little easier. That's a very important gift my mother has given me. Especially since I've been in California, the one thing I have going for me is that people like me, not in the way they like my mom—because they *love* her. Maybe it's her face, which is Mona Lisa-like.

She is spiritual but doesn't see herself that way—no confidence. She doesn't put herself down, though; she just doesn't see the gifts that she has. It's not so much that she's humble. Being black, my mother grew up in a time when her gifts were not necessarily considered assets. Perhaps, if she were middle or upper-middle class white, being charming would have been an asset. But "charming" is not the word, and "spiritual" conjures up an image of someone chanting in white robes and that's not what she's about.

Those assets, whatever we may call them, are more marketable now. When I took a job as a teller, the qualities that I have inherited from my mother brought me to the attention of the branch manager. Three years after I had quit that job, I got in touch with him about getting some credit, and he recommended me for a bank officer training program. Because I have only a B.A. and nothing outstanding in my background, I had to market that quality my mother had, a mix of integrity and character, perhaps. Let's put it this way: I would cash my mother's check.

Mother is truly feminine. She has the art of getting her way: She and I were discussing some man and I remember her saying something like, "They don't have to know everything." My friend Georgene and I were talking about men falling all over certain women, and Georgene said that her aunt, who's a little Greek lady, told her once, "They have The Way." So I guess my mom has The Way with people.

I guess it's that she's fair and objective—not judgmental. It's an attitude that I've tried to develop, but my mother has a real control that I haven't been able to master.

I'm almost forty, and there are few people in my life, aside from my mother, who have no negative qualities. I mean, she does, but it's mother stuff, not personality. I've been trying to analyze what makes her extraordinary, what the quality is, exactly. I have no idea of how she developed into the person that she is. When you meet her, you feel comfortable, as if you have an automatic ally. Danny [Mike's boyfriend] even got that over the phone. When she first called Danny "Sweetie," he got all excited: "Oh! that must mean something!"

## The Gift of Life

The hard work of a mother I have just recently, in the last ten years, begun to appreciate. Except for having to work for a living, I'm not unhappy. Since Mom always worked for a living, I said, "Life isn't all that great; why would you view life as a gift? Why would you want a child?" She said she just wanted to give the gift—to *me* (not someone else). If I were to adopt a child, I would have to feel as though I would want to give that gift of life.

I've gotten to the point where I can say, "You know, Mom, I've really begun to appreciate how hard you worked. I don't know how you did it." I've been fortunate because I've been able to tell both of my parents that I love them very much. I know my mother realizes I do, and I hope my father does.

You have to get out and pay your bills to see what your parents went through. They say, "Someday when you are older you will realize..." And they are right. That *was* the best time of my life, and I blew it! I didn't enjoy it, I couldn't wait to be grown, and now I think. "This is boring, I wish I were a kid and all the bills were paid, and I wish I were at that Money Tree. I'd like to have that Money Tree back."

# Moonlight, Candlelight

**V**IVIAN, age 72, the daughter of a Native American, was born in Syracuse, New York. Her family was very poor, especially when her mother had to raise many children alone after her father was institutionalized for alcoholism. Vivian's life was transformed through contact with her high school math teacher. As her daughters Linda and Rosanne say, their mother is a charming and sophisticated woman. Linda, 40, is a bartender in Greenwich Village. Rosanne, in her early thirties, lives with her husband and daughter Erin in Manhattan and is a color consultant and hair stylist. These are three fiery, passionate women.

## VIVIAN BRADT PENOYER

My mother, a beautiful woman with long, black, straight hair all the way down to her hips, was a full-blooded Mohawk who lived on the Onondaga Reservation. I have pictures of her in the very nice costumes of the day—big round hats with flowers on the inside and busty dresses with big white collars.

Her name was Lena, but everyone called her Rose. The only ones I ever heard call her Lena were her mother and brothers and sisters. I used to know her Indian name but have forgotten.

I wish I knew more about my mother's life, but in those days they just didn't talk about themselves that much. There were many times I asked questions, but I must admit, my mother didn't tell me any stories about her Indian life, none at all. I remember asking my grandmother questions, but she'd say, "Oh, you want to know too much, you want to know too much."

*Rose Billings.*

*Rose Billings.*

Now there isn't anyone left to talk to. My mother was born in 1886 in Long Lake, but there are no records in Long Lake. As a little kiddo, she probably lived in a wigwam. Her father, like so many Mohawk people, migrated south for employment and ended up in Syracuse on the Onondaga Reservation. He worked where they grew hops.

My father, who was a redhead, lived in the village of Manlius, where he met my mother, who came from the reservation to work in the glove factory every day. Now my little granddaughter, Erin, is a redhead.

In those days a white man marrying an Indian girl was not totally acceptable. But so many people have told me what a beautiful couple my parents made. My mother had nine children all together. Her firstborn were boy triplets, but they all died. Next she had another boy, and I'm the oldest girl. I was born in Syracuse seventy-two years ago come December. After that I had two more brothers and two sisters. My oldest brother died about three years ago, but the rest of us are still here.

## The Reservation

I wish I knew more about the Indians, but nobody ever talked about being an Indian on a reservation, the discrimination, or that their land had been taken away. My grandmother lived in a log cabin, the last one left on the reservation. We spoke the tongue—that is, Mohawk—because my grandmother spoke very few words of English. My mother would use the tongue only when we'd visit Grandmother. After a while it was difficult for my mother to carry on a conversation because there was much that she had forgotten. Still, she could always understand. It is a shame; I don't remember any of it, not even a word. You do lose touch if you're not with people on a regular basis. You get out of the habit, and your interests change.

## A Ripe Old Age

Both my grandmother and her sister lived until they were 101. Indian women often lived to a ripe old age, even though they were the matriarchs of the family. However, my mother died much younger, at seventy-six.

My grandmother kept a family bible, which is now owned by a cousin of mine. If we want any information we usually call my cousin to see if there's anything written. In fact, when it was time for my mother to get Social Security, we got the records of her birth from the family bible. They were acceptable, since no other records of births and marriages were kept at that time. I have the names of my grandmother and my grandfather, but that's about as far back as I can go. Of course, my grandmother had recorded the names of her children and when and where they were born.

## School Days

I went to elementary school in Nedrow just off the reservation because when my brother and I were small, my mother and father lived there for a while. Then we moved into Syracuse itself and I went to a grammar school there. I must have been around ten when we moved from Syracuse to Manlius, where we've lived ever since. All of us went to the Manlius schools and graduated.

It was a big deal when we came from Syracuse to go to school in Manlius—a couple of Indian kids! Nobody ever really made fun of us for being Indians. It could have been because the Bradt family has been a name in the village for many, many years—and because my mother was so beautiful. Quite acceptable.

I just loved high school. There were only twenty-two in my graduating class, so everyone knew everyone else. Too large a class creates much too much competition.

I've always believed reading is the key to everything. The biggest influence on me was Marion Clapp, my high school math teacher. Marion was very kind to me, and although math was my best subject, she taught me many other things that have enriched my life. I like nice things, and she's the one who introduced me to them—such as a gorgeous sunset and good music. At eighty-five, Marion is still a bright person and a good friend whom I see often. We even took a trip to Europe together about four years ago. A relationship like that is priceless.

I wanted my daughter Linda to see the new pictures I'd taken and was telling her what Marion was like today. I said so many

*Marion G. Clapp, 1985.*

*Vivian, Rosanne, Linda, 1985.*

*Vivian and Linda, 1985.*

people are unaware of the beauty of nature. And why? It's all for free, all for free! We have a beautiful sunset, the glory of a new moon, a full moon. At night we close out the house lights and go into the dark of the night just to see the beauty of it all over again; or as I said to Linda, to observe a flower coming from a bud into full beauty. That I love! And I think my kids like it because it's something I've always done.

## Getting Married

I still keep in touch with other friends, besides Marion, from high school days. Don, my husband, graduated from my high school a year before I did. We really didn't start going together on a serious basis until long after we were through school. Don was Catholic; I was not. We had a very unsympathetic priest who would not permit us to be married at the altar or even *off* the altar. We had to go to the parish house. I didn't think a lot about it at the time because the wedding was simple and quiet, anyway, and it rained torrents that evening.

Sometime after our first two daughters were born, I always took them to church. On St. Blaise's Day, the Blessing of the Throats, I didn't go up to the altar to have my throat blessed. Before the services were over the Father motioned to me and said, "I want to see you." I stayed in the church and he said, "Why didn't you have your throat blessed?" I said, "Well, I'm not Catholic." Then I started taking instructions and became a Catholic, and the children were all reared in the Catholic faith. I liked it, but I think the most difficult part of the Catholic faith for me to accept was the Confession. There was a mess of big changes, and I liked things the old way when it was more private, a quiet place where you could meditate.

## Bootstraps

When I graduated from high school, I went to the village of Skaneateles to wait on tables. As employees, we'd have our choice of whatever we wanted to eat. I had fruit in the morning and always put whipped cream on top. It was a big treat for me.

We were not an affluent family and didn't have all that good food to eat, and I ate until it came out of my ears.

As for interests or hobbies, all I can say is we were poor, *very* poor. My father was a foundry worker most of his life in the city of Syracuse. Then he lost his job out there. That's why we had to go to Manlius to live, where he was able to work again in a foundry. My mother was a beautiful seamstress and also did domestic work. Like most children, I was not conscious of being poor. The Depression had to be horrendous for people who suddenly lost a great deal of money.

My mother raised us six kids single-handed most of the time because my father became ill. In 1929 he was put into an institution, where he remained until he died. Lee, the youngest, was probably about five or six at the time. The two youngest ones used to come and ask me questions about our mother and father—things I could remember that they couldn't. I guess Mother must have done a pretty good job because we've all done quite well for ourselves. Successful and rich none of us is, but we are respectable and well-liked in the community—never brought shame on anyone, so to speak, and we're self-sufficient. We had to be.

How would I be different without the mother I had? I couldn't even think of such a thing! That is something I couldn't possibly change. No way. What I got from my mother that I wouldn't want to live without is a sense of survival and self-sufficiency.

I don't know how my mother managed or how she instilled this self-sufficiency in us. We just brought ourselves up by our bootstraps, I guess. Everyone helped everyone else: when the older ones went to work, we helped. I think those who went through the Depression had to learn very fast if they were going to survive. None of us went to college. College in those years was really a big deal. What often happened is that families let the young men be educated but thought it wasn't necessary for the women. Imagine that! At the time, these women might not have resented it, but, depending upon how things came about with their lives, no doubt they did later on.

My mother and I were very close, as close as we could be. She never talked about her marriage, and she had to have a very unhappy life because of my father's alcoholism. Perhaps it was difficult for him to accept the responsibility of a big family. The younger boys, not having lived in the environment with my mother and father together, were sympathetic with my father and spent a lot of time visiting him. They didn't understand how difficult it was for my mother, how hard she had to work to keep us together, how unhappy a life she had had. Because I was older and saw what was going on, I sympathized with my mother, and my visits to my father were few and far between.

## Friends with the Family

I don't recall that Mother had any really good friendships the whole time she was raising her family. When her mother was still alive, she would go to see her on a regular basis, and she was more or less friends with members of her husband's family. I remember my grandmother on my father's side; she was an Eastman, but I don't know if she was a part of the Rochester Eastmans or not.

The only real lack I feel is not knowing our family history. I really should delve into it, but I don't. The kids don't have the interest that I have. They've been too far removed, although they both loved my mother. She spent a lot of time at our house as my two older girls were growing up.

## Children First

My children are the most important thing to me, over and above my husband. I'm sure Don knows that, as, I'm sure, most men do. My mother felt the same way about her children. Oh, heavens yes! No doubt in my mind whatsoever. As for her hopes for us, my mother didn't talk about that sort of thing, but I'm sure that unconsciously we all learned a great deal from her. In her silent way she taught a way of life, I suppose, which was keeping body and soul together. Some of that had to have rubbed off on us six kids. Even though we don't talk a lot or do a lot together, we're always there for each other.

Like my own mother, I don't know that there was anything particular that I wanted my daughters to learn from me. They would learn from living. I don't think I ever talked to them about being a wife and mother. Whatever they learned of love and marriage was just being there with Don and with me. It's not all a bed of roses, believe me, which they both well know because Linda was once married and Rosanne was married once before.

The girls went through high school, and Linda went on to college. I wish she had stayed in Syracuse to continue her college, but she went to Oklahoma. That was her choice, and she did most of that herself. We made it as possible as we could for her; we got her started. Rosanne didn't want any part of college but never said why.

## Doing Their Thing

After her graduation, Rosanne moved to New York City. I was not especially worried. Of course, Linda was down there, too. Don helped Rosanne move down the first time, but he would "never ever" go there again. He knows who he is and what he wants. I enjoy visiting the girls, and even though I wouldn't want to live there, I can say, "Don, you're not young like them and it's a different world today. They're basically the same people they were; they're just doing their thing. How can you deny them? They've done all right."

It wouldn't have occurred to me to live in the city. I love to go down to New York because I love going to the plays and have spent a lot of time going to some of the museums and art galleries. If I were living there, I would take advantage of all of that. I don't think my kiddos do.

With regard to my daughters, I don't have any guilt feelings. Rosanne and Linda, once they were all grown up, began to ask questions about sex, and I don't find it that easy to talk about sex. I am not interested in their sex life, and I don't expect them to be interested in mine. I'm sure my response wasn't all that good. Probably, my generation would have done better if we had been able to speak more openly about sex and the whole thing, but it wasn't done when I was young. Otherwise, I'd give an honest answer, but, then, they didn't always ask things. After all, the kids today know more than their parents do.

I had a rough time with my firstborn Andrea, who had epilepsy for many years, starting when she was a young teenager.

She did well for four years, when she met a young man who convinced her she didn't need medication. Naturally, the troubles all started again, and the engagement was off, as well. At the age of twenty-seven, Andrea died, apparently having a seizure. It was a big blow for us, probably Rosanne more than we know because she was still home and saw a lot of Andrea. And it was just a couple of weeks before Rosanne's graduation. There isn't a *day* that goes by that Andrea is not with me. Not a day. Unless you go through losing a child, you just never know. You just never know.

I can't imagine life without children. It's an experience that you can't possibly compare to any other. They're a great source of pleasure to you when you get older. I'm not saying one *should* be a mother; I'm just stating a fact, that you have to be a mother to know the greatest love in the world. The love of a man for a woman, a woman for a man is different. A mother is going to consider that child before taking care of husband. That's as far as I'm concerned, and I think most mothers will say that. Biology must have everything to with it—*everything* to do with it. Yes, I would die for my children. My husband would very likely come second in importance. What would be third? I'm stumped. Well, my independence is very important. That's uppermost in everyone's mind—or should be.

## Money Aside

I haven't always had my total independence. It's too bad to have to equate independence with money, but it certainly has helped me a lot. From the day I started to work, I started putting a little money aside for my use as I saw fit, without having to depend on someone to dole it out to me. With the three kids, I couldn't always have that kind of independence; but when my children were old enough, I'd get back into the market again to earn money.

When the NRA came through in '33, I was working in the five and ten cent store earning eleven dollars a week. Then I haunted the office of accounting at Ma Bell in Syracuse until the man finally hired me. Oh, but I did lots of other things, including selling the first group of Tupperware that came out.

The very first thing I bought from that money was a piano so the girls could have lessons. I always had a little set aside that no one knew anything about, and as time went on and things got better as far as earning money was concerned, I just kept adding to it. Today I'm very happy to say I don't have to spend Don's money for what I want: I can get it myself.

When I was a child, I'm sure I didn't dream about what I wanted to be. Because of the financial situation there was nothing. How could you dream for something? I never resented that I didn't go to college; you might say I made that choice myself. We had the family, and that's about it: you have to take care of the children. But my life would probably have been a great deal different if I had chosen to go to college.

# LINDA PENOYER

All I know about my mother's early life is that they were very poor. My grandmother worked very hard because my grandfather, even at a young age, was rather inept. Shortly after my mother was born, something went wrong, and he disappeared, to return only to produce five more children. My mother was considered the black sheep in that family—outspoken, protective of the younger ones. Early on, she got out and earned money. They all did. They had no choice.

God, I don't even know what her first job was. I think she was selling something. I know that at a very young age, she went to work at a phone company, but I don't know whether that was before or after high school. In any case, she did work while still in school. She started becoming a clothes horse right away and was also spending a lot of money on her mother. She always loved nice things, and even though she was poor, she figured out a way to have them. My mother can get so excited about a silver candelabra: It's gorgeous, glorious! As far as I can see, the basis of her whole life was working. You want it? You can have it. You must work.

My father was a very good provider and supporter of his family, but my mother wasn't happy unless she had her own money. She managed, even with three children, to put money away.

## *Love of Life*

Her kids were important, too, of course, but boy, her independence! Her theory she's passed on to me was that if you pay your own way, you don't have to answer to anyone.

In terms of life in general, she has an incredible reverence. I think that's why she was so deeply religious at one time. She has loved life, and that's more important than anything. It's also why she's growing old so gracefully. She's not afraid; she's dealt with things right on, right up front.

This morning she was lying in bed with me, and she said, "Why don't you put your bed over there beneath that window?" I said, "Well, I don't want it there because the moon travels on this side of the house, and I love the moonlight shining on my bed." She giggled—and I know why. It's because I got that from her. Just this morning she said, "Do you realize how many people are walking around out there in this world who have never watched a flower bloom? There are so many little things, like moonlight, that give solace, but most people are oblivious to them." She wandered in the back yard last night to follow the full moon.

I feel that my mother never really had an opportunity to do and to express all the things that she's capable of. She wants one of us to do it, and we don't. She has class and style and sophistication and an understanding of people. I can't say that I know what her influence on other people has been because I have not lived in her community since I was seventeen years old. I'm forty now so that means I have been away from home for twenty-three years. But I know mother is loved and respected. She's very good about being there for someone who is in need and is a loyal friend.

Living in today's world, she would be a great businesswoman or a terrific saleswoman. She never got to do any of that. I think it's terrible that she didn't. Her teacher and friend offered to send her to college, but her obligation was elsewhere. Like me, she's much more comfortable giving than receiving: "Why would you do this for *me?* I'm not worthy." In her time college was for rich people only. Maybe she didn't think she could compete because she was raised in such poverty. Every now and then, late in the evening, I've heard her say, "Oh, I made a big mistake in not going to normal school."

I remember when I was fourteen years old I wanted a kilt and some Nina Ricci "L'Air du Temps" perfume for Christmas. My mother knew I wanted it. She said, "Okay, if you want it, you can have it, but you're going to have to work for it." I was scared to death. I wanted her to go and take a job interview for me. She said, "No, no, you get *yourself* a job."

So I worked when I was in high school, and I started buying myself clothes. I was doing exactly the same thing she was doing. I don't think she realized how much she passed that on to me. To this day I don't have any respect for someone who doesn't work. God, if you're not working, you'd better be doing *something*.

I've never, ever thought of her as being dependent on my father. He was a laborer, a wonderful, jolly, entertaining guy who drinks like a fish. But, my God, he worked, and he'd do anything for us kids. Whenever he'd say, "For poor people we have a lot of fun," it would really bother me: Are we poor? Is that what it is? From my mother the hidden message was, "If I weren't working, you wouldn't have any nice things, the fringe benefits." My mother carries herself like a wealthy woman. Maybe it's in her stars, but she has aristocracy in her—and a lot more dignity than Rosanne and I or anyone else in her family. I'm more hanging out, like my father.

## Follow Your Heart

My mother sat down with me and said, "Look, your father and I have done everything we can do. This is it; you're on your own." I said, "Okay, fine," because I wanted to go to college.

I'm forever grateful to her for that. She sent me off on a journey. She released me and did me the biggest favor of my life, a favor she never did for Rosanne. I don't think she even realizes she gave me my independence. I adore her, I love her, I respect her more than any person on this earth, but I don't owe her any money. It's not like, "I sacrificed everything for you." She never laid any of that trip on me. She let me go.

I had the problems that everybody else had dealing with life, but I followed my heart and was willing to experience new things, all the things that she would have done. Follow your heart, be adventurous, take on new experiences, embrace the world as much as you can—that's what she's been trying to do all her life, and so have I.

My mother never approved of any of my relationships. We parted company because of it. At that time, it was largely over the issue of the Church. My mother was an extremely devout convert. I knew she couldn't handle it when I left the Church, though I was too young to know why. When my sister Andrea died, something happened to my mother vis à vis the Church. I'm sure she still believes in God because the woman has faith in the world and the universe and love and nature like nobody else. But she relaxed her devout practice and absolutely refused to discuss it. I've had a million theories since. I was living in Oklahoma and she was here. I was very involved with a man I ended up marrying, and she did not approve of him at all. At times she expresses what seems to be a regret that she set me so free—because when she said I was "on my own," I took it literally.

I haven't talked to my mother lately, and I need to. I'd love to talk about how enriched my life has become from the people I have loved, regardless of what she thinks of them. Working as a bartender and waitress, I don't even have a career she can embrace. Yet in spite of it all, I know she really adores me. I'm absolutely nuts about her.

I don't make time to spend with her alone. The last two times I went home there were too many people around. She has said, "Oh, I can't stand it. I want you to come home when nobody's here."

Sometimes I'm confident that she will be accepting, and other times I'm not. See, I'm not afraid of her disapproval. I want her to know that I've gone on and learned despite it. But what she does (and I understand this) is to say, "Linda, you've always done what you wanted, and I want you to continue that." There's a finality in even that.

But I would not invade her privacy. If she says, "I don't want to talk about it," I won't press the matter. She is not causing my life any grief. My god, she's seventy-three, I'm forty. The best that I can share with her at this point is how grateful I am to her, how much I care about her, and I want to make sure her older years are comfortable and loving. I'm not interested in sending her into any kind of catharsis at this point. I want nothing more than to look her straight in the eye and tell her how happy I am. In her heart of hearts she *senses* how much I try to grow. But I want to *tell* her, I want her to really *get* it.

## The Red Tutu

My mother taught us simply by being who she is, by example. We've always respected who she was, the way she spoke, the way she regarded life. Along with that reverence for life, integrity, and the value of work, she wanted to make sure I knew about worldly sorts of things, and she gave us a taste of class and loveliness. She used to take Andrea and me into the city, always making sure that we were in lovely dresses in lovely surroundings. At home she wore lovely dressing gowns, and we ate by candlelight. In my own place people will ask me, "Why are you lighting the candles? What's the big deal about tonight?" I say, "The big deal is we're together having dinner." And that's what my mother always said.

She made the comment yesterday, "Linda, you've always lived in a fantasy world." I was laughing because she was the one who exposed me to the drama and glamour of things, shimmering silk, the exaltation of Bette Davis. My mother thinks she's ordinary and I'm some sort of weirdo. In reality she's quite unconventional. One night she put on this red tutu we have here, and she danced all over this house! If you were to go down there right now and ask her about it, she'd play it down, but I'll tell you, that night my mother was the prima ballerina of the New York Ballet. I love for my mother to get wild and crazy! Friends say, "Linda, you're so melodramatic. Where do you get all this bullshit?" I say, "Aw, I get it from my mother." I've got a whole drag closet, and I drag out all kinds of things. In fact, I was a theater major. I'm not an actress, but everyone thinks I am.

You see, I'm really outside of my mother and am able to see her as a person. What I like most about her is her individuality, her privacy as an individual. She says, "Each of us has a private cathedral that no one can go to." She's very private, I'm very private. We don't have any big investment in being well-liked.

That's integrity. My mother's loaded with it. The women of her generation had *such* integrity—not that we don't but they had even more. They would never lie, never try to get an extra dollar for work they didn't do. My mother does not burden anyone, takes care of her own business. I learned that from her. I will talk about my joy and the beautiful flowers but not what's wrong in my life.

Still, I hope she lives long enough to talk more about herself, maybe with the grandchildren. I have a feeling that nothing but wonderful things are going to happen to her as she gets older. I don't think she's going to get any kind of disease. Her life is going to be one mellow journey from here on out. Before she dies, I really want her to know how much I admire her. Yet I think even if she died right at this moment, I would not experience regrets about her because I feel such an affinity with her, a real connection. We have been through the mill together. I've done all the worst things that I could possibly do to disappoint her, but I don't regret any of that because I feel good about what I've learned, and I think that my mother does not want for me to feel guilty. Rosanne gives me more static about going home than my mother does. I have not been home for Christmas since my sister died fifteen years ago. I've been at my own place in New York or Poughkeepsie. My mother respects all of that, even though it's very different from what she had in her life.

Now that she's retired, I worry about what she's doing; I suspect she's pretty bored. A few years ago she went on a cruise. My dad had no interest in going. I said, "Mother, I hope on your cruise you'll meet some guy who is fabulous and you'll go to bed with him," and she says to me, "How can you say that with your father still alive?" She adores my dad. I said, "Don't be a martyr, Mother. You're going on a cruise by yourself, you're a sexy seventy-three-year-old woman who is really fifty, you've got a beautiful wardrobe, you're going to be dancing and hanging out and having a wonderful time!" Goddammit, if she had a man in her life who would show her attention and take her around, she would live another twenty years. Instead, she's sitting in Manlius reading books while my father sits and drinks and watches football on TV.

I would like to see her fall in love, have an affair, experience that abandonment of love. I'd like to see her experience youth and aliveness once again. I want her to live all those romantic things she's read about, fantasized about. She's not at the age where she can start up a business. What could she do that would be new and different? Find a man to travel with! Listen, my mother is the type who, if she were in Vienna dining in a lovely restaurant and wearing a lovely gown, would love to get up and dance to the music of violins, experience the luxury of lovely evenings in a beautiful foreign land. Yes! That's what I see for her.

I can see her now, in a sequined gown, on a trip down the Nile River, moonlight hanging over, a handsome man coming over and bowing: "Vivian, would you like to dance?"

# ROSANNE PENOYER

I don't know that much about my mother's childhood. I guess I heard more about that from my father than from my mother, but that's probably because he was more of a country person than my mother was. I know she was on the women's basketball team at Manlius High School. I've got pictures of the team. I don't think we ever discussed what her best subjects were; I have a feeling it was English. Recently, I have realized that my mother has a wonderful writing talent. She has written a few things that have brought me to tears. Linda has that gift, too.

## Keeping Up

Mother is so aware and alive, and she keeps up. That's one of the wonderful things about her: she's just all there as best as she can be, as much as she can handle, stuff that my father never even found out about, so it was strictly hers to deal with and accept or not accept. People of all ages can communicate with her because she's real; she doesn't block out half the world.

Mother missed out on a lot because she was born in the wrong time. With women's liberation and all, Mother's life would have been a lot different if she'd been born even twenty years later than she was. Mother is very worldly, and my father is very much a homebody.

She was twenty-six when she married, which was probably considered old in that time. Marion Clapp offered to send Mother to college, and she didn't do it. I guess she fell in love. Personally, I can't say it's for the better to give up for the sake of marriage—at least, not in my mother's case. My mother tried to persuade me to wait to get married, but not with any pressure. I was too young, but, of course, when you're twenty, you think you know everything. As you find out later, you don't. Nobody can live someone else's experiences. I'm not looking forward to going through the same thing with my daughter Erin. I want Erin to grow up feeling free to speak her mind. That's definitely a value I got from my mother. If you think differently than somebody else, it's okay. Moving to New York right out of high school was one of the best things I ever did for myself. I could be wild and crazy and different without worrying what people think. I wish my mother hadn't lived in a small town, so that she could have gotten away from that, but she says she would never have wanted to live in New York City. She'd certainly fit right in, though. She's definitely cosmopolitan and has always been different even now at her age.

As a new mother, I can relate to Mom more as an equal. Linda can too, but she has no way to share being a mother, and it's amazing what that can bring to a mother-daughter relationship. There's just no other experience that can serve that same purpose. If you have had a bad relationship with your parents, I don't know if you'd feel this way, but I have a new respect that I didn't have before. For example, when I was a young adult living at home, I'd come home at two or three in the morning, and there was Mother sitting at the table. I'm feeling guilty and she's telling me, "I was so worried about you." At eighteen you say, "Mother, there's nothing to worry about. I'm okay." Well, *now* I understand exactly where she was at.

My mom and dad knew each other in high school, but they didn't date until a few years later. It was a double date, and they ended up falling in love. My father is a very good-looking man. None of us looks like our mom, unfortunately. I could kill for the Indian nose and hair. Her own mother's hair was long and dark; it never got gray. Mother had her own hair long until a couple of years ago, when I finally convinced her to cut it off. She started growing her hair after Andrea died. Later she told me all that hair must have been her "mourning veil." I noticed that in general Mom seemed more relaxed without the weight that had been on her shoulders for fifteen years. Now that I have my own daughter, I can imagine how hard even a child's *illness* can be on a mother. Mom didn't talk much about it, but just a year ago she told me that the Church refused to bury Chic [Andrea] in the same cemetery as the rest of Mom's family because it's not a Catholic cemetery.

I really hate to say this, but I think Mother values her children more than anything else. It's what keeps her alive and up on things because we are always zinging her with outside stimuli—not that she doesn't seek on her own. I fact, if she hadn't had children, her life would be totally different. She'd have a profession or a business—something glamorous like a modeling agency. Without Mother I wouldn't have the good taste that I have. She always had dress-up drawers for us, and we were encouraged to be dramatic. She never pressed us to do anything, and it's hard to put into specifics what she had in mind for us. You can say all the usual things—honesty, morality, blah, blah—but I don't know that Mother actually thought that out in her head. *I* don't; I had lots of ideas before my daughter was born, but they all went out the window. You just lead your life in deference to your core being and hope that will impress your children.

I've come to know Mother quite well, having become more inquisitive since Erin's birth. If we're in a comfortable setting, Mother will answer almost anything. As children, if we wanted only a "yes" answer, we'd go to Dad. I don't think Mom knew her father very well, which is not unusual even for our generation. Fathers were there to bring home the paycheck, and that was it. I do hope it will be different for Erin's generation.

Materially, I had more than Linda because when Linda was little, Chic was growing up, too. By the time I was eight, Linda was away at college so there was more money at home. Without question, Linda resented having to pay for college; then, when she married, there was a definite rift between Mom and her. They love each other and get along fine, but I hope Linda can work things out because she'll regret it if she doesn't. It seems to me it's something she's got to work out by herself, not even with Mother. Maybe if she had a child, she would understand. My own understanding is a recent development. Because of Erin, I do get to spend more time with Mother, which has a lot to do with it. Personally, although I feel funny saying this, I believe I have a better sense of who Mother really is and what she really wants than Linda has. I may be entirely wrong. Someday Linda and I might talk about that, but it won't be very soon.

I would have to say, because of Mother's need to be self-sufficient and independent, that health is second in importance. She's had too many limits through life to now be limited by ill health. She worked very hard to have her own money.

She gave my father a big surprise when they retired. He thought they had very little money. They both get Social Security, but we all know none of that amounts to very much, and Dad doesn't have a very large pension. He was getting ready to knuckle under, when she presented him with her secret nest egg. That's what keeps them in the comforts to which they have become accustomed. And Dad was taken aback when he found that out. He says, "You *what?*" He thought it was wonderful, but... she had pulled something over on him. She wielded more power than he ever knew. Everything we had was because of Mother—the extras, the things that make life wonderful and fun. Always candles! Women are amazing.

*Beth and Nancy. Beth is going off to camp.*

# Olympic Material

**N**ancy Thomsen Heiden, 50, herself the athletic daughter of athletic parents, was a big force behind her son Eric and her daughter Beth, both of whom won medals at the 1980 Olympics. Nancy lives with her husband Jack in Madison, Wisconsin, where she was raised. Beth, 26, lives with her husband Russell in northern Michigan, where they both teach mathematics at Michigan Technological University. Whether consciously or unconsciously, Nancy made it possible for her daughter to lead the still untraditional lifestyle of a woman athlete. It is a gift for which Beth is very grateful.

## NANCY THOMSEN HEIDEN

When the children were competing, they were always referred to as "the children of Dr. Jack Heiden." I thought, what the heck? Jack goes off to work in the morning, and I'm the one driving them to Milwaukee, driving them around every night, arranging the meals, calling people to make sure everything runs smoothly.

Olympic athletes aren't just born. It's like a good violinist starting young in a family who played a lot of music; or a good mathematician in a family who played math games when they drove around in a car. We have plenty of stories about our kids putting on skates and going out to grandma's.

### Activity, Activity

My parents live on Lake Mendota in Madison where I grew up. We always shoveled a rink, had lights for night skating. So

Beth and Eric started when they were very small. Eric was only two and a half when Jack laced his skates and took him out on the lake. Eric kept falling down. Finally, he looked up at Jack and said, "I'm too little to skate!" Jack said, "We'll take you back in another day or two." Skating is what we all did and the kids wanted to be with us. Our children could have been very naughty if we hadn't done a lot with them because they had so much energy. We had no plan; we were just active. In fact, Jack and I met skiing. When we lived in university housing, we'd pack our lunch and meet Eric and Beth at the school rink, skate, and then go home. We made time for activities like that.

The kids were self-motivated. Of course, you subconsciously motivate others, too. Grandma and Grandpa were active, so Eric and Beth had two sets of adults who did things with them. Eric and Beth learned to depend on their grandparents for emotional support and direction.

I come from a background of athleticism. For thirty years my father was professor of physical education and Director of Intramural Sports at the University of Wisconsin. He had the biggest intramural sports program in the Big Ten. My parents were both athletic in a time when most women—and men— were not athletic. My mother was a diver, and my father, a competitive swimmer who won international awards, even swam against Johnny Weissmuller. He also played hockey and was a three-letter athlete at the University of Wisconsin.

Unlike most cities, Madison has a lot of open space; kids are free to move around. Madison is an ideal place to raise children because of the opportunity to pursue anything and everything. We have great running groups, the University Natatorium's fifty-meter indoor pool that the swimming club used, and the kids trained at the University track. The tennis stadium with twelve indoor courts was only eight blocks from our house.

I grew up in an active household. Sunday afternoons were reserved for hiking. We lived on the far west side of Madison, where there was open woods. We swam a lot, and I went to a private girls' camp in Saugatuck, Michigan. We did a lot of working on our personalities and our characters, so that we'd grow up to be the wonderful wife for some wonderful husband. I was sent away to become a "lady." Did I become one? Well, no. The training did not affect me, though. I'd be very comfortable when I sat down to a bowl of soup with the king of Norway. I knew which spoon to take and how to smile politely.

My mother must have considered Madison an outpost because my parents went back home to Milwaukee to have me, then took me back to "the outpost." So I spent a lot of time in Milwaukee with all my relatives scattered over the northeast section of Milwaukee. My mother, who's of Yugoslavian descent, still identifies strongly with her ethnic group and siblings in Milwaukee. Even though my father became more entrenched in Madison, he gave my mother a lot of space. Since Milwaukee was only seventy miles away, she would go there quite often.

## Mom's Influence

My mother influenced my life less than my father did. Mom was in the background. I was firstborn, too. That's hard, since the firstborn must break the way. Parents new to raising a child are always nervous. Mom knew what she wanted me to be like, but I don't think I really satisfied her. She has always favored my brother.

My mom was kind, good, and demanding, and I was proud of her. Both my parents were active community people. My mother is a college graduate, which is unusual for first-generation immigrants' children. I admired that and the stories my mother tells about paying her way through school and still feeling obliged to send money home, which is a European tradition, and about studying late at night and getting up and tutoring other people's children. Dad, of course, was able to work in the athletic department at the University, so he had regular hours. Men athletes were taken much better care of than women students. My dad was a big entity on campus; doors were open for him that were not open for women. My mother influenced me to go to college, have a family, and conduct my life as a middle-class lady "should." It's significant that my formative years were in the forties, and my high school and college years were in the fifties—directly out of the Second World War era, when girls were girls. Peripherally I followed that, but Madison is a little different and its schools are different. You're given a little more space to express yourself. In grade school, the girls could play on a softball team at noon if they liked—and I did. In

seventh and eighth grade, I was a cheerleader because I wanted
to be a part of the In Group. I *was* in the most important clique in
high school. We were the ones who ran the school. My mom felt
good about that because she liked my friends. I was president of
the pep club. Beth went to the same high school but turned off
that scene because of the Yuppy young ladies who didn't
participate in sports. Beth was part of an athletic group who were
all pals.

My mother put her foot down on cheerleading in high school
because it wasn't ladylike. We've about cancelled the
cheerleaders now. We were convinced that if there were going to
be cheerleading, it would have to be for girls' athletics, too,
which is producing just as many state champions.

When Beth was at school, I didn't like the high school tennis
program and wrote letters about upgrading it. After Beth
graduated, the principal called and said, "OK, put your money
where your mouth is. What would you do if we hired you?" For
the last seven years I've been coaching varsity tennis with
another lady, and we continue to work on women's attitudes
toward sports.

## Joining In

When Eric and Beth were growing up, I did what they did. If
they swam, I swam. When they played tennis, I started upping
my tennis skills. Beth and I went off to Harry Hopman's in
Florida a couple years with another girl and her mom. We went
down for about ten days in the spring and geared up for summer.

Here's how the kids got into speed skating. One Saturday,
when we didn't have anything else to do, we decided to go to the
city races. Eric and Beth did well in the speed skating competition, and people were telling them to take up speed skating. I
said, "Over my dead body! We're not going to do anything that
unrefined. We're going to figure skate."

Nonetheless, figures were a little too confining for my kids.
Within two years they were into speed skating training and
having fun. We had good coaches in Madison and a good active
club. Kids came from all over for training. Our house was the hub
of activity because we kept all the national team equipment in
our gymnasium. It was important to get the Europeans here

because Eric and Beth would only see them when competing in Europe in the winter. Many of their parents came too. My food bill! Incredible!

## Heavy Commitment

As I look back, I think I would say no to committing that kind of time. Is that what one should do with one's life? It took its toll on the kids—and on me. The public just descended on us. It was grim. People with suitcases stood at our door at seven a.m., expecting to stay.

Afterward, both Eric and Beth were pretty good at getting their act together. They put their skates on a peg on the wall in 1980, and that was it. Speed skating is nothing but going around in a circle. It's not a recreational sport.

## Going North

Now, it's six hours from our house to Beth's in Upper Michigan. We don't even consider that traveling. I get lonesome at seven in the morning: "Are you there? Fine, we'll come up." Then we hop in the car with two bikes, Jack's racing scull, and the kayak on top and all the different sets of clothing and my tennis racket in back. And we ski a lot. Compared to the kids I'm not competitive. I get on a bike, and I say, "Look, there's a hawk up there!" and "Wait a minute, you guys, there's a trillium down here!"

I like the idea that Russell and Beth live in a small town up north because they're both so trusting, and I would fear for them if they lived in a big city. Beth is dauntless, and there are people who play with a different set of rules than she does. In Madison, when I'm alone outdoors, I get so angry that I have to take a chance or even *think* I'm unsafe outside. I say, "Leave me alone, I'm birdwatching," or "Leave me alone, I'm taking a walk."

I do express my fears to Beth—especially now that she's older. You don't do that with young children because you might frighten them. You have to give them a pretty secure, insulated life so they don't run off with all sorts of neuroses. I often tell Beth I love her. We're not a family that ruminates, and there's always somebody's activities we're talking about or what is going on in the bike circles. Jack doesn't like to dwell on the emotional side of things.

With Beth I don't want to be oppressive. It's up to her to take from me what she wants and to do what she wants with her life... but I wish she could be more feminine. She loves to sew, and I'm always showing her patterns. She could wear makeup once in a while. It's a nuisance, I know; but when you get to be fifty, you have to augment what you have. I wear makeup when I go out in the evening or if I go to lunch or downtown because there are some slick nifty Yuppy ladies walking around in the capital. I remember raising the issue that I would like her to wear lipstick for her wedding, and she did. We're getting there, but Beth is a late bloomer. Just a week ago she said, "Everything seems out of perspective." She had grown an inch this year!

## Feminism

Women growing up in my time were told to go to college to make a better home, create a more intellectual environment, and make a better mate. But I had other intellectual desires and career motivations that were hard to put away. I taught for a while, and I would like to have been a school administrator. It's hard now to look back and say, "I could have been that." On the other hand, I'm lucky to be where I am.

I never encouraged homemaking. I made it clear to Beth that washing dishes and cleaning her room were not as important as studying and carrying on with her life. Yet it was very important to me to make sure that things were all tidied up so that everyone could function. It's a real dilemma; there seems to be no way to have a relationship, a loving family home, and everybody producing without a housekeeper to run the show. Two power heads in one family can create a very stressful atmosphere. But, then, why educate women only to put them in a house to clean toilets? It was necessary for the active feminists to irritate the system, but now it's *everyone's* responsibility to *keep* things moving in an egalitarian direction. So far things haven't been kept moving very well.

It's easier now that my time is my own. I do more than play.

I'm involved in environmental issues and legislation in Madison. This past spring, I've been in meetings a lot, working on a $400,000 fundraising for the Dane County Natural Heritage Foundation. I'm not happy doing it, but I feel it's necessary. I also work as a naturalist for the University Arboretum, so I do have some credentials in that area. I'm embroiled in an environmental issue right now. After I figured out that I couldn't teach any more, I started taking classes in environmental issues, and my work at the Arboretum is inspiring. And I can get on my bike and go. That helps. I couldn't do that until my kids were gone.

Anyway, I do talk to Beth; in fact, she's more frank with me than I am with her because I come from a background that taught women not to let everybody know what's going on. You talk to other women, but you don't expose yourself to your children or your husband—which I'm learning to do now whether they like it or not.

## BETH HEIDEN REID

My mom grew up differently from me, and once I was out of high school, she'd often say, "Oh, you're doing everything I wish I'd done." I thought, "Oh, no!" I was surprised since I wasn't very sociable. I didn't want to go to the mixers or the proms. That had been a big part of my mom's life. All along she'd say, "Well, don't you want to do that?" or "Wouldn't you like to have a potluck here for the girls in your class?" I think she was concerned that I wasn't interested at all.

One year at prom time Mom thought, "Beth needs someone to go to the prom with." When I found out she set me up with a friend's brother, I was so mad. I said, "Mother, the reason I'm not going is I don't want to go." Then when I was a senior, I was nominated for prom queen. I went through with it so people wouldn't think I was a snob. Anyway—I guess because they all knew me from the '76 Olympics—I ended up being queen. I didn't tell my mother. I was so embarrassed. No way I wanted her to know. I didn't want anyone to know. When my mom found out from her friend, she said, "Why didn't you tell me? It's just wonderful!"

*Beth, University of Vermont ski team. (Copyright © 1983 Nancie Battaglia)*

## *The Clothes Problem*

I'd never shopped for clothes. Mom would come home with stuff for us. Of course, when you're little, your mom will lay out the clothes you're supposed to wear for school. Well, my mother did that all the way through junior high. She'd say, "Isn't this nice, Beth?" and I'd say, "No, I don't need it." Poor Mom! I really feel bad now because she probably spent a lot of time on it. Once she quit, I wore only slacks. I think that was my brother Eric's influence. When I had to go to the prom, I had to have her pick out my dress.

Ultimately, she accepted the way I was. I don't think she minded that I wasn't conforming to the normal role. It was just, "Don't you want to go to Homecoming?" Since she would have wanted to go, she assumed I would, too. Socializing must have been important to her. She married a doctor, which is a social thing, I think. Why else would anyone marry a doctor? They're always working. We saw very little of my father, except that he did spend all of his free time with us. Maybe it was part of Mom's identity to have social status. I've never asked her about that—and I don't think I will.

I don't know how much other mothers talk to their daughters, but Mom was always there when I needed her. She was always consistent in her affection and being behind us. All the training for my skating plus studying was tough. I'd be ready to fall apart, and she'd be there.

I'm just realizing: I know lots of stories about my dad and none of my mom. That's amazing. Maybe it's just that I ask my grandparents and not her, but anything I know about her has come from them. Mom did tell us a few stories about her various boyfriends, Billy Daggett and so-and-so, and about getting pinned. She always took the straight line. She went to the University of Wisconsin but lived at home. She studied art and education; in fact, she even taught kindergarten for one year before we were born.

## *Stealing Apples*

I do remember her saying that at a skating party one of her buddies went through the lake. But that's about it. I'm sure she's told me about canoe trips, and my grandparents told me about the kids stealing apples at the orchard.

If I have kids, will I tell them about me? I might. When they hear about my brother's skating, they'll find out that I skated. I don't want them to feel they have to be an athlete. So I might be a bad mom and not tell any stories.

In Madison my grandparents bought the land on Lake Mendota where they still live. It used to be much different there when my mom was little—fields all around—and now it is the west side of the city. As Mom was growing up, she went to a lot of camps. I have a photo of us the day I went off to Red Pine Camp for Girls in Minocqua where Mom had been a camp counselor.

## Gingerbread Men

Now that Eric and I have left, Mom has more time to do what she wants. That's neat. She's going to be fifty this year, I think. I don't even know—maybe forty-nine. She was considered active for her time. In fact, they called her "Tommy"—and here I think of her as "sociable." I know she liked hiking. She knits a lot, and I know she liked art when she was in college. In fact, Eric and I ended up in art class; obviously she was responsible for that. She painted when we painted. She was always real good with making construction paper into something fun—things that kids like to do. When my parents first married, she made all their Christmas tree ornaments. One year she made little origami round-shape things and hung them up on the trees. Another year she made gingerbread men, which after a while were all gone up to a certain level on the tree. Mom said that we'd leave half their bodies. That was as high as we could get our teeth.

Mom never expressed any regrets to me about her own life. She talked about politics. She was really involved with the abortion issue and spent time lobbying for family planning. She worked at the local Planned Parenthood clinic serving the whole county and helped with fundraising dinners for local candidates. She liked Mondale-Ferraro. So, she let us know her opinions, and as a result I was a staunch believer that abortion is okay and two kids are the right number and that environmental issues are so important.

Mom's into birding and is a guide at the University of Wisconsin's Arboretum in Madison—a true naturalist. She's converted our own yard into a prairie by bringing in all the native prairie specimens. She also works for the Natural Heritage Foundation which acquires land and sets it aside for preservation.

## Competition

Our main sport was speed skating, and I did well in a lot of other sports too—track and tennis and biking. I heard about women not being equal in sports, but I myself didn't encounter discrimination. It was probably a case of all the feminists paving the way before me. So there wasn't a girls' soccer team? I didn't care: *I* got to play with the boys. My mom made it seem so acceptable, the natural thing to do, so for me it wasn't even an issue. And my dad always treated Eric and me alike. Maybe that's why I'm a tomboy. I remember how my mother first got involved in running, when we were eleven or twelve. The Madison speed skating club couldn't find a summer coach, so she agreed to guide and run with us. Oh, and she's a good tennis player and bikes lots of miles each week—a lot farther than I can. Well, maybe not, but her butt could take it. My mom lost a lot of weight once Eric and I were no longer her main focus. I never could understand why she didn't want to compete. She would go running every morning with a neighbor, always at the same leisurely pace—never faster, never farther. On the other hand, she has ranked in state tennis tournaments. Still, she'd rather just go for a bike ride.

I'm not nearly as competitive as I used to be. It was hard to go to school, get a university education, and skate at the same time. I quit when I was only twenty. Skating didn't exercise my brain much. I skated internationally for five years, and that was enough. You have to be in shape to enjoy skating because you're in that crouched-over position. Now I enjoy skiing and biking and running on trails, but I don't feel I have to be in training for some upcoming event. This past winter, I skied only two out of three days because I'm a graduate teaching assistant at Michigan Tech.

## No Preaching

My parents always wanted us to go to college, but they never had to push us. Maybe I knew subconsciously because I don't remember Mom ever saying, "I want you to do this and I want you to do that." Preaching's not her style.

I don't think my mom ever complained about marriage and motherhood. She just seemed to love little kids. All the little kids come to the Arboretum, and she takes them around and shows them all the little bugs. Her family is most important to her—as well as to be open-minded. She wanted me to treat people equally, not to have prejudices. Behind the abortion issue was "Hey! People have the right to choose." When Eric and I were growing up, our grade school was adjacent to university housing where there were families from Japan, South America, all over. She'd say how important it was that we'd have the opportunity to meet many different people.

Oh! Things would have been so different without her. She treated Eric and me so similarly, got us involved in everything. Piano lessons. Modern dance. Soccer. Speed skating. Diving. Swimming. There was no way we could have thought of doing them on our own.

She was probably *the* major influence in our becoming good athletes. She's still a good athlete. When we used to cross-country ski a few years ago, I remember teaching her a couple of ways to ski and she picked it right up. I couldn't believe it. She's not afraid of the trails, and that's a lot different from alpine. Most people are scared to death.

She did express some concern when we were bike racing because it can be pretty dangerous. In fact, I crashed one time on a training ride and came home with a broken collar bone and a brain concussion. I don't remember, but they tell me I kept saying, "I'm sorry, I'm sorry."

When I was a student at the University of Wisconsin, I fell from the balcony railing. I broke my arm, my collar bone, and had to have my spleen fixed. That wasn't bad. I could ride a stationary bike. I've broken my arm a couple of times, too. But all in all my mom was no worrywart, and when it came to changes, she treated Eric and me alike even though I was a girl. That's why I never felt discriminated against. Of course, I was in modern dance and Eric wasn't, but, then, I was in everything he was, except hockey. On second thought, Eric did take modern dance. Mom thought it was good for coordination. I'm sure she learned that from her dad.

My parents would take us biking when we were still too little to ride our own bikes. They'd put us in little seats on the back or on the handlebars. For vacations my parents would take us canoeing or backpacking. They took us hiking on Isle Royale when we were three and four. Imagine going hiking on Isle Royale when we were three and four years old. It's obvious both my parents had a huge influence on us. As my mother says, "You do all the things I wish I could have done." I'm sure it's because she programmed me to.

Every now and then, I really miss my mom. Sometimes I wish I would have talked with her more in the past. I kept a lot of things inside me. I think she would have liked it if I'd shared more with her, and I feel kind of bad I didn't because it was nice when I did. Of course, when everything would fall apart on me, *then* I'd talk to her. She was always available. But, then, I think about how I don't really know her stories. I guess I talk about her a lot with my husband. Just talking makes me appreciate her more. Now that I've been married for over two years, I've started thinking about her a lot more because maybe I want to have kids. Maybe I shouldn't: I couldn't be as good a mother as my mom.

*Jack and Nancy Heiden. Nancy is wearing a jersey Beth gave her from a race she won.*

*LaVerne and Paula.*

# The Zimmerman Dynasty

*L*aVerne Zimmerman Sloan (also called "Essy") reminisces about the Zimmermans and other German ancestors, including her own mother, Florence Delfs Zimmerman (deceased). La-Verne lives with her husband, a retired physician, in Houghton, Michigan. Their fourth child and only daughter, Paula, 40, lives with her husband, three daughters and three sons in Rockford, Michigan. Kara and Lee were adopted after having been their foster children. Paula's daughters Sloan, 17, and Shannon, 15 (brother Brett is her twin), extol her as a mother and a person. Theirs is a very close family, and now Paula must watch her firstborn go off to college.

## ALTA LAVERNE ZIMMERMAN SLOAN

My mother, Florence Christine Delfs Zimmerman, was born in 1887, and she died in 1984. Mother told very few stories because people were reserved in those days. Our mothers often didn't have a friend to call by his or her first name.

Mother's father was a baron from the Schleswig-Holstein area in Germany. His vassals were about to be inducted into service in the unpopular war against Denmark, so in 1869 he brought with him to the United States all those who wished to leave. He dropped his German title, and Joachim von Delfs became John Delfs. He married my grandmother, Ida Wadsworth Tanner, a cousin of Henry Wadsworth Longfellow. One of our favorite stories was that she "thought" she had "Indian blood," but if she did, we're not sure that it was *legitimate* Indian Blood!

183

Even though my grandfather had become a citizen and was fairly Americanized, his heart remained in Germany, and he still ran his house like a German baron. I still remember his voice when he spoke to his children or one of the maids. He was a martinet but never cruel. My mother was the only one of his four daughters strong enough to defy him and to get a college education, which was hard for a girl to do then. So that's the kind of mother to have.

Since people were not wont to recount conversations, the most she ever said to me was, "LaVerne, almost all my life, until he died, I thought my father hated me because I won. But he didn't hate me; he was just proud." I expect that old German was afraid to be warm about his daughter's victory because it might lead to more insurrection.

My mother was terribly, terribly proud of her mother. She was a tiny little thing but another martinet who protected and sheltered her family to the death but also ruled them. When my grandfather died in 1920, the sons all said, "Now, Mother, we'll just handle everything for you." She said, "Children, I am capable and will handle myself." They thought that it was a little whim and that they would take care of her inevitable mistakes. After a year or so, they found she was doing quite well, having invested heavily in Akron rubber and made a fortune. The sons couldn't stand it.

## Oberlin

My daughter, Paula, encourages me to be more assertive. When your husband is working at full peak to attain his professional goals, you get into the bad habit of making decisions about the children which would be best shared. Paula, who has a great sense of sharing, would say, "Oh, Mother! How could you do that?" I think I inherited this female protectiveness from my mother. I'm lazy and inconsistent, but I was certainly influenced by my mother. We lived in Oberlin, a town which was full of Boston conservatives and Negro liberals. Mother was one of the few women who were able to live comfortably in both camps because she was unbelievably honest. They had pretty rough times, but Mother had friends on all sides—white, black, Chinese—and just calmly went along. She was a rather gently reared person of privilege whose father had sheltered her. Nevertheless, she became so strong in Oberlin. I would be *ashamed* to be my mother's daughter and be a bigot. That's the greatest thing I have from her. If I waver, I am ashamed because she would not have it.

## A Love of Courtesy

My mother was sweet and calm. Within certain limits she created her own role in the family and was proud of it. She could be dictatorial, much stricter than my father, who was a lamb. Whereas she had absolutely inflexible standards for herself, I can equivocate over the least little thing—unless it's a matter of honor. When she was ninety she was interviewed on television. When the host asked her what she considered the most serious lack in this generation, she said, "Poor manners. If you have good manners, you will behave quite well." I myself think general courtesy makes for a much pleasanter world.

My father was an educator, a school superintendent, but since that didn't yield enough income to educate nine children through college, he became an editor and promoter of books. Although it was certainly more lucrative, he preferred being an educator for the direct contact. Although Mother regretted the switch, she agreed it was necessary and felt it was selfish of her to feel that his travel for promotion was hard on her.

My sisters and I were good friends, and we ended up with different personalities. In a family as large as ours, it was essential that you maintain a sense of self apart from your sense of family. Since it's impossible to have enough space for nine children each to have a sanctuary, you have to make space within yourself.

I was the oldest. It gave me a good spot with my father—a lovely, fine man—because I had more time with him than the others did. Here's one of my favorite stories. After Dad was found to have inoperable, untreatable cancer, Mother, my next brother, and I decided that he was not to be told. He was not going to suffer any great pain for a while and probably had about six or eight months to live in peace.

I was coming down to see him (mind you, long distance was not taken lightly then), and Mother said, "LaVerne, this is hard

for me to ask, but I hope you will not argue with your father."
Dad and I used to have these rip-roaring arguments, and we'd
end up with encyclopedias to prove our points. It was great, great
fun! I said, "Mother, of course. I'll promise not to say one
controversial thing—not even about Existentialism."

I'd been there two days, when one night Mother knocked on
the door. "Verne," she said, "I have a distressing apology to you;
and then I have a distressing request to make." She said, "I'm
sorry I asked you not to argue with your father: now he thinks *you*
are terminally ill because you're not arguing with him. Every
time we're alone, he says, 'Florence, you've got to find out what
is bothering her. She is not herself at all.' So please, LaVerne,
I'll do anything, if only you'll carry on as usual."

## Anklets

Paula and I had our normal periods of antagonism, but never
too prolonged so that they would erode our basic relationship. It
was pretty much a question of whether she could wear anklet
socks in zero-degree weather. I presume that as soon as she left
the house she'd remove the long socks and put on ankle socks—
exactly what I would have done. I'm sure we did not communicate perfectly; no one does. But we had a fairly good base of
honesty and trust. I've always considered Paula a person of great
integrity, as I do my mother, and I can communicate with
someone I can trust. That integrity was passed along from
mother to daughter to daughter. It's a way of life. If you see it,
you can approximate it.

Because of Paula's daughters, we've talked a lot more about
my own past and have learned a lot about each other through
them. They're curious and like to get our albums the last night of
Christmas vacation. They got absolutely hysterical over my
picture on the Castalia High School Girls' Varsity Basketball
Team—knickers, knee sox—I wasn't a star athlete, but I
participated and was a tomboy.

## Curly Hair

I remember a Maypole Dance, one segment of which I was to
lead. Then came the question of hair. I was a lanky, freckled kid

with the same straight, wiry, thick hair I have today, and I remember my mother trying to curl it with different solutions like soap suds and starch. She must have used brute strength to wind the hair around. Anyway, I had stiff ringlets. If I'd scratched my neck, they'd have bounced—but Mother did get it curled for the Maypole Dance.

I had an average number of boyfriends, but no steadies. It was just more plain fun that way. I remember my first boyfriend, Richard Patch, very well. We met at a junior high school picnic and walked off into the woods holding hands, not even talking. I've shown Paula pictures of some of my boyfriends, though none of Richard.

At Oberlin, I studied political science. I was going to be a lawyer, but it was Depression times and there were eight of us children. Besides, by that time, Paul and I planned to be married. It wasn't realistic for me to be a doctor's wife *and* a law student. I made the choice without a moment's hesitation and don't regret it at all.

It was absolutely clear-cut that my dad wanted me to have intellectual curiosity and to never quit pursuing knowledge. Mother, a great believer too, would have fought to the death getting her girls to have equal advantage with boys for any intellectual experience, and she felt strongly that her daughters must carry on certain standards—not superficial—of taste and courtesy and fairness.

Chiefly, what I want for Paula is what my mother tried to teach me; and, second, to have fun. *Enjoy!* You don't have to be happy every minute, but life isn't worthwhile if it's not fun.

At this point, Paula is perhaps too busy. Still, she enjoys herself. I think she's looking forward, not to time away from her husband, but to taking some trips for herself. I encourage her because it was great fun for me when I could take a few days in Chicago and see some plays. I tried to give my children my undivided time when they needed it. They sense your sharing, and sometimes that gives them the ability to make their own decisions. Actually, sitting down and handing over your pearls of wisdom hardly ever works.

I would say to younger women, you can do anything in the world you want to do. The generation of ten years ago were fighting tooth and nail for equality. In another ten years they're going to be fighting for privilege because they're still going to bear the children. Now, don't get me wrong: Phyllis Schlafy is at the bottom of the list of people I would like to know, and I think the ERA can be safely passed. A woman should get every bit as much money for her work as a man gets, and I'll fight for that forever. I just don't want the movement to backfire.

## Regrets

I have deep regrets regarding my relationship with Mother. I wish we had cleared up some factual things that no one in the family knows for sure. We didn't realize that she was going to be physically there but unable to tell us, so we let the time slip by. I regret that we didn't straighten out a number of things, that is, clarify them historically. There are also some emotional things. Mother had her favorites—my sister Helen, who had polio, and my brother John; but that proved she loved the rest of us, too, and I just wish *I* had told *her* more often how much I loved her. I really wish I had.

# PAULA SLOAN BANFIELD

My mother was born in Ohio and was the oldest in a big family. Most of the stories she tells us are about her family. I don't know if that was the rule in her time, or whether it was just true in her particular family.

I only saw my grandmother, a sweet, sweet lady, once a year. My mom, however, talks about a stern, firm side we never saw. I had my own opinions about my grandma, so the first few times my mom said things about her, I thought, "Boy, I don't see that." But, then I was seeing a grandma, not a person. My mom always called her mother "Mother" and said she was a disciplinarian. She didn't talk as much about her dad, my grandfather, except to say he was not a disciplinarian. She was always proud of him. I'm wondering now whether he had something to do with Oberlin College.

I remember my mother telling me it was expected that one wouldn't have black people in one's home. Nevertheless, her family had "The Walton Family" atmosphere, and they would

*LaVerne in school.*

*Paula in a cast when she was about 14 years old.*

*LaVerne, Florence, Paula, and baby Sloan.*

*Left to right: Sloan, Shannon, LaVerne, Paula, and Kara.*

have black people over. With my grandpa being an educator and a respected figure in the community who had made this bold choice, there was pressure. That was really hard on them. Even in Ohio this racism persists.

I don't know if she'd say this, but my mom had this big conflict with her sister Helen. As adults they became close, but I don't think my mom liked Helen a lot when she was little. Helen had polio, and my mom said her mother would say, "Don't do that to Helen because she's sick," or "Let Helen go!"

Besides Helen and several brothers, my mom had a younger sister who died of cancer when she was only thirty-six. Her two children are still close to my mom's family, and her husband comes to all kinds of family gatherings with his second wife and their child. I always tease him: "Once you got in on the Zimmermans, you just couldn't get away."

Food must have been a big thing in my mother's family. She told us a lot about what her mother would prepare and that everyone had special duties. It sounded as if all they did was cook and listen to a scratchy radio after dinner. There were fights over cooking because it was such a big family and everyone would try to sneak out of his or her job. She said there was a great deal of responsibility for the oldest daughter in a big family. I don't think it bothered her; that's just the way it was.

## "The Zimmerman Dynasty"

In fact, she was so responsible for her younger siblings that, because she and her sister got married a week apart, in order to help her mother prepare for the next wedding, she took the two young boys on her honeymoon. My dad said he put a sheet up between the beds in their little cottage, and he remembers the boys peeking over it. He said, "What an indoctrination into the Zimmerman family!" The spouses and in-laws of all these nine children kid a lot about "The Zimmerman Dynasty," how once you're in the family you're caught forever.

My mom never singled out one parent in terms of intellectual influence, but, of course, her mother was grooming her to be a housewife and mother. My grandma was always playing word games. My mom talked about Oberlin and its wonderful libraries and about how she wanted to go into law. I really don't know much about my mom's interests because it seems that school was important to her, and from that to having her family things went very quickly. I've said all I know about her growing-up years—except she told me about sneaking lipstick, which they weren't allowed to wear in high school. That was a huge secret her mom would never find out.

She talked more about college than high school because then my dad was in the picture. They went together many years, while my mother was still in college, and then all during my dad's medical school. They got married the same night my dad graduated at the University of Michigan. The internship and their marriage is the period of which I have the most vivid memory. There are lots of funny stories about how little money they had and how they couldn't pay to have my brother Eddie when he was born. Not many interns in those days had babies or even were married; my parents were a one-in-a-million couple. Maybe a few of the fellows would come by for beer on the weekend. I can't ever remember hearing about a girlfriend coming over. It was always people my dad was connected with in med school or at the hospital.

As for my mom's messages and what I feel about her as a woman, she was a gutsy, confident *person*, even though she never had a career or did what might be expected of someone of her capability and intelligence. Nevertheless, I don't think she felt trapped or restricted. She's very complimentary and boosts me a lot, but what she has given me has to do, not with being a wife and mother, but with becoming a woman, a *person*.

All my kids have a super relationship with my mom. She senses who needs a boost. My mom sent a special letter to Lee [Paula's third son] the year we adopted him:

> The very best thing this year, the very best year in ages and ages, was having you become part of our family. When we met you, we really didn't know then that you were going to be special to us, but we kind of suspected.

She went on about how proud she and "Grandpa" were. Mom does things like that. For instance, she said, "Aren't you proud of

Brett for being so sensitive?" That's something so special about her—so warm and honest.

And she has such a good attitude about dying. We were teasing one day about funerals, and when my parents got home, she wrote a note about how my dad wants a great big "pity party." She said, "When you're at our age, death could be close, but it's not a terrible thing. I'd rather be around than not, but that's the way it is."

## Regrets

There are a few times I regret, such as when my mom wanted me to go with her to visit a friend when I was a teenager. Even though I was too old for a tantrum, I remember having one: "You can't make me! I'm sick of going around to see your friends." What an obnoxious, self-centered outburst. I'm sure I was probably a real snot at other times that I don't want to remember.

But I have no regrets as far as communicating with her goes. I always felt I was lucky having the mom I had. If I wanted to ask her something, I'd ask her. She still gets emotional talking about my sister who died. She didn't talk about her when I was a kid, and if she did mention her, we were all kind of quiet. Since then, we've talked a lot about her, and I ask questions.

I always thought I had the perfect home, and people told me I did, too. I sometimes felt guilty when I compared my mother and family to other kids'—and lucky I was the only girl. I don't know how good I would have been about sharing because I was kind of self-centered.

Everything revolved around our family activities, especially sports, since I have three brothers. I don't know how he did it, but my dad did a pretty good juggling act to appear to be with us a lot, even though he was so busy. My mom would pawn off the discipline to him: "We'll see what Dad has to say about that." I remember the torture of sitting and waiting to get spanked. One time my brothers put a book under my pants, so Dad cracked up. But our real motivation was to avoid disappointing our parents. I mean, that was absolutely the only reason for not getting pregnant. I don't want my kids to worry about what I think; I want them to do something because it's what they want.

We do a lot of the same things now as when I was a kid, especially at Christmas time, which we spend with my parents in Houghton. Same house, same stairway, and it seems my dad wears the same cozy pajamas. I remember once nearly cutting my brother Eddie's toe off. I had chicken pox that Christmas, and Ed, who was babysitting for me, was stretched out in the hallway with his feet sticking out and talking to his girlfriend on the phone. I wanted him to get off and play with me, so I stomped on his toe—with my ice skates on! I knew I was a brat, but nobody ever told me I was.

In those days we didn't have girls' team sports, but with me it was all physical, anyway. With another girl I set up a girls' hockey game. My dad had warned me not to play, and I was hit with a stick. I think he gave my broken nose an extra good crank when he set it. I hated cooking and couldn't even successfully prepare a box of pudding. Boys! I liked boys, and my kids love to hear about all my boyfriends, especially Norm, and our old songs. I loved my English teachers. Mrs. Vizena was a sweetie, always wore little silk dresses and big, black shoes. When one of her "pupils" would yawn, she'd say, "Oh, a cavern! Cover it up so I won't fall in." And Miss Vivian was a big help to me. She gave me a lot of compliments I wanted to live up to.

Even in high school, my ambition was to have kids. Then it came time for college. I went to college mostly because I felt my mom wouldn't be happy if I got married too early, and I did want to go to school a little more. I liked every course I took, especially child psychology, not because I was planning to use that when I had children; it was just that such things interested me.

## Prejudice

I don't know whether my kids know this, but when I was in college in Missouri, there was a girl in our dorm who was "half" black and "half" whatever that white half was. In Missouri she would have been too light to be black. She went out with a black fellow and got into a whole lot of trouble because the house-mother said she could not date a black fellow. There was actually a rule that you could not date someone of the "opposite race." All of us got in a tizzy and said, "Then who *can* she date?" I mean, she couldn't date a white fellow; she could really only date someone "half and half." Actually, she was from France, so we said, "She will have to find a fellow in Missouri who's French and black."

The school was going to ignore this problem so we said, "You've got to get that rule off the books." A black fraternity at the University of Missouri and our dorms held a date-in. We had all these black fraternity men call on us at the dorm, and after we all went out, we brought them back to our parlor. Our school did change their policy.

## Hard Work and Hurts

I'd like my daughters to learn that everything worthwhile is hard work and often accompanied by things that truly hurt. You may develop a relationship that lasts and lasts. Eventually, one of the partners will die, and that hurts. Likewise, having foster children is so wonderful, but it hurts so badly when they must go, and you wonder about them. To my mom our having all these kids is temporary insanity. She'd forgive us for that, if only we would get out more—but what we want to do is stay home more. Mainly, I like what I'm doing, and if my children decide to create a family, I hope they will make a real commitment. My daughters and I talk a lot about relationships. I'm honest and tell them, "Don't settle for something unless it makes you feel comfortable and happy." It's hard to talk to kids, but I try. I'm having to learn to hold back a little; still, the kids will beg for advice. They are realizing I can't always tell them what's best, but I don't hold back on feelings. As a matter of fact, I can't think of anything that I wouldn't feel free to talk about—if the kids brought it up: drugs and sex and feelings about my own parents and theirs about me.

Even now as a daughter I talk quite freely to my parents. My dad's just not as interested, and he falls asleep when the talk gets heavy and it's too quiet at night. But my mom and I talk about a lot of things.

\* \* \*

*The following is a composite in one voice of an interview with two of Paula's daughters.*

## SLOAN AND SHANNON BANFIELD

We don't know anything about our mom's grade school days, except she did show us her report cards. Like all naughty little kids, her grades weren't very good. We were surprised; you always think your mother's perfect, even if she is a brat. She said she came home crying once because her teacher said that her dad, who's from Tennessee, must have had "slaves." Mom loved walking home from school. Slowly but surely everyone would drop off, and in no time at all she was home. Just the other day she told us how small her class was—only about eighty kids. Every Christmas vacation it seems we find a new yearbook or photo album to go through, and she points out everyone she knows.

She told us about Zephie, their dog, and how she broke her leg when she was running with him through a field. In a picture of her in her cast she looks like Shannon, or so our dad says. Everyone else says, "Paula and *Sloan* look so much alike." It's really weird because our mom's friends and side of the family always say, "You look so much like your mother." But then my dad's friends and family say, "Oh, you look exactly like your father." We think our mom looks good, but everyone says how young she looks. When you live with her, you don't notice because she's *Mom*, you know? One of the men teachers has "the biggest crush" on our mom.

### Twin Lakes

In the summers her family would spend the week up at Twin Lakes, and Grandpa, who was a doctor, would come up on weekends—with merthiolate up to his elbows. Grandpa got so busy that the family would have to get up real early Christmas morning to open the presents before Grandpa would have to leave.

Twin Lakes was a lot of fun with everyone getting together to play cards or eat at someone's house (her favorites—chocolate-marshmallow sundaes and cherry Coke) or sleep overnight in the boat or the small cabin or waterski and swim. She was always a daredevil, putting the waterski rope around her neck or getting the boat going really fast, then jumping out of it. She'd hope she wouldn't get caught because Grandpa would get so mad. She's still like that: just last spring in Florida she went parasailing two-hundred feet in the air! One summer she was a lifeguard, and although she didn't have to save anybody, it was fun because, like all of us, she loves to sit in the sun. She talked about how neat Grandpa's sailboat was and how nice Grandpa was to donate it to the Sea Scouts.

When they would drive back into town, she'd pretend she was asleep so she could get carried into the house. Essy would say, "Now, boys, carry Paula in." One of her brothers would say, "Mom, she's just faking," but Essy and Grandpa would still make them carry her in. They spoiled her.

In eighth grade she met Norm, our dad, that summer at the lake. She used to appear to be cool, casually sitting on the dock when he would come by in his boat. It seems so weird that she's known our dad since she was thirteen. There was also Johnny Schaefer, the fantasy man she didn't marry. One time when we were about en, we were sleeping in our motor home up at the lake. Our mom went outside with her pajamas on, and there was Johnny, working on the telephone line. She came running back inside to get her robe and said, "That's the John Schaefer I always talk about!"

She also talks a lot about our Uncle Dick, how when Essy and Grandpa had parties, she and Dick would help out in the kitchen. They'd put the tail end of everyone's drink in the blender and drink it.

We went up to Twin Lakes for our grandparents' anniversary in June. One day it was icky, so we went into town with Kara. It was a neat day together because she took us up to see her high school. She said she didn't like debating but liked to do plays. In her scrapbook there's a picture of her on stage. When docksiders became a fad, she said, "I think it's so funny. That's what we used to wear," and she dug out this picture of herself in docksiders. Just yesterday she told us about the "Teen Center," where everyone used to hang out. She never got to go until she was a senior because Grandpa thought it was too rough. When Norm (our dad) would be over, Grandpa would stand at the top of the stairs leading to the rec room and say, "Paula, its twelve o'clock," and she'd say, "Okay." Soon he'd be back: "Paula, it's a quarter after twelve." This would go on and on until, finally, he'd say, "Norm, time to go home!" Paula and Norm went to two proms together; she showed us the photos.

She talks a lot about Essy and Grandpa. But mostly what we know about them we get from Essy because our mom doesn't always have the answers to our questions. When our brother Jason was eight, he asked our mom how Essy and Grandpa met, so she made up this hilarious answer. According to the tale, Grandpa was in a motorcycle gang, wore leather and had tons and tons of chains. He had to chain-fight this other guy for Essy. Jason thought it was a true story and said "Wow!" Now we always tease Grandpa about the time he won Essy.

Our mom has talked about how she and our dad didn't have any money when they were first married. We were looking at pictures of them when she came home from the hospital with Sloan and also when she came home with Brett and Shannon— and she had the exact same outfit on. There's a picture of Sloan in a pathetic outfit that looked like it was made out of curtains or something. Why did they get married when they were so poor? Supposedly, they didn't want to take a chance of having an "early" baby. Even so, Sloan was born with a month or two— that is, ten or eleven months after they got married. One time when Sloan was about twelve, she heard our mom in the other room saying to a bunch of ladies, "So many times before we got married I'd think, 'What if I get pregnant?'"

## A Real Pal

We talk quite a bit to our mom—not lately as much, though. Ever since Sloan's graduation, they haven't been that close. Sloan's boyfriend got on our mom's bad list. She's with it, though, and knows more about people at our school than we do. In fact, she's friends with all our friends. She's president of the PTA, works at the children's agency, on parent advisory boards, does everything for us, and is always either going to Jason's basketball game or Brett's wrestling match or our cheerleading practice or track meet. She could be her own ladies' aid society. One of our parents attends every single time. If two events overlap or there are three at once, they'll spend equal time at each one. Mom will sit in the bleachers from nine in the morning until four in the afternoon to watch Shannon run. She'll be out there to watch us cheer at football games when it's freezing. We take for granted how lucky we are. Even Brett's friends think she's neat, even though she's kind of strict with us—the "Goody Two Shoes Banfield Girls." She asks us where we're going and when we're coming back. Other kids can just say, "I'm going out. Back at midnight." Sometimes we think our mom's a brat and we get mad at her, but most of the time we get along pretty good because we know how much she cares. Sloan's going to college in a few months, and our mom feels bad that the family is breaking up. She's trying to hold on, which is understandable.

Sometimes you look at your mother and think she's perfect. Yet sometimes when she yells at you for being self-centered, you get to thinking, "Well, *she's* not perfect." It's so hard to tell if she's right, and you get confused. Sometimes you have to make a choice between, say, your mother and your boyfriend. Or you wish you could just sneak away without having to ask her permission to go out with him. If we're mad at our mom, we'll decide not to talk. But it never works because she's always so friendly. Adults seem to forgive and forget sooner.

Sloan went with this one kid for almost two years. One time our mom said, "I know you can sometimes get carried away; but whatever you do, just be careful." That was it. She's told us everything about sex, but she never *asks* us anything. Does she wonder but doesn't really want to know? Maybe she *wants* to know but thinks it's better that she doesn't.

She's our mom, but she's still our friend. We respect her advice because she's straight with us and tells the truth. Some kids say that if they ask their mom a question, she won't answer; or they won't even dare to ask. It's nice to be able to talk to her, and it's hard to imagine not being able to. Sloan might be having a bad time with her right now, but it's not horrid, and they still like each other. A lot of girls don't get along with their mother. They love her, but they don't like her.

Our mom is no fuddy-duddy. She plays guitar and sings— even songs that are risqué. She and our dad chaperone our dances, and people say, "God, do you like your parents watching over you like that?" They're not "watching over us"; they just like to be there with all the young kids. Unlike other chaperones, they come out and dance with us. You can leave them in a room with our friends and not have to think, "Oh, God, I've gotta hurry back," or "Oh, no, John's gonna meet my dad." Other kids say, "My boyfriend's coming over tonight because my dad's not going to be home." That seems so funny because it's not like that at our house.

Family is most important to our mother. She loves her mom and dad and brothers, but we probably come even before them now. And she respects and appreciates us. For instance, most parents *assume* their kids will babysit. But our mom always *asks* if we will; in fact, she pays us! We say, "No way, I'm sure! You don't have to pay us to stay home to sit in the sun and watch our own brother and sister." She says, "I want to. You spend your whole day for me." We help her out, so we don't have to feel she's running around like our slave. Even when we do a simple favor for her, she somehow returns it.

She's been very effective in impressing her values upon us. She'd probably like us to learn how to be like her, how to go out of our way to care for other people and to give of ourselves. She's not a mushy ga-ga person, but she really, really cares a lot for us, the foster babies, our school. Some of our friends even like to call her "Mom" because she's the person who's with it. One time Brett's friend said, "Your mother and I had a really good talk. She's smart. She gave me a lecture about drinking and drugs that really scared the shit out of me. I'd never thought about it in the way she put it, but I know she's right." She can relate because of the way Essy and Grandpa were with her. Speaking of mothers and daughters, there is a lot of Essy in our mom—the way she talks and the stories she tells. Our mom said that the nickname "Essy" comes from "Mrs. S." Some little kid couldn't say "Mrs. Sloan."

It seemed that Shannon was Essy's favorite, and that although she loved Sloan, she maybe didn't like her. Then Sloan got the nicest letter:

Dear Sloan:

Sometimes a person who is outstanding in many areas is not appreciated. The overall excellence is not acknowledged. Everyone (us included) just naturally expects Sloan Banfield to excel. Sometimes we neglect to say how proud we are and how much we love you. Darling, we are and we do.

Love to everyone,
Grandpa and Essy

Sloan says, "I'll keep that note so I can ponder and treasure it."

*Baby Mary Linaford and mother.*

# Some of My Best Friends
# Are Liberals

**L**yn, her husband, son, and two daughters live in Vermont. Just as her daughter Sarah switched careers in her early thirties, Lyn in her mid-fifties started work outside the home. And, as the years go by, the values and politics of mother and daughter have become more closely aligned.

## MARY LINAFORD ("LYN") BASSETT

Sarah knows this: I was born in Wichita. My parents were from Kansas, but they were living in New Jersey at the time. They went back to Kansas on a trip to have me. My brother is ten years older than I am, and my sister is seven years older, so it was almost like having a different set of parents, although we were a close family. As the baby, I was considered by my brother and sister to be "spoiled"; but my father was better off financially when I came along, so I think it was just a matter of having more wherewithal.

One of the reasons that I married my husband Glenn was that he was one of the first people with whom I felt I could really be myself. I was not as religious as my parents, who didn't allow smoking and drinking. I never established my persona enough to do that in front of them. I used to say it was because I didn't want to hurt them, but it was really because I didn't want them to give me grief. My father would lecture and try to reason with me. Mother, more emotional, would be distraught.

I just can't emphasize strongly enough what an impact it made on me when I decided that I did want to smoke and drink. I wanted to do it with someone who didn't say that it was bad. My mother drank coffee, and I cannot in my whole life remember her ever having a cup of coffee in peace without my father telling her that it wasn't good for her.

## Born Quaker

I was married in Quaker meeting in Montclair, New Jersey, which we attended for years. You marry each other, speaking your own vows. There is no minister, only the Committee of Overseers, who sit on the side benches. In our Quaker wedding anyone could speak, and because my father was a well-known Quaker, many people spoke, and one man felt moved to speak twice. The marriage lasted an hour and a half. That's unusual.

As a Quaker, you can think what you want; your conscience guides you. It's hard to be a good Quaker because there's nothing to fall back on. You don't have Confession to absolve you.

My mother was born Quaker, and all her ancestors going back to Wales and England were Quakers. One of her ancestors, Morris Llewellyn, received the first grant of land from William Penn in Ardmore, Pennsylvania, and the house he built still stands—although not owned by our family—and Sarah's middle name is Llewellyn.

I went to Quaker meeting until we moved to San Francisco. There the Quaker meeting was held in a room with a two-story-high blowup of Joan Baez. This was not my idea of what Quaker meeting was all about. We traveled around to various churches and wound up in the Episcopal Church but not for too long. It was really the end of our formal church-going as a family. When my regrets come up in the middle of the night, sometimes I feel I've neglected that part of my children's life.

I consider myself a Quaker, but I'm not what you'd call a practicing Quaker. Quakers are liberal and activist, and my feeling is that Sunday worship is a place in which to be inspired, not a place to be told to go down to El Salvador. There is a deep division in the Quakers between the liberals and the conservatives.

I have very few friends who think the way I do. Most of the people I like are liberals; yet I don't share their tenets and beliefs.

My father, Howard Kershner, a conservative and very forceful person, was well known because he was a great public speaker. At twenty-six he ran on the Prohibition ticket and came very close to winning a seat in Congress. During World War I he worked in Washington on the War Production Board, saving pulp and paper for wartime use. Father has written a lot of books. He was invited to the White House twice under Roosevelt because the administration had a habit of trying to get people who spoke out against them into their fold.

## Plenty More

Mrs. Roosevelt always had scrambled eggs and sausages for Sunday night supper. When it came to Daddy, there were only two sausages left, and Daddy hesitated to take them. The waiter whispered in his ear, "Take them both. There's plenty more in the kitchen."

Another time Daddy was sitting by Mrs. Roosevelt, who noticed that he didn't have any lamb chops. She said, "Mr. Kershner, don't you like lamb chops?" Daddy replied, "I like them every time I'm offered them." They had neglected to pass the platter to him.

Food has always been my downfall. Our plates were never really taken away, and we just kept picking. Also, whenever Mother wanted to do something nice, she would say, "Well, let's go and have a treat. We'll go have an ice cream cone on the ferry going back from New York," or "We'll go and have tea," or "We'll go have lunch there." Mother and I liked to shop at Altman's in New York and eat lunch at the Charleston Gardens, and I wanted to carry on the tradition with my daughters. I remember one time I went to New York with Sarah when she was on a diet, and I was really upset that she didn't want to go to eat with me.

## War and Peace

My father wanted to do something. Quakers often do some kind of service abroad, such as feeding the hungry in war-torn countries. My father was sent to Europe to direct the American Friends Service Committee work in Spain between the two sides of the civil war. When he got to England, he was also made head of the British effort. Then there was an international commission; he gathered steam as things went on. They had the headquarters in Paris because the war in Spain was rapidly ending and spreading northward.

France got a lot of refugees from Spain. My mother's job was to scour the countryside and find places to feed and house the children. At one time she had twenty different colonies.

I went over to France with my parents because I was in seventh grade at the time and too young to send away to school. We went in '39, and in the first half of that year I studied with my seventh grade books from New Jersey, and my father gave me my exams.

The next year, because the war had started on the border between Germany and France (as a matter of fact, the night that war was declared, Mother and I were outside Paris in the children's colony that Mother had named Pax Colony), we had to drive back to Paris in a total blackout. I'm a person who never gets lost, whether I've ever been there before or not. At twelve years old, using a flashlight to look at the names of the streets on the curb, I guided Mother back to Paris.

Then they sent me down to an English boarding school in southern France. On all my school vacations I would go around with Mother to deliver supplies to all the colonies.

## A Lot of Hoopla

The spring of 1940 my parents went back to the States to report on how the work was going, to make speeches, and to raise funds. While they were in the States, the Germans broke through the Maginot Line and were headed toward Paris. I was still in France, and my parents went through all kinds of machinations to get me on the last American boat to leave France. It was the S. S. Washington, which left from Bordeaux.

After picking up more Americans in Lisbon, we were on our way to Galway, Ireland, to pick up more Americans, when at five o'clock one morning we were stopped by a German submarine! I was on the other side of the ship, so we couldn't see the submarine, which, of course, was not submerged. The captain didn't tell us anything, but word came around the ship. They got us in the lifeboats, swung them over, and I remember thinking, "If this lifeboat ever gets lowered, who's going to row the boat?" There wasn't a single man in the boat, only children and older women.

As the boat was swung out, it tipped a little, and the woman sitting next to me lost her pocketbook overboard. It contained all her jewelry, papers, and money; she was absolutely hysterical. Here I was at thirteen trying to calm her down, putting my arms around her to comfort her.

The captain said, "We have been stopped by a German submarine. He said he was going to torpedo us, but I told him that this is an American ship with nothing but people leaving Europe. They have apologized, saying they thought we were a Greek freighter." Now, the American flag was painted all over the ship and completely covering one side, the American flag was flying, and all the lights were on every night. I think the Germans were just being menacing.

The captain said, "We can proceed now. Everyone who is on deck, stay there. Everyone who's in a boat, stay there. We're going to start up and go full speed, and we'll get you aboard as soon as we can." We went for a whole hour while swinging in these lifeboats hanging over the side. It was a while later that he slowed down and they brought the lifeboats in.

I took it in stride. Traveling around France, we'd carried our gas masks like people carrying cameras. The first time I had to put one on, my father helped me. I said, "I can't breathe." I ripped it off. He was cross with me, and I said, "But, Daddy, I can't breathe! Something's wrong!" Then he realized you have to pull the stopper off so that air could come through the filter.

Meanwhile, my mother was scheduled to speak at the Women's Club that afternoon. Someone called her at two o'clock and said, "Mrs. Kershner, we're waiting for you." She'd totally forgotten about it; she'd been glued to the radio. Here they were, trying to get me out of Europe and out of danger, and instead they'd gotten me into this.

All together it took about two weeks to get across. When we landed in New York, there was absolute silence as we slipped into the pier, on the boat and among the people on the dock.

Usually there's a lot of hoopla. It was a truly moving experience I'll never forget.

Certainly, I have told my children that story.

## Potato Peels

I loved my mother. I would say I was closer to her emotionally and to my father mentally. Mother, I always felt, gave me good taste. She liked beautiful things and good things, whereas my father liked to save his money and considered Mother's charge accounts his worst enemy. Mother would point to some thing in the house and say, "This is a nice piece," but what she'd really wanted was such-and-such, and we couldn't afford it. I always felt that we could maybe have had nicer things, if my father had agreed to spend the money. It was not that he was mean or nasty but just that he made do with what was all right; you didn't need anything special.

My father was dominating, but Mother always had her way of getting a word in. If she spent more than he wanted her to spend, we would be told not to tell Daddy right away. Of course, I've continued this practice with my family. I don't keep things from my husband, but I do choose my opportune moments to tell him.

Mother had a lot of jealousy. Being faithful was something my father valued. Nevertheless, women were attracted to him all the time and were the bane of Mother's existence. Daddy delighted in the fact that he was attractive, as anyone would.

I had a culturally enriched life. Mother always had books on art museums and on famous artists. We went to Carnegie Hall and the Metropolitan Opera in New York City almost every weekend. When we didn't go, we listened to the opera every Sunday afternoon on the radio and the New York Symphony every Sunday afternoon. Sunday nights we listened to Harry Emerson Fosdick's sermons. He was a famous minister at (I'm not sure about this) Riverside Church.

If there was any deprivation in my life, it was because of my father's belief in not spending more than you had to. My husband's background was similar, so when we got together, we were pretty good spenders because we both felt we had not had all we wanted.

My mother's father, a teacher in a Kansas Quaker school, had to make ends meet by farming. My mother tells the story of raising turkeys but never tasting turkey until she left Kansas. Every turkey brought one dollar, a dollar which could not be spared because they had to buy staples. In all the time that I knew her, my mother made lovely soap that floated just like Ivory. Mother kept all these saving habits through the years and put them to use in the colonies in France.

College was always a foregone conclusion in our family. Father had graduated from Friends University in Wichita. Mother, who majored in Home Ec and piano at the University of Minnesota, taught the women in the colonies that most of the vitamins in carrots and potatoes were in the peels. She also taught sewing and other skills.

## Constant Care

My father kept my mother alive by sheer willpower the last ten years of her life. He took her along on trips, taking care of her incontinence and keeping her oxygen tent with him. He provided constant care. She was senile and wouldn't know where she was. Sometimes she was as loving as a child, but then if you did something to make her angry, she could be difficult. Generally, though, she seemed happy. Daddy put her in a home and visited her every day for supper.

For a while, another woman kept coming into Mother's room and getting into her bed. When I visited one afternoon, I was so touched to see Mother tucking her in as if she were her child. One time my father found my mother, all nicely dressed, sitting on the couch with an older man who had his arm around her. Daddy didn't like that. He could flirt, but she couldn't. It didn't take him long to get Mother home. I thought it was kind of a nice little turnabout.

My mother passed away in '76. My father preached the sermon at her funeral, and I don't think there was a dry eye in the whole church, the church where he had become a minister in his eighties.

My mother was never fond of my father's mother, who told my father that you should not enjoy sex and should not have it very often. My mother told me about sex so early that I don't even

remembering her telling me. It was a very natural thing. I never
had to ask anybody; I always knew, so I don't remember being
curious. My mother did very well with that subject.

Mother was a servile sort of housewife and mother. She slaved
over the garden and the house. I don't remember her resting or
enjoying herself very often. At our cottage in New Hampshire
we got our water from the lake, and we had a refrigerator that
needed ice. Then, of course, we had a woodstove. In later years
when I'd say how much I'd enjoyed New Hampshire, she said,
"What you thought of as a vacation, I thought of as slavery
because I had to everything without the conveniences I had at
home." I said, "Mother, why did you do it? Cookies from the
store would have been just fine." I honestly think that people
get in the habit of doing things.

I, too, was a servile housewife, more than I am now, and
certainly more than today's young woman. Yet I have found it
easy to relax my housekeeping standards. I kept pace with my
mother when I was younger but not anymore. My husband told
me before we got married that there were two things he didn't
want to do—shop for food and make a bed. I found out there
were dozens of other things.

Now we live apart during the week. He works in New York
and has an apartment there. Since he's been living alone, he's a
little more considerate when he's home; he's quite apt to get
breakfast and he brings me coffee in the mornings. Glenn has
always traveled during our marriage. I don't think he's ever been
home for any major crisis, like the cellar flooding or the children
having measles. I'm always very sad when he leaves Sunday;
but, I must confess that when I come home from work Monday
night, it's kind of nice not to have him there.

I don't mean this unkindly, but I don't think widowhood
would be very hard for me. I'm not the helpless woman that
many wives are. Many friends who have become widows don't
know how to manage a checkbook. It's quite ridiculous to keep
the woman helpless and unknowledgeable. The loving husband
is the one who really prepares his wife for his death.

I'm not embarrassed to tell my girls anything. I do remember
two lessons that my mother taught me that I'm not sure I told
them.

# A *Lesson Learned at the Five and Ten*

One time I was shopping with Mother at the five and ten. The counters were divided by glass, and things were just lumped together. At that time a lipstick called "Tangee" was supposed to take on the color of your mouth. I reached in and took a handful of the little tubes from the bin. Mother didn't see them until I got home, when she said, "What are you doing with these, Linaford?" I said, "Oh, they were free samples." She said, "Linaford, I don't think they were free samples, and we are going to take them back." This was maybe twenty cents worth of goods, and we drove five miles to take it back. I had to tell the manager I had taken them. That was quite a lesson I've never forgotten.

In third grade a bunch of my friends and I were playing in the schoolyard, when out came this second grader who was a little smaller than we were. She was beaming away. I can still see her face. We took away a paper she had gotten an A on—I guess *I* took it away—and we were teasing her and dancing around and wouldn't give it back to her. I tucked it into my book, and we ran off home. She was crying when we left. My mother, standing at the back door when I came home, said, "Linaford, I think you have something that belongs to somebody else, and they're waiting for you. You can leave off your books and walk down to Nancy's and take it to her." That was one of the longest walks in my life. When I got there, they opened the door and smiled at me, took the paper, and asked me to sit down and have some brownies and milk with them. I found it very difficult to swallow the brownies: I was crying and saying I was sorry. I don't think I ever bullied anyone after that.

I was always looking in my sister's things, wanting to know about her life and what she was doing, and I found this little decorated sugar cube that had icing on it, the kind they used to have at fancy teas. I popped that in my mouth and ate it. My sister went to my mother and said that I must have taken it because no one else would have taken it out of her purse. Mother asked me if I had eaten it. I couldn't bring myself to say I'd eaten it, but I said, "I ate *half* of it."

As a child, I wanted to go to dancing class because my boyfriend went, but my father wouldn't have paid a penny for social dancing. I did study interpretive dancing for three years with Anita Zahn, one of Isadora Duncan's pupils. I always felt that helped to give me rhythm, and I think I'm fairly well coordinated.

I also had a piano teacher whom I admired. She was a lot of fun and humorous but quite strict. When I went to France with my parents, I'd reached a crucial point in studying piano, and she wanted them to let me stay there and live with her and continue studying. My parents didn't want me to do that. I don't think I really wanted to, as I was intrigued with going to France, and I had the opportunity to study at a famous school in Paris. Being a concert pianist is not something I "gave up," for I truly do not think I had the ability or even the motor facility, and I always had a terrible time memorizing.

## The Opposite Sex

In some way I must not have been happy as such because my second grade teacher sent a note home to Mother that said, "Is Linaford happy at home? She seems to sigh so much." I don't remember lots of gaiety because I was born into a fairly serious family. Yet I do remember a fairly happy, normal childhood.

I think I was normally happy. I went with the same boy, Charles Highley, throughout grade school; we sat together and walked home together. When we got to seventh grade, something had happened during the summer, and we weren't close. I never knew quite what happened. Then I went to France in seventh and eighth grades and after that to boarding school in Poughkeepsie and in Pennsylvania.

I had always been reinforced and told by my family that I was lovely and great. When I got to school, I didn't feel the opposite sex shared this opinion. Oddly enough, going around to the colonies in France, young men older than I enjoyed spending time with me. I played chess with one and wrote to another one for years. But in boarding school I wasn't popular. I don't recall being troubled by it; I just assumed I would never marry. At sixteen, I went off merrily to college thinking I was going to conquer the world and become a doctor.

I started out pre-med with extra courses and piano. I never had any high school chemistry nor the pre-requisite math—and why they ever let me in and got me into those courses I will never know because I flunked both math and chemistry.

But the great thing was that I found out I was popular, so there was never any thought of my not marrying. *Everyone* asked me out. I changed my major to English but mostly studied dating and bridge. I regretted that I was kind of wasteful; but I had a great time, got a good liberal education and a great education in art. In traveling all over the world with my husband, I've enjoyed seeing the things I studied.

I fantasize about being a concert pianist or a great doctor. Actually, I get queasy at the thought, and I'm absolutely a basket case when I have to go into a hospital.

We were living in Cuba when Sarah, my first child, was born. She was born with cerebral palsy and a very rare skin disease. By the time she was three or four days old, she was close to fifty percent without skin. The disease involved blisters, and when the blisters burst, no new skin grew. Sarah was born with two of these blisters, and as she grew older, they increased.

My parents were living in New York, and they described the symptoms to a Viennese doctor who had worked in the Far East and had seen this disease. No one in Cuba knew what it was. It is called Ritter's disease, named for the Austrian doctor who discovered it. The cause is unknown. It's not hereditary, and it occurs about once in every million births. The doctor flew down to Cuba, and within twenty-four hours, with his changes in treatment, skin was growing.

I'd had a Caesarean because I had labor pains every minute for, oh! I don't know how long, but I would go to sleep and wake up and the clock hadn't moved; this happened all day long. Finally, at midnight, they decided to operate. Waiting too long very well might have been the cause of the cerebral palsy. Sarah was trying to be born and had no way of getting out.

Fortunately, Sarah's intelligence was not at all affected. Very intelligent, lovely friends said, "Oh, is she brain-damaged?" I said, "It's the motor part, not the intelligence. We were very fortunate."

Glenn and I went home that night and decided right then and there we would tell those who asked that she had polio, and we wouldn't tell Sarah the facts until she was about nineteen years old. When we did tell her, she was quite surprised. She wore a brace on her leg until she was six or seven, and we did exercises together.

Sarah likes to magnify the fact that I did these exercises with her every day. She now thinks what I did was incredible; but any mother would have done what the doctors said would help her daughter. They wanted the bone and muscle to grow with the leg, or she would have been like someone who had polio—with the tightened heel cord or back of the leg.

Sarah was very precious to us. Until she was seven, she was not very well. She was out of school more than she was in, but she was always a top-notch student. Sarah always had good grades until sophomore year in college, when she decided to have fun—which I can well understand. I had the distinction of being on dormitory as well as scholastic probation every semester of my college career. I'm not terribly proud of that but find it a little amusing. I had to buckle down and get A's the second half of each semester to counteract the E's so I'd wind up with C's. When I graduated, the Dean of Women said, "Linaford, you are two points short of a C average," and she said, "I talked the committee into graduating you because I didn't think I could get through another semester with you." She was very fond of me and told me I was the prettiest girl she'd ever known.

My children know about that, and I told them that I would never put up with anything like that from them. Sarah had a very gay sophomore year and came home, and we said we would not send her back. When she vacationed with us in Canada, she decided to go there to school.

## Private Enterprise

Sarah is a communal person: she thinks what's hers belongs to everybody else, and what's everybody else's belongs to her. This has always been a little bone of contention because she'll take things out of my closet to wear, even though she knows I don't like that. Sarah also has problems with money. She thinks every twenty-four hours has thirty-six and that the spending power of a dollar is ten dollars. No matter how much reinforcing these things get, they're lessons that Sarah has trouble learning.

Sarah is more conservative than she once was. She married an Englishman who was quite a socialist. She sold her stock that was given to the children by their grandfather when they were young because she didn't believe that people should own stock. I think she's lived to regret it. I suspect Sarah believes in capitalism now—certainly, private enterprise!

As a lot of people measure "success," I don't think my children have it. Sarah knows, perhaps, that Dad would be interested in seeing her become an urban planner, what she studied to become. I believe that she will be successful in massage therapy, but she did not have much support from her family; we didn't think she would really make it. Now it looks as if she'll have a very happy, productive career. I would like to live long enough to see my children settled in their life's career. Twenty years ago I never, ever expected that I would have a wood turner, an astrologer, and a massage therapist. The only thing I can think of that influenced them in their choice of career is that, although I'm conservative in belief, I have not been the typical parent. Certainly, I was less rigid than my parents were.

When I was fifty-four, I decided to get a job, and I looked for a whole year before I found someone who would even take a chance on me. I might have started doing something like this a little sooner. I was idle long after the children didn't need me, and I let about ten years go by when I could have been doing something. Someone asked me why I'd gone back to work, and my husband said, "She felt worthless." That was the gist of it. Part of it was not thinking my children were happy and success-ful: if I hadn't been good at that, maybe there was something I was good at. People laugh at me because I'm always telling my age: fifty-eight. I'm more proud of it every year. I'm the oldest one in our bank, and I have to laugh because women in their forties don't want to tell how old they are. We should be proud we survived. I don't look at life as one jolly road. That you can be reasonably happy is a great triumph.

I think that people, not things, are the most fascinating subject in the world. From my own experience, I would tell young people to spend a little less time on physical things. You want your home to look nice and be comfortable, but it should assume only its proportionate place in life. I know people who are never satisfied with the way their house looks. My children already know that acquisitiveness is an awful trap.

It was a source of great joy that my mother lived long enough so that I was able to convey to her how thankful I was for the upbringing I had and for the many things she taught me—which I didn't realize and fully appreciate until I had children myself. How satisfying to have the opportunity to come to a resolution, a turning of the whole circle, just to be able to say with all your heart, "Thank you, Mom." I was able to say that many, many times.

## SARAH LLEWELLYN BASSETT

My mother was born in 1927. Shortly after her birth, her parents moved to Montclair, New Jersey, where she grew up. My grandparents were both from Kansas farming families. In fact, her mother was so poor that even though they raised pigs, she was twenty-one before she ever tasted pork. She'd watch the trains go by and just longed for the day when she would be on one, heading out of there.

My mother's father, a teetotaler who ran on the first Prohibition ticket in Kansas, was a driven man—religious and sober. My mother told me that her mother taught him a lot about sexuality.

My mother grew up in a house where her father was constantly in his study working. They did a fair amount of entertaining, but my grandfather would say, "My family will now entertain you. I'm going off to my study." That's how my mother got to be confident in talking with adults because she would be left with her mother to entertain the guests. My mom has a bit of ham in her.

When she was twelve, which was during World War II, her parents worked for the American Friends Service Committee, and they had all sorts of adventures in Europe. I know a story she has told about leaving Paris on an oceanliner. Since she got very seasick, they had a steward follow her around with a mop and pail. And there was a submarine scare! I think she was mostly excited and thought it was neat.

*Mary Linaford (13 years old) with her parents.*

*Lyn's parents.*

*Sarah Llewellyn Bassett and mother.*

*Lyn and Sarah.*

## Indulgences

I think my grandmother indulged my mother, who was a little spoiled as a girl. My grandmother was the kind of mother who would do everything for her kids. My mother has memories of their family vacations at Lake Winnepausaukee, where they would go every year. My grandmother would be slaving over a woodstove, cooking pies and bread and roasts; it was no vacation for her. It was worse than being home because of cooking on a woodstove, and my mother vowed she would not repeat her mother's experience. When we went vacationing at Lake Winnepausaukee, we ate very simply, which was, of course, fine with all of us. My mother has memories of her mother being totally devoted to her husband and children and also of her being a somewhat jealous woman. I really don't know much at all about my mother in the early part of her life. I know that she, as the baby, was the funny, lively one of the family. It makes me sad that I don't really know who her friends and mentors were. I intend to ask her that.

I do know she studied piano at the Eastman School of Music and that she wanted to be a doctor. Because of her academic probation and her squeamishness, she didn't. She has some regrets that she didn't do something more "serious" or "substantial." I think she sees her life lived largely through the success of her children, and in a lot of ways all three of us have disappointed her, which is a source of sadness for me and also for her.

## Men

As I recall my mother's life, more than anything else, I remember the men she has told me about. My mother didn't think of herself as attractive. She was quite studious and was raised in an incredibly strict house with no alcohol or cigarettes. Somehow my grandmother managed to impart to her knowledge about sex.

When she went away to the University of Rochester, men began asking her out. She was just so thrilled that men found her attractive that her studies suffered. Finally, the Dean of Women said, "Oh Linaford, just... go. We just want you to graduate."

There were several men who wanted to marry her, one of whom she didn't marry because he was Catholic and she was not. It was important to this man to raise Catholic children, and she did not see how she could. (We were raised as Quakers.)

Then there was an actor, whom we now see a lot on TV. They had a strong physical attraction, but she didn't want to marry an actor. It was important to her to have a successful and exciting man because of her own father. My father fit all of those criteria. Just the other day my mother told the story of how they met, and I know how my father proposed. Mom was talking about what she wanted to name her children, and my father said, "What do you mean your children? You mean, our children!" My mother said, "Oh?"

Once when they were going out together, my mother said, "Glenn, I can't go out. I have to study for this test." Then she finished studying and someone called her and she did go out for coffee or a drink. My father or one of his friends saw her out. He was furious. He marched over to her dorm, grabbed up all his books—I think he even took his fraternity pin back—and stalked off. How they resolved it I don't know. My father does find it difficult to apologize.

Much of her life with my father has been lived vicariously through his travels. She would like to have been married to a writer because she reads so much herself, and there's a part of her who would like to be a writer. She reads adventure stories about the settling of the West, about people taking dangerous kayaking trips, and about bush pilots. If she had been born in another time, she would have made a hell of a pioneer.

## The Debt

My mother's pregnancies were extremely difficult; we were all Caesarean births, each life-threatening. Yet she truly enjoyed being a mother. She never talked directly about the challenges of motherhood, but maybe we got it on some level since none of us wants children—a source of sadness for her even though she knows one can't live life through children. There were times when she seemed to be lonely or struggling, and I would pick that up, not that I ever felt I was a burden. She admires me a lot, but I do feel I've let her down; she would like to see me married and financially secure. She will shake her head and wonder how I could be her daughter.

I feel I owe my parents something because they incurred a massive debt when I was born with a rare skin disease, as well as cerebral palsy. My mother worked twice a day for about seven years doing physical therapy with me. I feel sad that I don't let my mother know enough how much I appreciate her. Thanking her for the therapy is my way of telling her. She thinks it was just like putting dinner on the table, but the impact was quite amazing.

## Backbone

My mother would always—nicely, genteelly, but assertively—get her way. She's steely, she's got backbone. No one could ever make her do anything that ran against her principles. I admire that immensely and wish I could be more like her. I can't imagine my mother ever doing anything dishonest or being hypocritical. My father is an extremely witty, life-of-the-party type, and I think sometimes she feels overshadowed by him. But when you talk to her one-on-one, she is incredibly articulate, and I think I've gotten my love of words from her.

One Christmas all I got was books. It was awful at the time, but I did read all of them. When we traveled, she would forever point things out ("Look at that view!"), and we would become impatient: "Oh, Mom, come on!" Yet today we all have an appreciation for beautiful things and places, and she's instilled in me a love of travel. She'd always send us detailed accounts—on postcards!—every two or three days from all over the world.

Whenever she was going away on a trip, she would always make sure we were well taken care of. We had good babysitters, and she would wrap up our lunch money in little labeled packages, lay out our clothes and make lists of what we should wear. I think she felt a little guilty about traveling, but I'm happy it didn't stop her. I went into the closet to smell her clothes because I missed her. The babysitter discovered me and thought it was really weird, but my mother was touched.

My father has always been the expansive one, whereas my

mother puts the brakes on. Although she has resented having to play that role, her influence has tempered my own tendency to believe that a day has forty-eight hours and a dollar is ten.

On the face of it my mother appears to be stolid and conservative and phlegmatic, but she's got an incredible spunkiness, spark, and sense of humor. She's outgoing and makes people feel at ease. In exchange for the heightened self-esteem from being employed, there is a loss of contact with people and some of her other interests. She used to give wonderful parties, all beautifully orchestrated. I remember her always cooking lovely meals for us. We had a lovely home and she did a lot of business entertaining. I wish I'd learned more from her: how to cook, how to clean, the houselore that gets handled down from generation to generation. I feel ignorant about all of that—not because I didn't have a teacher, but because I didn't really take the time to learn or ask.

I greatly admired her going back to work at this age. I admire her calm outward demeanor though I know she worries a lot. I admire her passion (I don't mean sexual passion, although that, too) and her physical stamina. She's robust and never seems to quit; she seems to get by on almost no sleep. I think she'll have a long, long life.

My mother also had a certain seriousness about her. They traveled a lot in Latin countries, and upper-class Latin women dress up a lot. Because of her simplicity, natural beauty, and rebelliousness, my mother never wore makeup, which she thought frivolous. I know I picked that up. Along with that, she talked about flirting, that it was more important to be known for my mind. And who knows? With a different mother, I might have been thin!

She can get along with very different people, although she certainly knows where her own values lie. I mean, she can sit down and talk to a gay person or a Lesbian friend of mine. She gets along with people who have quite divergent views from her own. She's tolerant that way. I guess I got that from her, too, although I tend to be much more judgmental than she is. She's learned how to listen to me without overreacting to what I say. My friends have said they wish they'd had her for their mother.

My mother is a big worrier. She worries about financial security, that she hasn't been a good enough mother, about her weight, her health, about not having made a big enough mark in this world. I think there's a part of her who feels she would like the value of her life to have been based on more than her attractiveness and relationship to men, and that's why this job she has been doing the last two and a half years means so much to her. She is so conscientious and works hard and long hours and is good with customers. She's so grateful that anyone would hire her at age fifty-six that she just felt she had to do a good job. The truth is she's probably the best bargain they've got. There's not a whole lot hidden between my mother and me, except some resentments I feel it would be unnecessarily cruel to talk about. I save that stuff for my therapy group. I don't think that I withhold appreciation from her; I know she doesn't from me. Neither one of my parents initially supported what I'm doing, but I think they're quite excited about it now. My mother has said they're proud of me. My reservation is that I think she would really like my life to look different. I don't think she holds it against me that I'm divorced, but I think she wonders: "Don't you ever wonder what's happening with Ian?" She liked my ex-husband a lot, and it is a little bit of a chiding.

My mother is a funny mix: some things she's expansive about; others she won't talk about. No doubt she thinks, "Sarah, why do you wear your heart on your sleeve?"

I'd like to find out more about her dreams and her perspective, but I avoid asking because I get the idea from her sleepless nights and the worrying that she does that my mother has a lot of pain. I don't want to stir things up for her. I just want her to be happy.

*Audrey Jasper (front), her grandma Betsy Salk, and mother Gertrude.*

# A Tough Old Bird

**A**udrey, 58, recently earned her Master's degree in Stillwater, Oklahoma. She and her husband Robin uprooted a few years ago, and as Audrey began a new career as a therapist—one small step at a time—she and Robin separated. Now they are trying a new marriage, wherein Audrey can be a full and equal person; they have moved to Dallas to be close to their daughter Tia, grandson Bryan (a new grandchild is due in a few weeks), and son-in-law Randy, who is an art director at the University of Texas in Arlington. Because Tia is modest, Randy is the one to reveal her many talents: she is a poet, lyricist, musician, and she teaches music to children at an alternative school Bryan attends. After some difficult years. Tia and Audrey have become fast friends—on a first-name basis.

## AUDREY JASPER PADORR

My lineage is of really *strong* women. My mother, Gertrude Salk, did not finish school because her father was a very stingy man and she had to go to work. The "tough old bird," as we three daughters call her, still has a back of iron. She calls *her* mother a "saint."

Mother does not express regrets. I tend not to worry about what was, as there isn't anything I can do about it, anyway. Nor do I look too far into the future—except my mother and I have a similar interest in the occult; she was the one who gave that to me. She had a dear friend who used to read tea leaves. I myself used to go to my mother's friend for readings.

My father died when Mother was thirty-eight and I was nineteen. She raised all three of us and then got married again herself, when she was fifty-one.

## Big Steps

I think I had an advantage that most women do not have. It has to do with something I read in Carol Gilligan's book *In A Different Voice*, which says that women need to learn to be individuals. Men have the opportunity as young boys to go out and try different things early on; women don't get those choices. I was an exception because my father had wanted a boy. Because I was firstborn, I was raised as a boy. I played baseball better than most of the guys, and I often came home with torn clothes because I was always climbing things. One time my mother found me on the roof of a three-story building. My father threw me into the lake at seven, and I quickly learned to swim. Because of that I taught swimming in high school.

Mother gave me dolls, but mostly she just wasn't going to be bothered with me. She'd say, "Why do you have to take such big steps?" When I was sixteen, I wanted to make the transition to the feminine world, but it took a long time. The male world was fun!

My mother's mother was divorced in a time when divorce hardly existed, and that, of course, colored my mother's life. She had to go out and do for herself. So I could, too, but at the same time, because it had not been important to my mother to get involved with her kids, I must have felt cheated. I thought, I'm not going to do that to my kid; my kid is going to have something different from what I had. I had been given so much freedom, only to turn around and become a traditional, overly involved mother.

I admire my mother for her strength and ability to survive under adverse conditions. When she lost her husband, she had not worked in twenty or twenty-five years, but she found herself a job, was almost fired, and stood up for herself with her back to the wall—all while raising three really neat women.

I went to work at fifteen. My father had said, "My daughter is not going to work," and my mother said, "Leave her alone. It'll be good for her." I worked for the magnificent sum of three dollars a day at Goldblatt's. Later, at Saks Fifth Avenue, I worked every single day after school, and then Monday and Thursday evenings and all day Saturdays. That was to help pay for college.

## A Woman's Career

When I graduated from high school in 1944, I wanted to join the WACS, and my mother said no. I wanted to become a nurse or a social worker, and my mother said no. In those days it wasn't acceptable to do anything except get married. Fortunately, I had an uncle who manufactured dental X-rays, and that's how I got into dental hygiene.

Dental hygiene turned out to be a marvelous career for women. I was in the first class (1946) that was licensed in the State of Illinois and was a pioneer in that field. It was hard to get work in those days because the dentists had an underlying fear that, perhaps, the hygienists would take away some of their practice. While dental hygiene fulfilled some of my needs to serve, today I would probably become a doctor or go into a business because I've got a head on my shoulders.

## The Great Depression and World War

My family lost everything! My father was a pharmaceuticals salesman; toward the end it was almost as if he were another Willy Lohman. My father had one of his heart attacks when I was around fifteen. Mom said, "I gotta go," left me in charge of my two younger sisters and went down to Springfield, where they had taken him off the train.

It was a lot of fun being in dental school during the war with the naval students. I became interested in one young man and wrote to him when he was out to sea, but when he came back, I wasn't interested in him any longer. He looked different out of uniform.

My husband Robin and I had grown up in Rogers Park and gone to high school together. At fifteen I nudged one of my friends and said, "That's the guy I'm going to marry." I had a friend in the office at school and was able to get Robin's program. Robin never understood why I just happened to be standing outside the door as he was walking out of his classes. I even asked him out for our first date. After high school, I wanted to be in charge of my life, so I broke up with Robin. I'd finished dental hygiene school, when Robin called and we went out again. A couple of months later we were engaged. Neither one of us was ready for marriage, and neither one of us knew how to tell the other. Our marriage was pretty stormy that first year. Two years later we had Chuck, and twenty-two months after, we had Tia.

## Going Bananas

I reclaimed my "femininity" by buying the traditional package. I tried to emulate both my mother and my mother-in-law and to become very much a part of that Jewish middle class, which meant staying home and taking care of the kids and working for the League of Women Voters and the temple. I was going bananas.

I started working two half-days and ended with four days a week. I juggled home, children, house, job—an absolutely typical "Supermom." Would leave the office in my uniform and go to a school play on my lunch hour. Then I'd run back to the office. Or I'd leave the office during a snow storm, go home, drive the sitter home, come back and shovel the driveway. Or go home from the office, get rid of the sitter, start dinner, and go to the train to pick up Robin. I had to prove I was still part of that middle class, even though I was working. It was not acceptable for middle-class women to work in those years. Oh, boy, did I get flak. "Poor Audrey—her husband can't take care of the family."

## Switching Gears

By age fifty I decided that I was going to go off and do my own thing. I knew the only way I'd get off dental hygiene was to move out of Chicago. It was pretty harrowing at fifty, but I had the guts to leave. Once we moved, I wouldn't have changed that for the world. What a marvelous way of living!

I didn't care whether Robin needed me to take care of him. I was restless and had done a lot of self-evaluation. Before we left Chicago, we searched cross country. At Fayetteville, Arkansas, I said, "This is it." We took another trip to the northwest, including Alaska, just to make sure.

After three years in Fayetteville, we moved to Stillwater, Oklahoma. I'd finished my undergraduate degree and then went down to enroll in a Master's program. Soon Robin decided that he needed to find someone to take care of him, and he did—the old poop. That was a tear in the gut. I'd made the erroneous assumption that, since I had done all the taking care, it was my turn. Still, I went on—which amazes me when I think about it—and finished my graduate studies: 4.0.

## Success!

I knew that I needed to do that for myself. I was going to move myself up to the top—no friends, no sisters, no children, no husband in the way—and that's exactly what I did. I put my toe in the water and took it one step at a time. It was the best thing that I ever did in my life.

Robin has accepted my new way of life and has finally decided on a recommitment. He and I share the housework now. It's a whole different marriage because I'm as important as he is.

Oh, I'm so proud of myself! Along with school, I've gone through therapy. The important part is knowing myself. If I don't know myself, then I certainly can't help other people.

I don't know how Tia or Chuck stood me, but they were marvelous. Tia gave me telephone privileges: "I don't care if it's three o'clock in the morning, you pick up that phone and call me." I soon realized that, since my husband was also her father, she didn't need all this nonsense.

My relationship with Tia is very special. Tia has been willing to share, even though it's been difficult: she had to overcome a steamroller mother. She has the guts to tell me to back off, but she also has allowed me in her world.

Tia may be my daughter, but I had nothing to do with the marvelous woman she has become. She's taught me an enormous amount, and I'm willing to listen. It's been a two-way, give-and-take with both of us. Tia always marched to a different drummer, and it took me a long time to accept who she was and what she needed to do.

Tia kept saying, "Mother, you got the wrong daughter at the hospital." I'd say, "Tia, you're absolutely wrong." She sure wasn't Nancy. That's what I named her. When she took the name Tia, it helped me to see her in a different way. Nancy no longer existed as what I had hoped for her. Even her dancing—I don't even know if she knows this—is something I wanted to do. *I* wanted to dance. Tia took ballet lessons very early on. Then she decided not to do that anymore. She was in the process of making some changes in her life, and that's about the time she decided to move away. Lately, she has let me know that a lot of the bumpiness in her life was her own responsibility.

## A *Babe* in the *Woods*

Twenty years ago I was probably self-effacing but not any more. I'm going to be fifty-nine in September. One of my idols is Maggie Kuhn, the head of the Gray Panthers. If she at seventy-five can do what she does, then I'm only a babe in the woods. If I can, I'll live to be 102, so I'm just now hitting middle age. There's probably a *third* career down the road for me. It freaks my clients out when I say that. I'm real proud about my age, and I've never wanted to lie about it.

Women have enormous potential. I'm hopeful that they will have the opportunity to realize their dreams. I tell my clients right off that I'm a "blazing feminist," and they want to know whether that means they have to burn their bras. I say, "No, it means you have the potential to do whatever you want to do, whether that's staying at home and taking care of your children; whether that's going to work and doing something like be a doctor; or whether it means juggling it all. You have the potential for going back to school at fifty or for going on to graduate school at thirty. You don't have to be hampered by gender or age." I hope that I will serve as a model for Tia to understand that nothing in this world is cast in concrete.

I've always tried to maintain some link with my children, no matter how superficial. It took me forty years before I could accept my mother and forgive her for what she wasn't. I'm grateful that Tia's been able to do that much earlier. For a couple of years she has been vacillating between calling me "Mom" and "Audrey." As long as she talks to me, I'll answer to anything— even "Hey, you!"

## TIA PADORR-BLACK

Audrey Jasper was born in Chicago. When? Good question! She's fifty-seven...I think. It seems that her family was close. I remember seeing many pictures of her with cousins and sisters. It was a protective environment, but it also defined and circumscribed her life. It was a long, long time before she could feel she had an existence apart from her family's perception of her. In one photograph she and a cousin are standing up on a chair together, and what I remember about the picture is that she seemed to be such a happy, radiant, adorable child. She lost that radiance, as we all do, in the process of growing up.

Audrey never said that she had a happy childhood. The sad and difficult times made more of an impression on her than the happy ones. The family went through some tough times together, and her parents' relationship was really difficult. Her parents, she told me, were domineering, demanding, and exacting. As a child, she had a hard time because of that.

One thing that stood out in her mind, for example, is coming home with four A's and three B's and her father coming down hard on her because she had not gotten all A's. Her achievements weren't ever appreciated or recognized, and she felt much less attractive than her two sisters. The youngest child was "the bright one," and the middle child was "the social one." As the oldest, she became their caretaker. After her father's first heart attack, her mother put her in charge of the house and her sisters. When she was twelve, her dad died and her mother had to go back to work to support the family. There were great pressures on Audrey to be independent as well as to help more with the family. Unfortunately, the night her dad died, she had had a big argument with him. For years she blamed herself for his death and had to resolve that with therapy.

*Audrey Jasper Padorr.*

*Gertrude and Audrey.*

*Tia and Audrey.*

*Tia Padorr-Black.*

## A Lack of Feedback

Audrey's assets were overlooked. She's a bright person in her own right, but without any feedback from others she doubted her own ability and intelligence. People who knew Audrey well didn't seem to look beneath the surface. At that time, internal qualities were overlooked. Audrey is a generous, kind, and thoughtful person, fiercely loyal to her principles as well as to her family and friends. Although she was ahead of her time in some respects, her values were not seen as being particularly remarkable or special. As she grew, though, she must have struggled to retain a sense of self-worth. Audrey has talked about playing piano and enjoying that. Yet in her family they couldn't do something just for the enjoyment. She had to play with the intent of becoming a concert pianist.

What made her different from her sisters? Well, maybe it was because Audrey was closer to her father—a real independent spirit—than her sisters were. I wonder whether she found the courage to be different by looking at him. She became a real nonconformist. Sometimes she calls it being a "loner." She never belonged to a clique and always felt on the outside of all that superficial social stuff, whereas her sisters seemed to plug into that easily.

## Gertrude

I remember Audrey talking about not having much money at all. I think her family was extremely poor. After all, her mom was supporting three children. Gertrude, my grandmother, was quite an independent woman. When her husband died, she seemed to come into her own personality. She had always been under Charlie's thumb. It was always "Yes, yes, yes. I'll do this and I'll do that." As soon as Charlie died, the family was taken aback by her sudden resolve and willpower. She refused to be supported by any of the other members of the family and wouldn't accept any help, or very little, with taking care of the children or with making ends meet. She just went out and got herself a job.

Gertrude tells a cute little story. "People would ask me how I managed during that hard time. The best advice I could give anybody is to talk to yourself in the mirror." This wonderful advice I follow myself. Obviously, Gertrude, an eccentric with a real strong character, had to have a lot of backbone to get her family through that hard time. I think she was a secretary for a while and then may have moved up to more responsibility. Waiting until after her daughters were all married, she herself remarried.

Her mother's strength greatly influenced Audrey. As soon as she was old enough, she got a job. She was young when she became a mother. When my brother was five and I was three, she went back to work. It gave her some control over her life and something beyond the housewife trip. She has thrived on the independence her work provided.

## Staying Home

As a child, I wanted her to be around more. It seemed that the job, even though it was only part time, required a lot of her psychic energy, and there wasn't a whole lot left for kids, who always expect more than they get. I did feel deprived. Because I missed my mother's energy and devotion, I tried to provide that for my own children. Still, I do understand my mother's choice. I surely can appreciate that, especially now, heading into the birth of my second child. There's something claustrophobic about staying home without an additional focus. It wears you down, just being in the house all the time.

Audrey didn't talk a whole lot about her high school days. She has talked about why she stayed in dental hygiene so many years. She didn't want to face the fears and the risks from admitting she ought to be doing something different. She had ambivalent feelings about her work. I don't recall her talking about her interests at that time; she must have been out of touch with herself. Robin, my father, got frightened during her discovery process, and for a while they separated. When Audrey embarked on her journey, she didn't know it could cost her her relationship with Robin. I think she's still paying for her accomplishments.

It was a real struggle for her, too, because the separation occurred during her last year in graduate school, and she continued all on her own, without his support and with his derision. She was traveling two hours to class and two hours back home, and then she did the graduate work on top of all that. She would not give up! They were still estranged when she graduated.

Audrey was proving to be so highly intelligent, so capable on many fronts. She went through a B.A. program getting mostly straight A's and then went through a graduate program with straight A's. On top of all her graduate work, she was doing volunteer work in counseling and building a fantastic reputation in the community. She was offered some interesting positions, including drug and alcohol counseling, in which she was recently certified.

## Special Friends

It was after she met a group of special women that she started to think about leaving Chicago. She felt that if she could physically leave that area where she had grown up and had made many associations, she could begin anew. Some people can do that right where they are, but she has said she needed that distance. Once she got out of that environment, she started to make rapid changes.

It was so neat. Suddenly she started making friends that represented her new self. Except for those people in her spiritual circle, the friends she had in Chicago seemed to have been in the static mode. The new friends in Fayetteville in the service professions were vital—warm, kind, generous people doing wonderful, innovative, progressive things. They could have been *my* friends.

It seemed to happen so quickly, as if she had simply stepped out of her skin. An amazing, beautiful thing! When I think about what Audrey has done, what she was before and what she has become, I think of Gail Sheehy's *Pathfinders*.

## A New Radiance

Audrey and Robin built a beautiful new home in Fayetteville, and there was a certain beauty and radiance about her, too. There always had seemed to be this big gap in our taste, in our thinking; suddenly there was hardly any gap. I connected with Audrey. I got so close with her because of my respect for her ability to step out like that. At fifty years old she was becoming a person. I never thought she'd have the strength to do that, and I'm so proud of her.

Periodically, Audrey says, "If I wanted to say one thing to all the younger kids and students, it would be: Life is not cast in concrete. No matter how old you are, you have to realize that nothing need be permanent. You can do so much more than you realize. We all have potentials and possibilities we are unaware of that we can tap into with some courage."

Audrey has been quite a role model, helping people to see that life doesn't end after forty. Also, she's been a good and loyal friend. She has an extremely hard time being dishonest or pretending that she's one way while being another way. I've learned some of those things from her. She must be quite an influence on the people she works with, too, because she herself has gone through so many experiences and has been in so many lonely places.

What I like most about her now is that she's starting to develop a sense of humor that's just really wonderful. Everything was so serious and intense before. Just the other day I told her I was very worried about having my next child in the hospital. "What if they take the child away from me?" Audrey says, "Don't worry. You take the baby and run, and we'll all be here to occupy the staff and stop the doctors. You make it out the back door!"

Gosh, when I was a teenager, I would say I pretty much hated my mother. She was very controlling and domineering. She was afraid to let me do anything. She would give me lessons, like ice skating and riding, and I would get to a certain point and she wouldn't give me any more lessons. I kept thinking, "What's going on?"

Just a few weeks ago she told me that's the way her mother was. She wouldn't ever let Audrey sleep over at anybody's house. I said, "God, Mom! You never got to sleep over?" She said, "Well, when I was in high school..." I said, "You had to wait until high school to sleep over? Were your friends' houses contaminated?" She said, "My mother was like that. She was afraid to let me ride a bike in the street."

In my opinion, what happens in some mother and daughter

relationships is that the mother has let the self die, and her daughter knows that and is scared. In my mom's generation getting rid of your own "maiden" name was part of the process. What a horrible moment of realization, when the daughter is trying to move toward life and realizes that there's no life in the mother to relate to, not enough life to spark the daughter. She has to find it somewhere else. As a teenager, I was sure that Audrey was dead and gone. I tried to get as far away from her as I possibly could.

That's the source of the great rift between mothers and daughters. Daughters are in a life and death struggle to find themselves. That's what being young is all about. That's what adolescence is all about. It's the search for selfhood.

# Sweetbreads

$S$ondra, 48, is the divorced mother of three daughters—
Mandy, Martha, and Leslie—and a son, Joel. Several years ago,
when she left her husband, Sondra moved from a wealthy suburb
to the country in a northern county of the state. Here Martha,
17, and Leslie, 16, discuss their mother's transformation from
fifties housewife Sandy Sands to Sondra Rowan (her maiden
name). They respect and adore the person their mother has
become but must also deal with her lingering rage from the past.
In contrast to Sondra's radical feminism, her mother's life was led
as the traditional wife of a professional.

## SONDRA ROWAN

After my mother died, I felt sorry I knew so little about her
history. At the time she was alive, of course, I never cared very
much. My mother, I know, was born in Philadelphia, and I just
found out a few months ago that her parents were born in Russia,
not America. Having my own children makes me want to know
more about my mother. My brother told me that as a young girl,
my mother lived with her family—quite wealthy people—in a
hotel penthouse in Baltimore. When the hotel burned to the
ground, they lost all their possessions.

So my grandparents moved out west and my mother went to
high school in the city. They lived in a very fancy area, which
was all gated in in the middle of the city. My mother grew up in a
huge house, which I saw as a child, and then her father lost

*Names have been changed because "Sondra" didn't want to censor her story.

everything in the Depression. He was flat broke. All this made me understand my mother's desperate need for security and why, for instance, she insisted I marry a professional man. From the time I was born, my mother knew exactly under what tree I was going to be married.

## Trial by Fire

I didn't discover all this until a year ago. I had vaguely recalled the fire and that Grandpa had lost everything in real estate. They ended up in a small apartment, and to me as a child they seemed destitute compared to us. We lived in a very well-off neighborhood. I felt sorry for my grandparents, but I'm sure they were just fine. They were, apparently, socially conscious, whatever that was in Jewish society, as was my mother. She chose a husband, my father, who was already a professional when at thirty she married him.

The perfect wife and mother, her goal was to build her whole life around her children and husband. I resented that until the last few years, as I have come to understand her situation. She was an extremely talented woman who never did much with her talent because at that time it wasn't acceptable for a woman. She was an outstanding public speaker and an actress. She went back to college to get her Master's in theater arts, and she acted in plays there. But the rehearsals took her away from my father too much, and he didn't like it, so she quit. She said, "Dad doesn't want me to do it," but I always suspected that she was looking for an excuse to stay home. In retrospect, I'm sure that even though he may never have actually said that, she *knew* he didn't want her to get her Master's. She *knew* he needed her to be the subservient housewife. Even now, he's into conventional roles for women. He calls himself a liberal, but I've heard him make horrible, sexist remarks about women lawyers and judges.

Until the last couple of years, I thought my father was God and my mother was the problem. Those were the days when the wife was seen as the complaining bitch who drove the nice guy to drink.

Imagine the confusion of being brought up in this kind of family, "tolerant of everybody"; yet when I went out with a Mexican guy, Lenny Gomez, my mom removed the picture of him on my desk, when a friend of hers came to stay in my room.

It was the same thing with sexism. Now I can understand my mother's duty to please my father by fulfilling her traditional role. I mean, that's what he liked about her! And when I veer from his view of the "right" kind of woman, he's frantic to control me.

My mother developed her talents within those limits, so a lot of her creativity came out in her needlepoint, and she's an incredible seamstress, too. She sewed my clothes, my children's clothes—little hand-smocked dresses; beautiful, beautiful things. "Crafts" are really art within the context of that one acceptable avenue for women, homemaking. In fact, Alice Walker discusses that in *In Search of Our Mothers' Gardens*. Black women in the South, while living in squalor, creating these magnificent gardens.

## Very Nice, Dear

So I can understand, when I think of my mother getting out there and trying to be an actress, how frightening public speaking was in the male world. If you weren't blatantly put down, then you were placated: "Very nice, dear, very nice. Why don't you go home now and do your cooking?" Hence the creativity in homemaking.

My mother had what they termed in those days a menopausal depression. It was a nervous breakdown that went on for years. She had a nurse around the clock and was afraid to go out of the house. Here was a formerly social woman. A lot of it had to do with that feeling of being "crazy," and I grew up with that, always thinking *I* was "crazy."

My ex-husband is a doctor, and he's got the brains. He knows better than to be the guy on the street who whistles at you. Instead, he's the guy who tells you how wonderful you are, how much he needs you—all those things that you need to hear, right? So I married a manipulating man who needed a woman to behave in a manipulative way.

And that is how my mother was with my father. That is, as long as my father was in control, everything was fine. An incredible thing about women, including my mother, is that they think the only way to get what they need is by manipulating or whining or ailing. You didn't *ask* for what you needed because the response would be, "How dare you need something!"

You cannot ever be intimate with anyone if you have this big wall inside. I realized in therapy that what people called my strength was rather a façade to keep myself alive, to survive. But I've learned that it does feel better when things don't sit inside and boil.

Both my parents were a hundred percent outer-motivated. Losing everything in her life made my mother's case even worse. She never asked me what would make me happy.

## An Awful Perfection

Here I was, the perfect mother of four perfect little kids in perfect clothes; the perfect wife with the perfect doctor husband and the nice little perfect house in the suburbs. My mother didn't even want to know what was going on with the marriage. "Don't tell me, don't come to me, I don't want to hear it."

When I became engaged, my mother gave me a lecture I'll never forget. She was standing in front of the kitchen stove and said, "When your husband comes home from work, if you're cooking dinner and he wants 'it,' you turn off the cooking. I don't care if you're in the middle of a gourmet dinner; you turn it off and you go."

Somewhere deep inside I knew this was wrong. As the separation started happening, I thought I was going to have a nervous breakdown. I lost twenty pounds. I mean, I had been married for seventeen years and had four children. I went through the divorce and therapy with incredible pain and change. But I guess the process of reclaiming myself really started after the trauma was over. It's funny. Martin used to call me "Sandy," and everyone he knew called me Sandy—and I *was* Sandy Sands, a different human being. Now I've changed by name back to Sondra Rowan. That's who I am.

## A Different Planet

And I'm not like my mother anymore. I feel as if I'm from a different planet than my family—in fact, than most people. I've never been happier in my life, being alone, and a man would have to be damn special to be in my life. But it took a lot of years. Before the divorce, I never talked to my children about what it was like for me. After all, I was still Sandy Sands, trying to appear as though everything were okay, trying to shield them from it all. I still get guilty over how the kids suffered.

One time I just started to scream and shriek. I had just sat down with my kids about two months before and really let them have it about supporting me when I'm angry with their father. I said, "I never ask you not to love your father; but you can certainly tell when I have a right to be mad at him, and I just need you to not run away from me as if I had the plague. I really don't like to vent my anger in front of you, but sometimes it just happens that you're here and he does something, and you all start acting like, 'Don't do this to me!' as if I'm doing something to you."

While this "primal scream" was coming out of me, Martha, my sixteen-year-old middle daughter, came running in the room and lay down on top of me and put her arms around me. My other daughter was standing in the doorway. She didn't know what to do, but she didn't want to run away. I mean, if I were she, that would have scared the shit out of me. But they were there. My daughter lay on top of me until I stopped. It brings tears to my eyes—talk about supportive! Then I was able to get up and deal with it, whereas before, I would have gone on for weeks.

## Emotions

I said to Martha, "That must have been pretty scary for you." She said it wasn't. With Martha it was real clear that these were my emotions. It had nothing to do with her, and she knew she didn't have to be afraid of them.

We women grew up thinking that our emotions "killed" other people. My mother taught it to me ("You are killing your father"), and I am sure I taught it to my kids the first half of their lives. That's when my kids probably had a confusing time because half their life they saw me one way and the other half another way.

Only in the last five years, say, have I been able to give my daughters some clear messages about the way things are, and I think they're confused. Leslie, my youngest, has really got the message because she has grown up with it. Mandy, the oldest, had it the least. Martha, my sixteen-year-old, is following in my Sandy Sands footsteps. I adore her; she's a sensitive, wonderful kid, but she's totally dependent on her boyfriend for her happiness.

Mandy's gotten a lot because we talk a lot when she comes home, probably more than Martha and I talk in the whole six months. When someone's been away, you're intent on catching up on things. But Mandy and I talk more politically, so she misses out on the personal. When she was growing up, I was much more closed, trying to present an image of who I was, hiding things I didn't want them to know. I don't do that now— although there are still probably things my kids don't know about me and I don't know about them simply out of lack of curiosity.

## Good Girl

I was born in the city where my mother was also born. My father was probably very early into his profession, and we lived in a little house in the west part of the city. We always had maids and nurses, even when my family had no money. That was my mother's thing; she was raised that way. We didn't have a live-in until I was seven or eight, when we moved to our new home.

I was a very good child. I'm sure I was the nicest kid in town. Really! I was cute, I was sweet, I did everything I was supposed to do; I was the perfect child. I adored ballet, and my dogs, and my parents always lied to me about what happened to them. It's hard to know how much I remember and how much is from pictures. We have no pictures of me roller skating; yet I remember rolling skating and skinned knees. I was also very athletic, and I loved to hang out with my brother, who didn't want me trailing him around.

Supposedly, I started having asthma attacks after I was four years old. I would go to school for days and days when I could not even breathe. There was nothing to do, except go on, and then if it got really bad, my mother would give me adrenalin shots. At any rate, I was never hospitalized, but asthma was a big part of my life. I seemed to outgrow it for a while, and when I had Mandy, my first baby, it came back.

As a teenager, also, I was the best little girl. I dated, probably more than I wanted, because of the pressure. Actually, I preferred to hang out with my girlfriends. I always had a crush on some guy, but dating, just to date, was not my thing. Saturday night you had to have a date. I hear it's not true so much anymore. Occasionally, I got hooked into going out with someone I didn't like and always regretted it. A lot of girls didn't care who they went out with as long as they had a date. I remember every guy I dated—even their names. Just the other night I even had a romantic dream about this guy I was fixed up with on a blind date in college. It turned out to be this jerk I had known in high school. He got drunk at this party, so I insisted on driving home—and got stopped by a cop. My date got out and started bullying the cop, so they threw him in the cop car and took him away. I still had his car.

When I was in fourth grade, a little boy who adored me kept putting things like melted candy bars in my desk, and I'd get so mad. His name was Ozzie. At a birthday party, the mother had the boys put lipstick on all the girls to play post office. Ozzie kept throwing me in the closet and trying to make out with me, so when my mother picked me up, I had lipstick smeared all over my face.

## The Boys Are Calling

After fifth grade and Albert Winslow, who came up to my belly button, it was seventh grade and Eric Jansen. I used to wear Eric's jacket. My best friend Sunny started liking Eric and wanted to wear his jacket, so she and I didn't talk for a while.

Then at a dance I danced with Eric. He was chewing blackjack gum, and it smelled so awful that I hated him after that. He probably thought he had good breath from chewing it, but it made me sick.

Then came Jeremy, my first hot romance. We made out and petted all over the place but not to get caught. I wore his St. Christopher medal! I think I still have it.

Next came tenth grade and Cal Gillespie. He was really cute and was the rowdy of the school. Cal came and got me one time to go to this party at his uncle's house. I was not allowed to go to a party unless an adult would be there. Well, his uncle was sixteen! These people were doing it in the bedroom and drinking beer, and I was petrified. I kept telling him to take me home, and finally I went out and sat in the car (I was such a good girl). I was so scared, and I told my parents. I always told my parents everything. Cal came to the house one day, and my brother told him never to come take his sister out again.

Then came Raymond Spenser. He was really cute, too, but he was a jerk. I always picked the really good-looking jerks because I was always attracted to them. Ray was a hot one.

## The Biggest Romance of All

My biggest romance, actually, other than Martin, was in eleventh grade, when I had a crush on this guy named Dane Barr. I liked his name, and he was a nice person. He really loved me, and it's probably because of that that I didn't love him, which says something about who I was. Never did we have intercourse, but we did everything else, and I would feel so guilty that I would cry and call myself a whore.

My mother would always say, "Now, you know Dane's a very nice boy. But, you know, socially your classes are different, and you'll *never* marry, and you'll only end up hurting him." This is how my mother always got me to break up with people, or not to get serious. Dane worked in a gas station; Dane was not going to be a professional—very similar to Martha's boyfriend, which is interesting. Nice, yes, but nice doesn't matter; professional matters. So what did I marry? A jerk who was a professional.

I broke up with Dane when I went off to college, and he was so upset. I think that's why I've always chosen men who would break up with me. Breaking up with Dane was the most painful thing I had to do. I remember crying and crying hysterically at home and my mother coming in. I felt so awful. But I got over it, needless to say, went right into college, got back in the swing. Still, I wonder sometimes what Dane is doing. I figure he's probably a very nice person to be married to. He probably treats his family right. Funny.

As a freshman in college, I met another guy I was hot for. I met him skiing, and he was a playboy and so good looking—Don

Vinciguerra, and my mother used to call him "Vinegar Boy." Of course, that name probably killed her. "Italian? She's going to marry an Italian?" All my mother wanted me to do was meet a nice Jewish boy. Here now is Don Vinciguerra, after Dane, right? Now she's really having a heart attack. Don and I probably went out for about five months, and then he dumped me.

## A Nice Jewish Boy

After that, basically, came Martin. My parents had bribed me with a '55 Thunderbird to go to a certain college so I'd meet a nice Jewish boy. I went to that college for one semester, re-met Martin (whom I'd known since junior high), started dating him and went back to a different college.

Martin was sneaky and horrid from the time I met him. He was cheating on his girlfriend who thought she was going to marry him. She was in the hospital with pneumonia when he started going out with me. He actually called me to get the phone number of somebody I knew to date, and then somehow we started going out. The good girl wouldn't go out with him as long as he was going out with the other woman (who loved him madly), but he'd lie and say he wasn't.

I was madly in love with Martin, whatever that means, which says something else about me. I once broke the engagement with him. I threw the ring at him and went home, and my father lectured me: "You don't threaten. If you say it's the end, then it's the end, and you better think of what you're doing." It scared me out of my wits. I mean, it had to be a *final decision*, and breaking off the engagement wasn't what I wanted; I was just angry. I quickly called him and apologized. Of course, he took me back. He had nothing to lose, only to gain. He was always trying to get me to go to bed, and I would never let him, until he threatened me with some other woman. I finally agreed and then ended up getting pregnant because I was so naive, and I had an abortion. Martin's whole motivation, as long as I knew him, was sex. Every time I looked at him cross-eyed, man, I was on the floor. I thought I hated sex because I was so tired of it; I thought I was "frigid."

## Dangers of a Boy's Lap

The other thing my mother said was the very opposite. This was the only other time we talked about sex: "Never sit on a boy's lap. You will excite him, and the poor dear can't help himself. It'll be your fault." That was her pre-marriage advice. I wouldn't give *my* daughters pre-marriage advice. How can I give them advice? Look at my marriage. If they asked me a question, I'd answer it. The message I've always tried to impart to them is to be peers of the man you're with. You have to know who you are, he has to know who he is.

## Relieved

My mother died in 1975, ten years ago. I felt a tremendous amount of relief (I mean, after all the trauma of her dying), and I'm amazed to this day that I was honest with myself about how I felt about her dying because that was a no-no to feel relieved. Yet I did, and I admitted it. I mean, I cried and was very upset and angry she'd left me, but glad she was gone in a lot of ways. She lived five minutes away and was always at my house. I would drive home, and there she'd be sitting in my driveway waiting for me to get home. Four kids and I'm trying to do my thing, and there's Mom.

But there were wonderful things about her. The kids loved her; she was a wonderful grandmother. She took Mandy for three months when I was in the hospital. (Isn't it interesting that Martin didn't take care of Mandy?) Mandy was three years old, and my mother was pretty old and fragile by then, and it's hard when you haven't had a child around.

Still, it was a relief. My life started when my mother died. I really believe that.

## No Life of Her Own

I don't know a lot about my mother, and part of it's my fault; I just wasn't that curious. I'd like to know more about her, if she were here to tell me, but I don't pursue that information, and I don't think my kids do, either. Well, we do sometimes talk about family—spontaneously. There's nothing in me to make me wish someday I could tell the kids about such-and-such, or anything like that. I have no need to know, for example, about Martha's personal relationship with Daniel or Mandy's relationship with Ron, unless they want to share something that they haven't brought up. That's their affair. I don't need to control them. My father is trying to control Mandy's choice of husband. As I told him, "That's for Mandy to decide. I married a man you chose for me, and look what happened." Instead of Dane, who inside was a genuinely nice human being, I picked the outside. I just feel that only Martha and only Mandy and only Leslie can really make that choice. If I saw anything that really bothered me, I would tell them; still, I have no need or desire to tell them what to do. Some of that, in my opinion, has to do with having your own life, your self-esteem.

My mother had no life of her own. We were her life, so how could she let go of telling me what to do, when it meant she would have to do something about her own life?

The whole message my mother gave to me was your life is not your own. It's family, community, temple. If anyone tries to take any of those away from you, you're losing a chunk of yourself. As a mother, I don't feel that way—at least, not yet!

## LESLIE SANDS

My mother was born April 8, 1938. When she was growing up, they used to take a lot of trips to the Grand Canyon, and she liked that. She's always told us lots of stories. When she was a teenager, she and her friend used to go with their dates when they would hunt grunions on the beach. She and her friend didn't like to do it.

She always dated the studs of the school, the popular ones. I haven't seen any pictures of any of her boyfriends, though. She was particularly fond of Dane.

She had a lot of girlfriends. One of her stories is they'd laugh so hard, they'd wet their pants. Once they laughed at one boy my mom was supposed to go out with because he was bald. Her mom made her go out with him; she was always setting her up with someone because she didn't want her daughter to become an "old maid," I guess. I don't think my *mom* was afraid of that. She was popular.

My mom was probably afraid of her parents. I don't know why I think that. Her mom used to try to force her to eat. I'm not sure, but I don't think they were that close; and her mom was kind of protective of her.

My mom wanted to be a ballet dancer; and she said when she was little she wanted four kids named Sandy, Dusty, Rusty, and Hank. Why she liked those names I don't know!

She talks, too, about what she was like before the divorce. At that age, you don't really think about what your mom is like. I suppose she regrets not doing something she wanted before marriage and the kids. I think she got married because it was the easier way. Back then, you know, you didn't have a lot of choices except to be a teacher or get married, and if you married a doctor, that was pretty good. You'd be rich. She wanted to make her parents happy. She must have loved my dad in a way, but I don't know what that way was.

## The Divorce

She's never told me what it was like when she first got married, but later, it wasn't too good. She was unhappy. I don't remember that, though. They were divorced when I was six, and then we moved up here. Well, I don't remember her being that happy when we moved up here, either.

She talked a lot more about my dad when we were older. When we were little and she was struggling with all of that, she didn't talk about what it was really like to be a wife. Only recently has she told me, "Don't get married." And she says, "Be careful, or you'll be sorry later. Be careful that you really want to get married, and make sure you have a plan set out for when the divorce comes. Marriage is a risky thing." I won't get married for a long time, and I think motherhood is hard. It's hard to be a single parent, a divorced parent. Without the other partner, you can't decide what you want for your kids. When the kids are with you, they do one thing; when they're with the other parent, everything you've taught them can get erased. As a result, the kids will act in a way you disapprove. When you have kids, you're bound to fight. You have something to fight about besides yourselves.

My life would definitely be different if I hadn't had her for a mother. She's had a big influence on me. She's always telling me bad things about the world I don't want to hear, so now I'm more aware.

It seems there's something new every day! I believe that the things she talks about are worthwhile, but sometimes I don't want to hear it because I already know it. My mom lectures a lot, always telling me the same thing over and over again; and when you tell her you already know, she gets mad. Mom will never admit she's wrong. She says I won't, either. When we do fight (rarely), we both get so mad. And I cry easily so it's even worse for me because I can't finish what I have to say. I'd like to be able to say to her, "Leave me alone sometimes. Just don't push me; don't tell me all the problems of the world." Yet if I didn't have my mother, I'd probably be just like everybody else in my school: dumb and walking around thinking only of myself. I feel I have a broader picture. In general, instead of being unaware, I'm aware. Maybe she lectures so we won't get into trouble; she'd rather lecture than have to ground us. She says her parents lectured *her* a lot, mostly about how it's important to be smart in order to make money and not be poor like them.

Mom offers her opinion, regardless of whether people want to hear it. Sometimes that can be very embarrassing. She's just never...quiet. It's always, "Well, I've just gotta tell you that..." Nevertheless, my friends like my mom. They think she's different. I like her too. I *love* her—even though she has her bad points.

What's most important to her this very moment is trying to keep Reagan from doing any harm. Trying to keep oil out of the Pacific Ocean. Now she's opening a store, starting a new career. She has to. If she doesn't, she's not going to make it in the world. If she had her choice, she wouldn't do anything. She's being pushed into it, now that she has that threat hanging over. In 1990, almost all of her present income is going to be cut off—all of it, actually.

If I had to sum her up in a couple of words, I'd say stubborn, honest; she can't lie even when she's forced to. She's pretty wimpy about that. You've got to be able to lie a certain amount to get through life. To sum up her message: Don't let yourself get pushed around. Stand up for what you think.

I don't know if I like my life in general right now, but I like my relationship with my mom. But do I like living with her? You bet I do!

# MARTHA SANDS

I've seen my mom's photo albums, and I know that she was a ballerina when she was little. One picture was all crumpled. She told me that she hated that picture and had tried to rip it up, but her mother got it away from her.

## Food and Cigarettes

Whenever they'd go on vacation or whenever she was in a restaurant, she'd order club sandwiches. But one time she told me that when she was in fourth or fifth grade, she wanted to order sweetbreads. My grandpa kept asking, "Are you sure you know what that is?" She kept saying, "I want it. I know what it is." When she got it, she says, "I didn't order this. This isn't what I ordered." The waiter says, "Yes, it is," and my grandpa says, "Yes, it is!" She goes, "No! this is not what I ordered!" "Sweetbreads" sounds so good, like a coffee cake or something.

Because Leslie and I always love a lot of sour cream on our potatoes, she said that when she was young, instead of putting sour cream *on* the potatoes, her mother would make a bowl of sour cream with the potatoes *in* it, and she loved that. Now she loves chocolate. I don't think she did before, but now it's taking the place of her cigarettes. She quit for a couple of years and then started again when we moved up here and the divorce was going strong. After everything settled down, she went to a smoking clinic. We all went to her graduation meeting. I was so proud of Mom; she said it was the hardest thing she ever did.

When I look at her pictures now, I cannot believe the change. I always say that my mom has turned around; she has become a different person. She'd blow-dry her hair straight, and she wore perfect clothes. She worked for J.C. Penney for a while at the mall. There is a picture of a party my mom did for my sister. Everyone came as a different country in the world. My sister was the United States. She had an Uncle Sam top hat on with little flags all around the top, and she was wearing a big flag. So Mom was P.T.A. Woman of the Year—well, maybe not P.T.A., just "straight," like a lot of other mothers. I don't ever remember my mom waking up with us in the morning. I have friends my age whose mothers make breakfast and their bag lunches.

## *Therapy*

We moved up here when I was in third grade, and by the time I was in sixth grade, everything was coming to a resolution for her. She'd gone through therapy, and things were flowing a little more smoothly. She was becoming more of who she is. If she hadn't come to know herself, we would never even know how much alike we are.

Before that, I was so young. She was just my mother. When you're younger you don't think of your mother as a changing, growing person. You don't care what your mom's doing. Your school life and your friends, man—that's all that matters.

But it's different now, and I know her better. We're not just mother and daughter, and I don't have to wonder what my mom's *really* thinking. I have a lot of friends who don't know their mother. I know mine, and I know that she loves me, and we can talk like friends. She's real open, and she never pushes anything on me. She doesn't say, "This is what I want and you do it." She just says, "This is what I think."

This is no big deal, but right now I can think of something that bothers me a lot about my mom: she lectures. Did Leslie tell you this? She doesn't really lecture about us, but she starts getting into something, one of her demonstrations or something, and man! I swear to God, Leslie and I have to sneak away. I start moving slowly away: "Well, Mom, I've really gotta go..." Not that I don't want to listen; but after a while...

There are things she's taught me, I'm sure, that were just from watching, such as, how important it is to know yourself and to be happy with yourself—and of course, you can be confident if you don't know yourself.

Even though I'm at a stage where I'm not as materialistic as most people, and I know that people get so greedy with money, still, I like it. I may not strive just to be rich, and I know that in my brain, but, still, I'm not as free of it as my mom is.

One thing I've learned is that you don't need a man around to raise a family. Mom doesn't say that too much, but she doesn't need to say it; I just know because she's so independent. I like that about her. Right now I'm dependent, as she used to be; I know, because she's told me.

When she talks about marriage and motherhood, she says that

we should make sure that we're happy with who we are. Don't just look for a handsome man with a lot of money. Make sure that he's honest. The truth is the one thing in her relationship that was missing. She also said that her mom pushed so much: "He must look good and be rich, and then you can marry him."

## The Divorce

When the whole thing was going on, Mom would think we were mad at her for talking about Dad, but we weren't. She'd say, "I'm always the bad guy." I'd say, "We don't blame you; it's just that we don't want to hear all that screaming." I know what a dick Dad is, but I wish she could let go of her anger—for her sake.

With her as my mom, I'll grow up happier with myself because I'll have resources to fall back on. A lot of people don't know that life can change with therapy. They strive and strive just to get a house and a car. Once they've reached forty and made it to their goal, they think, "Now what? Where am I?" From my experience with my mom, I know that you have to find things you like to do so you won't have to depend on other people for your job or money.

## A Mom You Can Talk To

I know people who don't even have *one* parent they can rely on. I may have a father who's not so great, but at least I have a mom I can talk to. I think everyone should be able to talk to someone, not necessarily a therapist, but just *someone*. People may have some problems in their life, but they don't take it seriously: "Oh, I don't need to see someone." Mom has given me books and articles for a new perspective on things, such as *The Kin of Ata Are Waiting For You*. I loved it! It just taught me so much about people and life!

I'm at the point in high school where I hang out with just a few friends and don't do what everybody else does. I get so mad at people who do because I know that's false. I'm not saying I'm confident because I'm not at all; there are so many things that I have problems with. After all, that's human to some extent. But some kids will do anything to be popular and even as adults are still excluding people, hanging on to their little society cliques. It seems weird to me because my mom isn't like that at all. Where *are* these people? Why don't they grow up? They're teaching their kids to be exactly like them: to never learn about themselves. I will never be like that, thanks to my mom. Even before therapy, she was always incredibly sensitive. She never excluded people or stepped on their toes. I'm sensitive like her: I cry over everything and can't help feeling sad when awful things happen. If I had a different mother, if I had their parents, I would probably be that way, too, and then I would in turn become that kind of parent.

## "*Warm, Happy, Loving*"

In creative writing we had to write a paragraph or two on our mother and a paragraph or two on our father, and at the end of each we had to write three words describing how we felt while writing it. During my dad's I felt "scared, nervous, uncomfortable." During my mom's I felt "warm, happy, loving"—absolute opposites. The experience of writing it was weird, and what I wrote about her was all good. (I don't know that much that is bad about her.) I don't know why, but I was embarrassed to let her read it. It's hard to give someone a compliment and to reveal something so emotional, so I left my mom alone. When I came back, I could tell she liked what she'd read. Then I was glad I had shown her because I did want her to know how much I look up to her.

I can't imagine, after having such a nice mom as mine, what it would be like not to be proud of my mom. Nor can I imagine being glad, like so many kids, to be away from home. Living with my mom, I have never felt I don't want to come home.

*Leila and Anita.*

# Brussels Sprouts

**A**nita, 30, a divorced single parent, talks about going through a transformation upon the birth of her daughter, Leila. Furiously educating herself, she became a more fulfilled person; now she is studying broadcast journalism. In order to "be there" for Leila, she has worked her life as a person around her life as a responsible and attentive mother. Acutely aware of the snags in the effort to reveal oneself as a person to a young daughter, she also talks at length about her own mother. On the surface they rigidly adhered to the mother-daughter roles; yet there was an undercurrent of a person-to-person relationship, which went unspoken and unacknowledged. Leila is 11, a striking child with bright blue-green eyes and copper hair. She and her mother live in Sonoma County, California.

## ANITA ARCIERI

My mother lived in Florida until her twenties. She went to St. Peter's College, where she met my father. She was a WAC and he was in the Air Force. My dad is from South Carolina, where they lived before moving to Staten Island. My mother went to NYU for a year and decided that she didn't want to get a degree in teaching, so she dropped out. She lives on Staten Island now where she's lived for thirty-five years, over half her life so far. I visit her, but I don't go back East all that often. I hope to have her come out here. When I go there, I'm at *Mom's*; if she comes here, she's at *daughter's*—and that's not what she wants so she resists. She's been to California only one time. I live up here in

Sonoma County, and I went to San Francisco to visit her at her hotel. It's always: "You come here to me."

While I was growing up I really didn't know anything about her. The little I do know I've learned since I've been away from her.

While she was in the WACS she was a USO singer. I'll never know why she didn't go on; that's her private memory. She once had an interest in law. That was the way she wanted to go, but she didn't pursue that, either. She got married and had kids instead. My parents got divorced when I was eleven, and I know that one of the issues from my father's point of view was the *kids*. It makes me wonder what my mother's point of view was when she married this guy. After their divorce, she dated one man for a year. I saw her happy then; however, it ended, and she hasn't been with anyone since I was eleven. My twenty-six-year-old sister still lives at home, and my brother lives close by. She's still in her mother role.

## Almost Equal

We didn't communicate much. My mother had an attitude that we were the children, and she was the parent who mandates and dictates; but I never, ever remember having a conversation with my mother until after I left home. It was years after and usually on my insistence. There are also three thousand miles between us. You can be very brave over the phone when you've got a lot of distance between you. I've lived out here since I was eighteen. There were many times when we'd talk and she didn't like what I'd say, so she wouldn't write or talk to me for two years.

Then my mom worked for twenty years for the New York Police Department in the courthouse. I don't know what she did exactly; she really didn't talk about that. I remember in 1968 she was working at a detention center for women in Manhattan. She got a bench shoved into her leg and ended up in the hospital due to a clot. She had a gun which she kept in a shoebox in my closet because she trusted me. I never, ever looked at it.

Whenever she was going to change the drapes or the furniture or buy a new rug, she would come to me. When we were operating on that level, we were almost like equals. But those times were few and far between. One time my mother had come home from work, and I'd made her something new for dinner. It was haute cuisine. We just sat there looking at each other while she ate more or less silently. It was interesting to watch her mind open up. Every now and then I saw that, but it was so unconscious and too rare to bridge the gap. As a policewoman and single parent, she was in a position of great responsibility and authority. She resented any challenge to her position as much as having to be in it in the first place. I sometimes go through that, too.

Every time I talk to my mother I tell her something from my childhood that I remember about her. A week ago I told her my earliest, strongest memory—the day she gave my favorite dress to my sister because it was too small for me, or so she said.

I don't ever do that with Leila. She's got things I'd love to get rid of. When she outgrows something, I'll say, "Why don't you give that to Molly or Sally?" and she'll say, "No I want it." and I'll say, "Fine."

I was close to my brother but not my sister, who was four years younger than I. I felt like her babysitter all the time. Mostly I remember sweet and pleasant things about my childhood—playing with lots and lots of kids; long, wonderful summers, catching fireflies. My parents aren't even in the picture much.

## Transformation

When I turned thirty, I gave myself permission to say "no," which is real hard for me to do. I had to teach myself how to say "no" to some things and "yes" to others.

My getting pregnant made some realities come into effect very quickly. My husband didn't want to have a child, and there was just no way I wasn't going to have one. I was moving in one direction: into myself. It was the first time in our relationship that I had something that was absolutely mine. Before that, he did all the great things with me at his side.

I remember being at a Thanksgiving dinner before the December birth of my daughter. Two little girls asked me what I was going to name the baby, and I said "Leila." One of the little girls said, "If I had a baby, I'd name her Suzie." I thought about that for days. Should I name her Suzie? Should I *really* name her Suzie? That was absurd, but it's where I was emotionally.

When I was pregnant, I went through changes and had new dreams. The morning after I brought Leila home from the hospital, I heard this voice of urgency in my head: "You've got to get it together now. You don't have any more time." Period. That was it. In the first week I read ten books—big, thick books on anything and everything. Slowly, I started to change, and it was almost like...war maneuvers.

I needed to learn how to survive on my own without my husband, and the birth of my daughter motivated me. Had she not been born, I probably would have floated along; she created for me an immediate responsibility. The sun was real bright in my life, and I've never felt that again. Leila's my only child, and at times I consider having one more—one of my "if the world were different" fantasies I keep in my "crystal bubble." My rational side (learned in the School of Hard Knocks) says I'd be crazy to have another kid right now. It would be five years before I could start thinking about doing something again; ten years to get back to where I am now. Children and family are such an *emotional*, wonderful thing. It's disgusting to have to think, "Can I afford it?" That probably has to do with men. It's been my experience that men don't want children, and I've finally decided it's too hard being a single parent.

## What About You?

Leila is the most important thing to me. Next, becoming an integrated person. In my relationships with men I've lost a lot of time adjusting my thoughts to theirs, giving up my own desires and goals. They don't say, "What about you?" Women have been brought up for centuries to think about everyone else.

The next important thing is what I'm doing right now. I really love what I'm doing, and I'm trying to make my studies a bigger part of my life. My pursuits show Leila what the possibilities are. That's something I never got from my parents. It was always "Be a kid, be a kid; be a teenager, be a teenager; follow the rules, follow the rules; got to bed, get up, go to school."

I would like to see Leila, who's very smart and naturally talented, think her own thoughts and follow her spirit. I want her to know that there are so many options and that they're all right there and she can do whatever she wants to do. It doesn't matter what, just that she stay with it.

Sometimes I regret that Leila and I have a certain closeness because that closeness can intrude upon my personal, individual life. Sometimes I feel, "This would never have happened if I were like my mother."

When Leila was about six or seven years old, I realized I could say to her, "Because I said so." I don't have to give this little person an explanation for why she can't have a dollar for ice cream before dinner. There are times when your daughter can handle information, and times when she can't. My daughter has a very hard time handling my relationships. If there's a man who's interested in me, Leila wouldn't like him if he were Santa Claus. On that issue, we've come through some pretty heavy times, and I try to say to Leila, "This is my life, and you have to respect me in it. All that's required of you is that you be pleasant in this person's company." Sometimes I wish I had never given Leila the choice to voice an opinion from the beginning.

I'm beginning to adjust my actions around the idea that something of mine may be part of her life, but it is not her business. I make arrangements for her to be with friends, and when I go out, I don't take her. But I regret that I have to be that way with her, and sometimes I really dislike her for it. I think, "Who is this person in my life, anyway?"

I do believe in being myself as a mother. As a person, I'm entitled to my privacy. Still, I consider my daughter first in, I would say, ninety percent of everything. When I went back to school, I waited until she was ten, when I really knew that she didn't need me here two hours every morning. Then as she got older, I saw that she didn't really need me for four hours; she could really handle that—she even likes it. It's her own space. For the past two years on Tuesdays, I go to work, school, and get home sometime around midnight. I never considered doing that when she was four or five: she wouldn't have been able to handle it.

## Talking to Daughters

Could mothers tell their daughters more about themselves as a person when their daughters are young? I think it's a good idea. I think some of my habits are bad in that area, and I should change that. I know only one thing about my mother's mother, and that is that she died when my mother was born. I don't know her name or how old she was. I don't know anything about my mother's childhood. I don't know songs that she sang. She never told me that, and I don't pursue it, either. Unfortunately, I do the same thing with Leila. If Leila's in the house singing, sometimes I say, "Oh, I used to sing that when I was a little girl," but I don't consciously tell her what I used to do as a kid. When a child is four through nine, those kinds of things can apply in their world of experience. I often wonder if I will talk to Leila about my teenage years, since they were pretty wild. I'll wait until she's a teenager because I don't want her to justify what she's done by what I've done. I've always been watchful for the appropriate time to say this or that.

Sometimes I'm afraid to talk to my daughter about myself. It's a certain kind of fear; I don't know what kind. As a child, I didn't get that from my mother, so it takes a lot of effort on my part to pass information along to my daughter. But we do spend a lot of time together, just she and I, which I like a lot.

Since Leila is an only child with a single parent, I never want her to feel she has held me up. But sometimes I express a soft regret by saying, "Oh, that would have been neat to do, but Leila was too young and I didn't want to leave her at that time in her life." It's not a concern because when I had my daughter, not only did I have this intense feeling of wanting to get my life together, but I also got ideas. Had I not had her, I would still just be floating around having a good time. I wouldn't have had a purposeful kind of life.

Marriage and motherhood is a big secret that no one ever talks about. Sometimes your grandmother can tell you things, but your mother can't. It's something that has been set up for centuries, and no one dares upset the balance. Men are taught to be talkers, women to be sweet and helpful. That will change, and I want Leila to assume, not hope for, it.

I do talk to her about my fears and anxieties. My biggest fear is that she'll be kidnapped. When we go into stores I say, "Don't go where I can't see you." When she reads the milk cartons, it bothers her that one of her kind, another kid, is in danger: "My God, that kid's been missing for a year." I think, oh my God,

I've put this horrible thing in her head, but then I think, no, that's her own concern because if she didn't want to know about it, she wouldn't read it.

I have always wanted to tell my mother that if she had taken more time to see *me*, I'd have been a really great person a lot sooner in my life. She didn't work with me as an individual or notice the things that I really felt were important. She gave into some things that I wanted, but only because she felt pushed up against the wall.

One year I wanted a camera. I really wanted to get into photography. She gave me a gold watch, instead. I opened the box and looked at it and never said a word. I've never worn it. Giving can be powerful. Because she didn't give me what I wanted, it became a bigger deal than it might otherwise have been, and I had to leave her to find the things I wanted.

I wish I could express to Leila that I'm going to be with her all of her life, whether we're together or apart, and that she can be secure and comfortable, less possessive. I want to say, "Let's look at life as a journey together. Let's travel forever." I really wish my life were *perfect*, whatever that means; then, our lives together would be *perfect*. That's my crystal bubble—and that's it!

# LEILA ARCIERI

My mom doesn't talk about her childhood very much. But I wonder about it, so I'll ask her. I think she liked to do sports. I don't know anything about when she went to school or boyfriends or anything. She told me what she wanted to be when she grew up, but I forget right now.

Her mother is nice. She has a younger sister and an older brother. She told me when the kids would have Brussels sprouts, they would hide them and put them in their napkin. I don't like Brussels sprouts, either.

When my mom lived in New York, she had never heard of an avocado, and when she came out here, she had her first avocado!

My mom works at TV 50. She was a producer for California North, and she goes out and finds places for it to be filmed and what would be interesting for it, and she writes stuff like "Good evening..." That's called bumps and glues. She really likes it.

*Leila.*

*Leila and Anita.*

## A *Nice Mom*

Right now she mostly works. She likes to dance. She visits friends a few times. I don't know what's most important to her. I usually hear about her feelings and stuff because she talks to her friends about it. I haven't heard about any fears yet, except, when she goes to work, she tells me if I go into town to come right back and not to get into anyone's car, not to talk to strangers, and to call her if I go to a friend's house.

What I like about my mom is she's usually nice. I'm like her in some ways. Sometimes I have a short temper, like with people who don't listen. And she would probably want me to not be as shy as I am.

# A Ton of Coal

**J**une,* 65, is a brave tough cookie with a deep voice and a beautiful Roman face revealing sleepless nights of planning and scheming. She would have been dependent on her husband but from the start found a way to get her kids a life she wanted for them. Recently, she gave her daughter Lisa the money to start her own bookstore in Vermont. Theirs is a story of the mother-daughter alliance within a family in which, on the surface, the father had all the power. Before opening a bookstore, Lisa was a social worker. In her early thirties, she has been undergoing a transformation as she struggles to accept life as it comes. A mature, aware, lovely woman, Lisa has, nevertheless, been unable to find a suitable partner.

## JUNE VACCARO TRAVANTI

I was born July 14, 1919, in New York City and raised during the Depression.

When I was sixteen, I met Mickey, but he died of rheumatic fever soon after we started going out. *Him* I really loved. Oh! Mickey was handsome with the most marvelous head of black, wavy hair and green eyes. Well, of course, when I was *that* young, I went for the good looks.

By the time I met Johnny, I was going for something else. Johnny was married and he wasn't that good-looking. When my girlfriend saw him, she said, "Why are you going out with him?" I don't know if I was madly in love, but he was very good

*Names have been changed.

sexually, and I knew he had a steady job. He was dance-crazy, and I loved to dance, too. Until I got married, I worked in a money-printing company as a feeder. I'd put this big sheet on the machine that would ink it up as dollar bills—foreign, not American!

I worked a two-to-ten shift, and in the afternoon my girlfriends and I would stop at the ice cream parlor. That's where I met Johnny. We started to kid around, and the next thing I know, it's "Let's go out," and from there on it all just happened. To tell you the truth, if it wasn't for wanting to have children, I wouldn't have wanted to get married.

I got married when I was twenty-nine. We're a late-marrying family. I had been going with Johnny for a long time. Then after seven years, I was thinking to myself, he's not going to marry me. I said to him, "Look, we're going no place. Let's break it off." I went home and was jumping all over. I got one terrific headache. "This is no good," I said.

## A Kick in the Stomach

So I looked for Johnny the next day and couldn't find him. The day after that, we met for a couple of drinks. That's the night we decided we'd get married. He and my mother didn't get along. She said, "June, I bet your bottom dollar that guy's married." I said. "Oh, no, Ma; he's not." So, sure, after six months he told me he was married. Oh, that was like a kick in the stomach. By that time I really cared for him. He got a divorce, and then we got married. My mother said she wouldn't come to our wedding. I said I didn't care. I never argued with my mother until I got married, when I had to be the peacemaker between her and my husband. I had to stick to one of them. It would have to be my husband.

In the first six months of marriage Johnny raised his hand to hit me. "Go ahead, go ahead, hit me," I says. "I'll call the cops so fast, you won't know what hit you." He turns around and walks out of the house, furious. I never did let him step on me: From that day to this, only once did he lift a hand to me. When I was about fifty-five, he slapped me across the face. Seeing I was so damn mad, he walked away fast.

I wanted children very badly. The *first month* I wondered,

"Why aren't I getting pregnant?" I got pregnant two months after I got married. Imagine, even though my womb is tilted and it's hard for me to get pregnant. I got my son. Boys run in my family, and I desperately wanted a daughter. When I went to the hospital for the second time I told the doctor, "I want a girl." He said, "Well, I'll do the best I can."

## A Quirk

The first time I'm pregnant, one day my husband and I come out of the Y where he always plays handball, and I've got a big stomach. He says, "Walk a couple of steps ahead of me. I don't want people to know what I did to you." He was *serious*. It was a quirk with him. For the nine months I was pregnant, he'd run around all over. The day the baby was born everything would go back to normal. The second time I told him I was pregnant, the same thing happened all over again. I figured the third time I get pregnant, I'm not going to tell him—because I had noticed the pattern; and I decided not to try for a third child.

I never asked him what the deal was. I knew it was something he couldn't help. If I had asked him, he would have said, "It's nothing, nothing." He's the type of person who thinks nothing's wrong with him; it's always the other guy.

Once I got the kids, I never worked. I *loved* being a housewife. All the young girls today want to work. What, I often wonder, do they get out of it? At home you're your own boss. A good husband and a good provider is the key. I guess that's what they can't find anymore, though. Things are completely out of hand. A young kid can't even buy a house. That's why I'm so protective of Lisa.

## Running the House

I would get thirty-five dollars a week to run the house. I was pregnant with Jack, and Johnny was running around. I figured, how does he afford it? One time I look in his wallet, and I see two-hundred-forty dollars in there. I think, "You bastard!" Well *I* was going to have *myself* a little kick. So from then on I used to take five dollars and put it in the bank. Then Johnny's first wife got married, and he wanted me to take their fourteen-year-old son. I took the son, but I said, "It's impossible for me to manage on the money you give me." I got a hundred dollars a week from then on. Then I could pack it away. Before we left my mother's house, I had five thousand dollars in the bank. Boy, over the years I saved thirty thousand dollars, just out of the house money. A hundred dollars a week was a lot of money then, and we ate cheap. I'd buy Spam and put pineapple and cloves in it and bake it in the oven with a can of sweet potatoes.

Anyway, I figured to myself very quickly in the first year of marriage, Johnny bets the horses and likes to gamble; I would never get much money out of him. How different life could be with my own stash of money.

Another big part of my life was dealing with my son, Jack. He was brilliant, outgoing—and a congenital liar. While I'm dealing with Jack's problems, my daughter Lisa is growing up in all this. For an eight-year-old child to be so thoughtful was unbelievable. She'd think about the old people—and kids don't think about old people, you know? Satisfied with her I was; she was no trouble. She was also a very studious child, always on the honor roll and the Dean's List. I wanted her to have better teachers than I'd had, so I sent her to Catholic schools all the way up to high school—all the while dealing with Jack's drug problems.

Lisa went away to school and was away from home for twelve years. I missed her, and to see her I'd drive out to Colorado and back alone. Lisa, unlike her brother, would listen to anything you said to her. You didn't have to tell her much, though. One time when I was out in Colorado, I'd given her money, and she told me she had loaned this girl fifteen hundred dollars. I said to her, "Lisa, you want to know something about lending money to people? Nine times out of ten you're going to lose your money, and you're going to lose your friend." Which is exactly what happened. I said, "If you learned your lesson, it was well worth the fifteen hundred."

When I was visiting Lisa, the same friend she had lent money to said, "Oh, I know what I'm going to buy you, Lisa—a little shovel for your cocaine." I didn't say anything at the time, but when I got home, I wrote her a long letter reminding her about her brother's life and how drugs run in my father's family: "You are more susceptible than other people." I had an uncle who sniffed cocaine, and all the cartilage in his nose disintegrated. Lisa said to me, "Oh, you didn't have to write that, Mom." I

knew she resented the letter, but she got off the cocaine, thank
God for that.

## A Loaf of Bread, a Can of Salmon

Johnny wasn't a good father, but he was an excellent husband,
a good provider. See, I had lived through the Depression. I
remember one time my mother had a loaf of bread and a can of
salmon for dinner for three kids and a mother and father. My
father must have taken some of the salmon, and my mother
hollered at him: "Let the kids eat first! We'll eat what's left."

We lived in the city only until I was seven or eight, when we
moved up to the end of the Bronx. Across from our little
bungalow, beyond a row of houses, was all grass and woods.
When they fixed up the bungalow, my mother worked like a man
all day and all weekend building that house. A very strong
woman, my mother.

I hardly knew my father, who worked all the time. As for my
mother, she was my whole life. Her children always came first,
too. My mother and I were extra-special close.

She taught us bridge when I was about twelve and my
brothers were ten (one of my brothers died, and my brother that
died and myself were very close). Every night we'd all listen to
"The Shadow" with her or play cards. Mainly, she would take us
to the beach because we had no money. That was it. But we'd
light a fire, and she'd let us roast potatoes in the backyard. Then
she got cancer of the esophagus. Towards the end of her life, she
was a drinker because she had arthritis of the spine. She used to
fall, and I was afraid she'd break a leg or a hip. But God helps
drunks and idiots: she'd always fall easy. The doctor told her,
"Stop drinking," and she did, just like that, the last two years of
her life.

## The Inheritance

Money never meant much to me, except to provide for my
children. One day Mother says to me that my part of the
inheritance was going to be divided among all the grandchildren.
Now, if she had said my inheritance was going to be divided

between my two kids, that would have been a different story. With my two there are ten grandchildren; they'd wind up with only a couple of thousand dollars. I didn't say anything, but I'll never forget that night. I was so upset over it that my stomach was churning, and I couldn't sleep.

One day a couple of years later I told her, "I don't think that's fair." I said, "Why should Lisa and Jack be done out of it, and Tony and Joey's kids get my money? Don't leave anything to me—that's okay—but at least give it to my kids!" She turns around and leaves me seventy-nine thousand and the house in Florida. Right away, I gave Lisa forty; I kept thirty-nine. Then Lisa had fifty thousand dollars. I told my husband that I was left thirty thousand and Lisa twenty thousand.

Then Lisa wanted to go into business; when she told me how much it would cost, I was flabbergasted. I had twenty-five thousand, so in a weak moment I said I'd give her this money to put in the business. But a little while later, I said, "You've gotta give me one promise. I don't want you to go into the twenty-five thousand for the business. Keep it for yourself because there's always the possibility that you won't make it. I want that twenty-five thousand to go into a house for you." She's a damn hardworking kid, but she'll need that little bit of luck with all this. Now there's the interest on the fifty thousand, and she can't take vacations anymore. I pray she becomes accustomed to it all. As long as Lisa makes a living and she's happy with her work, that's all I ask for her.

Like me, Lisa finds it hard to find a guy. I'd go a long time before I would let a man touch me. I told her, "What about artificial insemination?" She said, "Oh, I could get pregnant by somebody." I said, "Well, then he'd have an interest in the kid. You'd be pulling the kid between you. With an artificial insemination, the child is completely yours." I told her about this because to me a child is one of the marvels of living.

My mother comes from Wilkes-Barre, Pennsylvania, where her parents had a grocery store. There was a strike, and they continued to let people run up their bills, until they lost their business. Cousins had moved to New York, so then she and her family moved to New York.

Her father had the black lung, but he lived on a farm he bought himself in Delaware, and all of a sudden, after seven or eight years, my mother opened the door one day, and there he was. He and my mother never got along—because *my* mother adored *her* mother. Her mother was sickly; she had dropsy. My mother seemed to be the one her mother would rely on. The others were flibbertigibbets.

In New York, mother's oldest sister became a thread winder, and my mother, who must have been seventeen at the time, worked as a messenger girl for Western Union. Those two sisters got a room by themselves and became very close.

## A Skirt Chaser

My mother was married at eighteen. She was also a big saver, very big, and she also played the stock market. When I first started to work, I was making thirty-five dollars a week, and she said to me, "I'll charge you fifteen dollars a month rent, for room and board." Then I got several raises. When she bought the house, things were tight, and she says to me, "June, could you give me your whole salary? I need it to pay the contractor off." I gave her every penny I made, and she gave me seven dollars a week for carfare and lunch. That's how she fixed the house up. She got the house very cheap, but it was a shell. They had to put everything in it, but she didn't have a mortgage on it. My father made a fabulous salary, but my poor mother had a hell of a life with him; he was a skirt chaser.

When I was taking care of my mother for seven months, I was a nervous wreck. I pictured that she would end up screaming in pain. She had always been a very independent woman, and here she couldn't control her bowel movements. I would clean her off. She'd say to me, "To think that a daughter of mine would have to do this!" I said, "Ma, how many times did you do this for me when I was a kid?" The day before she went in the hospital, she washed her hair. She's dying, and she makes an appointment for a permanent! "Okay, Mom," I said, and I took her to the beauty shop. Ten days later she was dead of pneumonia. What a relief that was, that she didn't have to go through that pain that was on my mind for seven months.

I'll never forget a dress my mom made for me. She stayed up late so that I could have it for a party. It was red with white polka dots and had a big wide skirt, open in front, and a red slip. I was a big hit. They called me "Jezebel." That was really something.

But I never went to my prom because my mother said to me, "Well, it's a case of either getting you a prom dress or us a ton of coal." Naturally, it was the ton of coal.

## LISA TRAVANTI

Mom was born in 1919 in Manhattan (I think) and raised in the Bronx. With her New York accent, she's a New York lady through and through. My mother met my father in a candy store in the Bronx. I remember I asked her that. I remember saying, "Mom! You picked this guy up in a candy store?" He was six years older.

My mother was very practical. The way she saw it, here was a hardworking man who had a good job. That was important to her. And I remember asking her if she loved him. She said, "Well, yeah, I loved him, but more important than that, he was a hard worker." She wanted somebody who was going to support her family. With all these things we consider nowadays, we never would have married him. My father was a very handsome man, but I don't think she was swept off her feet.

I know how my mom got my dad to marry her. He was divorced, and she, at thirty, had never been married. She told *him* that she could not live without him. She told *me* she was convinced that his ego was just big enough so that he would be thrilled that somebody couldn't live without him.

### A Hot Dresser

Mom is the oldest. We never talked about her early childhood. My knowledge of my mother's life begins at her brother's death when she was sixteen. That was a very difficult time in her life and her mother's life. Then Uncle Joe, her brother, was born, so she's about sixteen years older than he. Strangely, they gave him the same name as the boy who had died. Her first stories were about when she was in her twenties; dancing, drinking, and partying all night long and getting up at six the next morning to go to work. She would tell me about how her mother would go all out making gorgeous dresses for her when there was no money. But my mother has a tendency to remember the good things, so I don't know that much about her life in the Depression, except that it went on for years, and they often didn't know where the food was going to come from. Her father was lucky enough to have a good job with the city, so they were okay—actually, better off than a lot of people. I think both my mother and my grandmother put a real strong value on financial security.

I know that when she got out of high school, she worked at a bank. My mother's never been outgoing, and her two friends, Fay and Annie, who were with her in the candy store when she met my father, are still her friends to this day.

Before that, in her early twenties, she had been going out for a while with a man who died. She loved him, *really* loved him. I've seen pictures of this man who *wasn't* as handsome as my father.

She always said she loved to go out and was a hot dresser. That was what my mother was into. She has these pictures of herself. I said, "Jesus, Ma, you didn't fool around when you dressed!" She said she and the girls would always go out together to this place in Manhattan known for ballroom dancing.

## An Urge for Family

I don't know exactly what my mother did with her life. She wasn't a deep thinker—not much bothered her. She never had an urge to educate herself, just to enjoy life, and she went out with a lot of different men. Apparently, men were strongly attracted to her. Later, when she was thirty, she as hit by an urge for family.

I guess because we lived by her parents, I got to know them well.

One time I asked my mother, "What did Grandma want out of life?" My mother said, "Well, I once asked Grandma that, and she said she wanted love out of life more than anything, and if she couldn't have that, then she'd have money." The Depression had given her a healthy appreciation for money. By the time she died, she had accumulated quite a bit of it.

My mother has no regrets about anything she's ever done. At least, that's what she tells me. How can she be so clear? Her dream was to get married and have children, and her children were absolutely the most important thing to her. *We* were her whole life, more important than our father, and she'll tell you, "He was never there. He was always off doing something else, and if I didn't have the children, well..."

## Purse Strings

My mother's relationship with her mother was difficult, although she loved her mother very much and was devoted to her. My grandmother manipulated purse strings because they had money, and at one point, my grandmother even threatened my mother, told her she'd cut her out of the will. I don't remember the reason for it, but I remember my mother got very upset about that. They didn't speak for a couple of years. Also, my mother told me that her mother never hugged her, never kissed her, never held her. She found out years later that it was because her mother thought she would give her tuberculosis. How sad!

My grandmother was a domineering person and my mother a people pleaser. She might look at herself as a peacemaker more than anything. The conflict between her mother and my dad was probably the second greatest pain in my mother's life.

Her truly greatest sorrow is my brother Jack. He was psychotic when he was thirteen, into drugs and sniffing glue. He was in a mental institution off and on until senior year in high school, and he's never pulled it together. He's been involved in jail and various crimes and drugs, and he's a street person. Mom, as a parent, feels this nebulous guilt and responsibility but has no idea of how she might have contributed in any way. We've talked about how she still loves Jack and wants to help; about their lack of relationship. One time he even set her up to be robbed!

## All in the Family

Over the years she didn't have too many relationships with family members or friends that were more positive and supportive—except for her brother Joe, with whom she's very close. Mom and her friend, Irene, go shopping on Fridays, but my mother is a very self-contained woman. She doesn't seem to need to be around a lot of people. She usually stayed at home with the family, reading or taking care of the kids.

My mother accepted whatever came and never thought about it; that's her attitude towards life: "My life is good. I have no complaints." *I* think she's had one of the most difficult lives. *I* could never have coped with such a life. My mother has this remarkable resiliency so that she can just pick up and go on—on the surface, anyway. She doesn't deal with the pain inside. She says she's not in pain, but I say, "Well, Mom, look at you physically." She says, "Well, what do you mean?" She doesn't see that her physical condition is related to her feelings and emotions. Her greatest fear is dying of cancer, and when she gets scared her blood pressures goes up. She gets heart palpitations and is somewhat of an insomniac. She has written out her will more times and has told me where everything is. Every time she goes to the doctors it's "The money is over there." I say, "Mom, would you please stop? I've had enough of this already. Write it down for me once and for all, or else you're going to bring cancer to yourself." I tried to be a little more therapeutic about it, but it's hard to do with one's own mother. I make her up some herbal remedies. Last time she was here, she actually asked me for a bottle of "rescue" remedy.

Still, she doesn't talk about the feelings associated with her symptoms. I would always openly express my feelings and emotions, and she'd say, "Gees, you're so temperamental and sensitive." I'd say, "Well, that's okay." Recently, when I was really angry, she said, "Well, don't be angry. That doesn't do any good." I said, "Don't ever tell me not to be angry again. It's *your* way of living to never express your anger, not mine. For once just acknowledge that I'm angry and let me be angry. Just comfort me." She held me, and I just cried and cried.

## To the Core

She couldn't explain it, but she has a way of getting to the core of the issue. For a long time she used to freely offer her wisdom, and I, of course, always rejected it. Now I ask her more often. Sometimes she'll say, "You know, I don't like to offer my opinion here." She's so smart with me because she knows that if I think she's telling me what to do, I won't do it. I'll just get real stubborn and thick-headed about it. Maybe that's one reason mothers don't talk more. It's that whole authority thing. But if I go to her and say, "Well, Mom, what do you think?" then she'll tell me her opinion.

I could see she was exhausted from the whole trauma of dealing with my grandmother's death. Since Italian funerals are very oriented around food, she made these two huge pans of ziti and locked herself in the bedroom for a while. Meantime, people just went through that ziti, and there was nothing left for her. When she came out, she absolutely blew up. "How can there be no food left for me?" It was one of the few times I've seen my mother get openly angry.

She manipulated things so that she got her own money. In the beginning my father was giving her some minuscule sum to run the house, like ten or twenty dollars a week. One night she was doing the laundry and found a roll of money in his pants, like two hundred dollars, and she began to realize that he was going out and enjoying himself, gambling and doing what he wanted to do, and she said, "I'm going to get what I want, too!" Then she immediately went and told him, "Twenty dollars a week is not enough. I need forty dollars a week." Out of that she would put aside a certain amount of money every week for herself. She also learned never to tell him the true cost of things. That's the way she lived her life with him. Pretty wild, huh? Could you live like that? I couldn't.

## Fathering

When my mother was pregnant with both my brother and me, my father wouldn't walk down the street with her, "Because," he said, "then everyone will know what I've done to you." But I think the real reason was that he didn't want to have children; he wanted to have fun. She told me he said, "I thought you couldn't get pregnant, since you have pernicious anemia." That hurt my mother a great deal because she wanted children more than anything.

Maybe it's because of my psychology orientation that I was able to draw things out of her, and as I've gotten older she's opened up to me more. We couldn't talk about sex when I was younger. I was probably in my mid-twenties when she started.

Most of the information that I've ever gotten from my mother I've had to ask her for, but I didn't ask her about her sex life. She freely told me about that.

## A Thirty-Year-Old Virgin?

My mother was not a virgin when she got married. I asked her that. She said, "Always be a virgin when you get married. That way your husband will have nothing to throw in your face." I was young at the time and didn't realize what she was saying to me. As I got a little older, I began to understand that *someone* had thrown something in *her* face. Well, she was thirty years old when she got married. What do you want, a thirty-year-old virgin? This is what she tells me: "People did it back then, but they didn't talk about it or flaunt it the way we do now. That's the only real difference."

She never gave me the impression that she was promiscuous, but if she had dated somebody and really, really liked him...Now, I didn't ask her and she never told me *when* she lost her virginity. She talks to me mainly about the sex life with my father. She said, "One of the reasons I married him was because our sex life was so wonderful." She said, "If he wasn't well-endowed, it would never have worked. He was not what you would call a good lover." But he was "well-endowed," and for some reason that satisfied her. And I remember she told me, "I'd always have to climb on top of your father in order to have my orgasm because your father would never really care very much about me."

Another problem in their marriage is that my father got hit with a handball. A handball is a real hard black ball, and God knows how fast that ball was flying. Apparently his great endowment was no longer, and she said, naturally, neither was her sex life. This was when she was around forty-five. My father wasn't willing to learn any other way to satisfy her. Now they sleep in separate bedrooms, and every once in a while, my father will come in. She's not into it because I don't think he knows anything about foreplay. She thought about taking a lover at one point because they were really having some problems.

## Generation Gap

I have been pretty open with her in most areas of my life. Most of the things I would withhold from her—and there aren't that many of them, really (I made the mistake of telling her I tried cocaine once)—are just because of the generational difference more than anything. She is one of my best friends.

I don't know how I would have survived without her. That's the God's honest truth. I thank God that my mother was there as the person she is during the family life and growing up—my whole life, really. My mother has been the Rock of Gibraltar, the anchor in the storm. Without her I think I would not have felt as loved as I do and as secure. Whatever self-esteem, confidence, and security I have comes from her.

My mother has been influential, not in grandiose ways, but steadily and consistently. I don't see her as a person with her own life because she doesn't have a life. Her life is other people. Going through motherhood, a woman is not the full person she once was, and my mother, especially, was not. A mother has to give up a whole part of herself. She has to be selfless. My mother is self-sacrificing. She says, "There is nothing I have that I really need, and I'll give it to you so you can enjoy it when you're young." There are the few times when she expresses her needs, and you are taken aback: "Wow, okay, Mom, okay." I remember one Mother's Day I called her when she was down in Florida. Some of the people in the condo had gotten some flowers, so she got real upset. I forgot what she said, but the message was, "Give me some flowers." So I immediately went out and sent her flowers. I said, "Gees, Mom, I'm sorry. I didn't know you felt that way."

## A Powerful Woman

Some people might consider my mother a real nonentity, but I could *never* look at her that way. My world would have been miserable without her influence. Yet she never really did anything according to the way of the world, what is considered material success or accomplishment in that sense. What she did people tend to ignore or even ridicule. She was a very powerful woman in my life. *Very, very powerful!*

I think one of the more touching moments for me and my mother was when I told her, "You've been a great mother, and I love you and thank you for being my mother." I think she was somewhat taken aback when I said that to her. She didn't know quite how to react because I don't think anybody's ever said anything like that to her. She just said, "Oh, Gee, I never knew how you felt about me." And I said, "Gees, Mom, you know, I guess I never really said it, but I think you're great." She had a real hard time taking that compliment, but I could tell she loved it.

It's funny. We do ignore our mothers. We create a lot of barriers, too. Not that the mothers don't, but it's the two of us together creating this situation. It seems that we daughters need to be the more flexible ones. It's a hard lesson, but I think I've gotten a little bit of it. There's some very strong karmic bond that always seems to manifest so negatively. I think the real key is to try to see what's positive about it. Believe me, for me to be able to accept my father, I've gotta learn something here.

## Acceptance and Admiration

My mother once said, "You're the one who's missing out having all the bad feelings you have." That jolted me out of my arrogance. At times I even thought, "Why can't my mom be someone else?" Now I can appreciate what's there instead of what isn't. Years ago I saw that acceptance was the key, but I didn't know how to do it. Recently, I have seen that the key to acceptance is forgiveness, including self-forgiveness.

My mother has a lot of qualities I greatly admire. She can see the true spirit and goodness in people and can let everything else be secondary; she has the rare ability to let people *be*. She's always been generous with those she loves. That's the only reason money is important to her. The only thing I don't like is that she doesn't stand up for herself. But, then, I'm sure she wishes I could develop some of her patience.

She'd probably also say she wants me to get married so I could experience the joy of having children. I learned from my mother that I wanted to be more independent, but now I want to strike a balance. I'm coming around to say it would really be neat to have a kid. As for my new venture, it's the best move I've ever made. I'll have to carefully manage the finances, but I know it's going to go. More than anything my mother wants me to be happy.

It's obvious I don't know much about my mother's past, especially her youth. To me, actually, those kinds of details aren't that important. But, geez, maybe to *her* they are; maybe she talks about what I choose to talk about—which is not about her. Only as she's gotten older has she been talking more. I guess she thought nobody ever really wanted to listen to her.

*Mildred Coon Hawkins as a young girl.*

# No One Can Take the Place of a Mother

**M**ildred Coon Hawkins lives with her husband, Lou, in Lake Linden, Michigan. Their daughter Lois, an active and busy feminist, lives just down the block with her husband and three young daughters, the oldest of whom I met when she dropped in on her grandma during the interview.

Raised on a farm in northern Michigan, Mildred went to school in New York City, where she lived with a rich aunt and uncle. Having lost her own mother at age fifteen, Mildred is a devoted mother and grandmother.

A mutual friend told me to interview Mildred and Lois because of their remarkably close relationship. I even thought the photo of Mildred as a little girl was the lovely, blond Lois, now in her early thirties. Mildred, in her early seventies, has a deep and sultry voice; unbeknownst to her, it held me spellbound.

## MILDRED COON HAWKINS

Although your children don't think about it, you *do* have a life beyond motherhood. Not that you mind, but you give up your life for your children. We said this the other day when we were talking about a cousin whose former husband was murdered by a stepson. First the stepson choked his mother, then hit his stepfather in the head with a hammer, then took them to the park and buried them both. When the mother didn't report for work on schedule, the authorities were called in. They found the car in the garment district of Manhattan, but the grave would never have been found if the son hadn't led them to it. It's terribly tragic for a child to murder his own mother. A stepfather I can understand, but his *mother!*

If the son had known his mother better *as a person*, maybe he wouldn't have choked her. You treat people as objects when you don't know what they're all about. I said, "You can hate a stranger but go home to get away from him; when you hate a relative and you're living with him, it gets worse and worse."

Sometimes parents don't talk to their children because the children don't listen. Even at Lois's age, children are so involved in so many things that they don't have time to listen. My grandmother lived next door to us, and we spent a lot of time running back and forth. Of course, we were close to our aunts and uncles, too. My dad was one of ten and had five children of his own. My brother had *fifteen* children. We've kept in touch with many of them. It's kind of fun when all your relatives get spread all over the world.

The most tragic thing in my life was my mother's death when I was fifteen. Even now it hurts. I think it's hardest when you're a teenager. My mother-in-law died when she was in her eighties. Still, we felt bad, but it made us realize that *we're* the Older Generation. Once, our grandparents were the "old people," even when they were younger than we are now. It seems so strange to realize you are getting old.

I was born in Hancock, Michigan. When I was about two years old, we moved to a farm, and I can still remember the horse and buggy. My mother had to clean all those buildings from top to bottom before we could move in. For my nap, she'd put me up in the haymow—the attic of the barn where the hay is stored— because, she said, the house wasn't clean enough. She didn't want us to get bedbugs. She'd put a blanket on the hay for me because the hay was so prickly. I still remember my naps; it was summer and it felt good.

My dad was a mailman in Hancock, and he worked in town. He and my older sister stayed in town with his mother, and the rest of us stayed on the farm. Sunday afternoons they would walk seven miles to town, even in the middle of winter. Cars weren't dependable then. They'd stay in town until the next weekend.

Since we didn't have telephones, my mother wouldn't know whether they'd made it into town. Lois is about to move to the country, and I think of our old house—two rooms downstairs, no basement, and upstairs just one big room. For privacy, my mother hung screens.

## TB

When I started school, we started spending winters in town. I got TB when I was twelve and was put to bed for five years, since there were no drugs in the early thirties. My sister, a nurse, told my mother, "If you put her in a sanitarium, she'll never come home." In spite of this drastic change in my life, I was lucky. Until December I lived out on the front porch, which became a real hangout for my many friends. What if I'd been alone all the time! I lost a year in school, but I had a part-time tutor, so the school let me skip a year. I was out the last half of the eighth grade and was told I could go on to the ninth if I was physically able to do the work. I'd go to school by bus, take a class, rest, take another class, and go home.

A boy down the street had TB. For treatment, I'd go walking and the boy would ask, "How come she's out walking and I'm not?" When he finally died, I realized how lucky I was. The only reason we found out I had TB was that Steve Condon's mother remarked to my mother, "I understand your little girl is sick." My mother said, "Yes, and it's left her with a cough she can't get over." Mrs. Condon said, "I don't mean to frighten you, but if her cough is persistent, you'd better take her to a doctor." Mrs. Condon probably saved my life.

## A Rich Aunt and Uncle

After I graduated from Hancock High School at eighteen, I went to live with my aunt and uncle in Brooklyn. My dad put me on the train, and when I got to Grand Central Station, my aunt wasn't there to meet me. I waited by myself—a dumb country hick. Pretty soon Aunt May came in a chauffeured car. While I lived with them, I went to beauty school. Sometimes the school sent us out on weekends to work. In those days beauty operators would do manicures in barber shops. My school was just a block from Minsky's Burlesque. The kids used to take off to go to Minsky's, because the humor was good. I don't *think* they went for the striptease.

## Subways

Aunt May's husband, my uncle, was president of a company and had a chauffeur-driven car so I got around New York in style. Quite a contrast to making hay on the farm. But despite this new ease of travel, I learned to ride the subway instead. In school, I met a girl from Vermont, and when Aunt May heard she was living at the YMCA, she said, "You should bring her home at least once a week for a decent meal." The girl didn't know how to use the subway, so I took her back by subway because I wasn't afraid to travel alone. Back in 1936, you had no fear in the subways, although one time a man sat down alongside me and exposed himself. I was shocked. The next time a man sat beside me the conductor came by and asked if he was bothering me. You could get anywhere in New York for only a nickel—and later on a dime. On Saturdays, my cousin and I often went into Manhattan by subway to Lord & Taylor to "shop." That is, we'd look, but we didn't buy.

After finishing beauty school in New York, I came back to Michigan. To get a beautician's license in Michigan, you had to apprentice for a while. While I was looking for an apprentice-ship, my sister got a job as a lab technician in Connecticut. She wrote that I could have a job in the lab.

## Greater Possibilities

The other day someone was interviewing a divorced woman and said her marriage had been a failure. The woman said, "I don't call twenty years of successful marriage a failure." That's true. People live longer now and want more out of life. They see greater possibilities and they're willing to struggle. We didn't ask as much as today's young people ask. There's no limit now.

In my case it was only by chance—because my mother was dying and the household falling apart—that I could go off and do the career thing rather than marry right in town. One sister was a nurse, as I said, and the other sister stayed home to take care of the house. But after the Depression she had the opportunity to go East to work. My father said she shouldn't miss her chance, so I was left alone at home. My dad was living out on the farm with my brother and his family, so there was no reason to stay. I went off to Connecticut to live with my sister.

Then I met Lou—a farmer, a non-Catholic *and* an Easterner. I had wanted to marry someone from Michigan because I wanted to go home to live. We made our home in Connecticut, and I didn't care if we moved back because the people in Connecticut were wonderful. I left the lab to have my first child, and after that, I worked as a receptionist in a doctor's office. I liked my job and the people.

## Married Life

My husband, Lou, had said, "No wife of mine is going to work," and I told him, "Well, *I'm* going to work." I did, until my oldest daughter was born. He didn't mean I wasn't going to *work;* he meant I wasn't going to get *paid* for working. A wife *should* get paid for working for her husband. It makes a difference in income tax and social security because if he pays you, it's a business expense. We often say we'd have been better off if we'd done it that way.

I just have girls, and I'm glad Lou wanted girls because I think he would have been hard on sons. Fathers expect their sons to do all the things they've never accomplished—and usually twice as much; daughters can do no wrong.

When my allergies got bad and the city wanted to take our property, we decided to move back to Michigan. To replace our business, it would have meant investing everything. Lou thought we should try Michigan to see if I liked it and if my asthma got better. So we came back and looked for a place to live. Hancock was too full of relatives and Lois wouldn't get used to a small town. After a city of 75,000, a town of 3,000 would be difficult to adjust to—especially with relatives reporting every move you made.

## The Taxidermist

I was only fifteen when my mother died, so I never knew her well. But in that short time, she did talk about her own childhood. Her mother, my grandmother, died when she was thirteen. She was born in Canada, the oldest of three, and then moved to Ashland, Wisconsin. Her father, my grandfather, remarried, and the woman he married tried to poison his children. The stepmother was a taxidermist so she had access to arsenic. When my uncle, my mother's brother, complained about the food, his father got annoyed, and the boy said, "Well, it tastes funny. You taste it." When my grandfather tasted it, he realized the truth. That was the end of that stepmother! There were to be two more; the fourth, Josie, was loved by all.

My mother *did* tell me about the Peshtigo [Wisconsin] fire. It's strange, but wholly by coincidence my father's family was at the Peshtigo fire, too. What a small world! They got into ditches to get away from the fire, and then the trees exploded. It happened the same day as the great Chicago fire, which overshadowed the Peshtigo fire. I *think* Lois has read about the fire in a collection of family letters.

## Life's Tragedies

There were so many tragedies in those days. My father seemed to be the most tragedy-prone. When I was fifteen, my mother died; when I was eighteen, my sister, a Red Cross nurse in lower Michigan, died. She was planning to marry a man from here and come back to live and keep house for my dad. She was a kind person, fun and good-natured. When she died, my father said, "I'll never count on anything again." I had planned on going to beauty school and living with her. She had come for my high school graduation, but she became ill and died.

My mother had a mastoid infection before I was born. It was common then. The surgery left one side of her face paralyzed— a tragedy for her. Except for a one-sided smile, it wasn't too noticeable, but she was self-conscious.

With all their difficulties, people didn't complain. Families were close and rallied when there was a tragedy. My sister died of a ruptured appendix, a common cause of death, and my cousin of pleurisy a week later. It was more unusual for a family *not* to experience deaths; it was expected.

## The Depression

Nowadays people think too much of themselves. They talk about being poor, but in those days there was no welfare to fall back on. The trouble with this generation is that it never lived through a depression. I remember when pork was six cents a pound and standing rib was twenty-seven cents. My dad worked for the postal service, and before the Depression, people would say, "The pay's no good. Why do you work there?" When he still had his job during the Depression, they said, "Why are you working when we're not?" Dad had worked for thirty years but was too young to retire; still, the government asked him to retire so someone else could have his job. Sometimes his pension would be several months late, and my sister would have to call our congressman. We did the best we could. I never bought clothes until after Mother died. She made everything—usually out of something else. When you've been through a Depression like that, frugality becomes second nature. Nothing is thrown away. In Hancock, people made do, but people who lived in the city without a garden starved.

Maybe I'd get more schooling. But I'd do everything else the way I have. My life has turned out better than I had ever hoped. I'm satisfied with my husband and never wished I'd had another one. I did enjoy working at the hospital. If I ever went back to work, it would be in a hospital because I like working with energetic people who think. When I was young, all we asked was to be free of debt. My husband felt it was asking a lot just to look forward to travel upon his retirement.

Lou recently commented on a newspaper item about older women marrying younger men. "Men age much faster than women," he said. "A woman of sixty is still young. Women keep going; they do things." I say, "Well, they *have* to. They can never give up housework. Men can retire; women can't." It's like the guy who came home and found the house a mess. He asked his wife. "What happened?" His wife said, "I just didn't do the things I usually do when you wonder what I do all day."

And no one can take the place of a mother. Mine has been

dead for so long that I don't know much about her anymore. So Lois and her girls can't know about her, either. I've always enjoyed my daughters and granddaughters. People say, "You shouldn't spend so much time babysitting for your grandchildren." My answer is, "In a few years those children won't have a bit of interest in us. For now, I get a kick out of them."

## LOIS HAWKINS ANDERSON

I know this much: When my grandmother was in labor her sister came in and said, "I should go get the doctor!" While she was gone, my grandmother delivered my mother on the couch.

Many traumatic things happened in my mother's childhood. When she was eight, her twelve-year-old sister died of a ruptured appendix. Then, when my mother was twelve, she contracted TB and had to stay in bed for years. She couldn't do anything except read. By high school she had read all of the required Shakespeare. When she was fifteen, her mother died. She went through all of these traumatic experiences in nine years. A fifteen-year-old girl needs her mother, and she didn't have one. But even though she's been through a hard life, she doesn't ever complain. Well, she does say she would never go through her teenage years again.

Instead of going downstate, she went to New York to live with an aunt and uncle, which was a real switch because they had a huge house, a bell for the maid under the dining room table, a chauffeur, and other such luxuries. Next she lived with a sister in Connecticut and became a lab technician in a hospital, and before she got married, she worked as a receptionist for a woman gynecologist. My mother, who was always fascinated with medicine, should have gone to medical school. She talks about the lab and about things they didn't know at the time, like RH factors.

### Meeting Lou

When she met my father, she felt sorry for him because he was "awkwardly shy." He was good-looking, but she said she wouldn't marry him because he was from the East and wasn't Catholic. He was a farmer, and she did not want to marry a

*Lois Hawkins Anderson (right) with sister Blanche Hawkins Knapp.*

farmer. While I was growing up, my mother helped my father in his dairy business but didn't work outside her home. She did the books and always filled in where she was needed. Still does. They just put an addition on their cottage, and she was out there with the hammers and ladders and concrete. She'll try anything: "If somebody else can do it, I can do it"—an attitude I learned from her. Her mother-in-law said that my sister was going to be born out in the pasture because my mother insisted on helping when the cows would get loose.

Yet some of the things she did were still pretty traditional. I don't know if she really did try to break out. She didn't go to college. I wish she would go to college even now, not to become anything she's not but just because she is hungry for knowledge. We share a lot of interests and are friends as well as mother and daughter. But I wish her life did not totally revolve around her husband and family. I guess she's untraditional in her ideas but not in some of her actions.

## Sign of the Dove

She teases my father that men are fools, and he jokes back. Still, she does cater to him, not so much because he is a man but because she will do anything to keep peace. My dad likes Mexico; she doesn't, but she'll go because she won't take a separate vacation. It makes her nervous for me when Rick and I do a lot of separate things, and that I don't have a hot dinner on a cleared table when he gets home. That is all part of her being. I'm not saying she is a woman dominated by their relationship, though. She's strong and knows what she's doing. In fact, she has said, "That's the choice I make." After forty-five years of marriage, she and my father have finally struck a more equal balance. She feels she gets as much as she gives, and they have been best friends all these years.

## A Rewarding Profession

On Mother's Day one year she said something about not being a success. To me that seemed odd, as I looked back on how much she had put into being a mother.

In summers at the cottage she would get up in the morning with my dad, leaving the sofa bed open until I got up. She and I would always head back to bed to read and cuddle. Then we'd picnic on the beach and spend the whole day together! She'd always hug me and say, "I love you. You're great, you're smart, you're wonderful."

She was so good as a mother that it's hard for me to think of living up to that. Yet one cannot feel like a success in the absence of feedback like money or recognition. Motherhood is such an unrewarded—although not unrewarding—profession. My mother has never talked about wanting recognition, but I sense she would like to have had a college degree, something to say, "I did this."

I think she wanted to be married and have children. However, when she was pregnant with my sister, she said to my father, "What if I don't like her?" He said, "It'll be your baby. Of course you'll like her."

You know, there's this whole conspiracy that you don't tell anyone how horrible labor is. The day I had my first child I called my neighbor to tell her. She said, "Wasn't labor terrible?" No one says that the whole time you're pregnant; they wait until you've had the baby to say, "Wasn't that the worst thing you've ever been through?" I try not to hide the truth; with five pregnant friends now we talk a lot about labor.

When my mother's sister expected her baby, it was a year and half after my mother had had my older sister. My mother told her sister that having a baby was like going to the dentist. Afterwards, my aunt aid, "What dentist do *you* go to?" My mother said that what she meant was that it's horrible, but it *ends*.

My sister is eleven and half years older than I am. My parents were just about to go out and buy a nice big sailboat, when my mother found out she was pregnant with me. She said, "I'm not raising a toddler on a sailboat."

When my mother was in labor with me, she drove us to church, drove back home, scrubbed the floors, and cooked a big roast beef so that my dad and sister would have something to eat while she was having me.

On such questions as abortion, she can see gray areas, but she does have strong opinions. Rapists should be castrated, at least! The punishment should fit the crime, she says.

Even though she rebelliously married someone out of the Church, she had me going to church every week, even when we traveled. If you were too sick to go to church, you were too sick to go anywhere else. One day she said, "Well, I've done my part for eighteen years. Now it's up to you." Now she doesn't go to church at all, partly because she's always been upset that the Church is "dominated by men."

I see my mother as a feminist. In her upbringing for us, there was no such thing as, "You can't do that because you are a girl." She seems to have a preference for women. It was nice to know as I grew up that she'd wanted daughters and never strove to produce a son. She has two daughters and six granddaughters—all girls. She wanted us to be married and have families because she thinks it's hard to be alone. When I gripe about my marriage, she'll say, "But you don't want to be left alone, do you?" She says, "You compromise, or you're alone." In many ways she is a contradiction—an extrovert who loves to be alone—probably a good balance. In San Juan, although my mother doesn't speak Spanish, she and a policeman somehow conversed with each other. She can talk to anybody, anywhere, any time.

## Reticence

She is very close to me and my sister Blanche and puts in a lot of time on all of her relationships, including a man she has known for sixty years. She said she had a wild crush on him when she was eight. All along, no matter what was going on with her—dating another man or being married—they have still gotten together up here every summer. He has always called her "Duchess." One time he came to pick her up and said, "Come on, Duchess, we'll knock 'em dead."

She has good friends but not a confidante. Maybe it's because she's been so close to my dad; or maybe its because so many of the people she was close to died. Whatever the case, when it comes to personal subjects, she is rather reticent. She seems to prefer intellectual discussions. It's funny because even though she wasn't very open about sexuality, she was casual about nudity. She and I used to go skinny-dipping, and it seemed I took baths with her forever, drawing on her back with soap. I've told Rick that as soon as all the children are finally in school, I plan to start going to the bathroom alone. I'm not going to be reading a book to anybody, I'm not going to have anyone sitting on my lap or peeking in the shower. Just the other day up at the lake the subject came up because my mother talked about picking berries with her mother in summers at the farm and how her mother would put little cans of kerosene under the legs of the beds to keep the bedbugs from climbing up. My grand-mother was super-clean, especially when it came to the out-house. She'd dump ashes in and burn holes on the two-seater. That made me think how bad it must have been for my mom and dad when I'd accompany each one to the outhouse and sit right alongside.

Still, my mother is not confident about her looks and is upset about her body shape, how all those stomach muscles go. She would like my dad to be more complimentary and to say, "I love you." He does pick out romantic cards for her; and in his burial vault and septic tank business he'd go out to hell and gone to get her armloads of trilliums to transplant.

## Nonviolence

My dad spanked my sister once, and he never did again because my mom said, "You're too strong to do that to her." They're both very nonviolent, and my mom is nutsy about animals and little babies. While I was nursing my babies, she would lean close: "No one can explain that bond to you." She was sharing in the bonding. She's loving to my children, which surprises her; she didn't think she could ever be as close to anybody as she is to her own children. She puts a lot of time in with her grandchildren and gets it back a hundredfold. I have a Brownie troop, and for Mother's Day I had the girls make cards in which they would write their feelings about their mothers. My daughter said, "Mom, can I do Grandma? I don't have to give you one because you already know." I said, "I do not. You never tell me what you like about me." So she made us *each* a card.

Besides being a busy grandmother, she's on a commission for senior-citizen and low-income housing. She stays because there are only two women on it, and she knows if she got annoyed and quit, Dolores would quit, too. She says, "You've got to have women on that commission." The men wanted her to go look at drapes or furniture, and I don't think she liked being taken for granted like that. She wouldn't take a board presidency because she wants total freedom to travel with my dad. She said, "I'd rather never go anywhere, but since your dad has worked all his life and wants to travel now, that's what we'll do." The way I see it, she didn't choose her way of life because somebody said she should or because that's the way she was brought up. I think she did it because she truly wanted to have kids and my father in her life.

## In Trust

If she were widowed, she says, she would never remarry. She's sure Dad would marry within two months of her death because he couldn't live on his own. Now she's setting up a trust: "I want my kids, not his new wife, to get everything." Her father left some things to his sons that she felt the daughters should have. Although she keeps saying, "Don't be like me: throw things out," she does want us to have the meaningful things that have been handed down from her mother's family. We dug in the cedar chest just the other day. She said, "When I'm gone, you should take this, and Blanche should take that." Careful to be fair, she is torn between giving her Grandmother Emilie's necklace to my sister or to my daughter, Emilie's namesake.

When I look at the tragedy and illness of a life like my mother's, I expect to find a bitter person. She's not. She doesn't blame her life on anyone or anything. She's an intelligent woman, and I admire her.

# Ruthless

**R**uthann, 50, is married and the mother of two grown sons and a daughter Elena, 22. A cheerful, soft-spoken but assertive woman, Ruthann has been active for two decades in the politics of a small community in upper Michigan. Along with a handful of women, she founded an early chapter of the National Organization for Women. She is mentioned in *Megatrends:*

> Our biggest concern is the government's interference in land "use," says Ruth Anne Ruehr [sic], leader of a Michigan residents' group. The object of their protest? A Navy Seafarer communications proposal to bury 500 miles of low-voltage cables in nearby forests.

Elena has been accepted to study music composition at Juilliard. She says, "I'm mostly interested in classical music right now, but I do write pop music and am trying to sell some songs to Cyndi Lauper and people like that so that I could support myself while writing my art music. Certainly, I don't care about becoming famous."

## RUTHANN RICHWINE RUEHR

My mother, Mary Elizabeth Wilson, was born in 1915 in Detroit. She was the oldest child of a family which eventually had, I think, eight children. She could play piano by ear and taught herself to play other instruments as well. She was

---

*Megatrends*, by John Naisbitt (Warner Books), p. 115.

*Ruthann's mother, Mary Elizabeth Wilson (center), with her mother, Beulah Buchanan Wilson, and sister Ruth. After Mary Elizabeth died, her husband (Ruthann's father) married Ruth.*

planning to go to the University of Michigan and study piano, when she met my father. I was incredulous: Why would this woman marry this man? I just couldn't figure it out. I'd say, "Mommy, why did you marry Daddy?" She'd answer, "Because he was the handsomest man in the world." She'd tell me over and over that he'd brought a rose on a blind date, that she just took one look at him, and that was the end of her plan. They were only nineteen when they got married.

My parents were pretty poor when I was born in 1935 during the Depression. They sold meat from a panel truck with ice in it and had a hotel candy store. For three years we lived in my grandparents' house, where my mother gave birth to me and later a set of stillborn twins. I was closer to my grandparnets than my parents for that period. My grandfather was like an artisan. I loved to watch him carve flowers on the saddles that he'd made, loved the smell of leather. On the side of the gas station he owned, there was an ice box with pop in it, and inside was a candy showcase. I could snitch chocolate pop and candy bars whenever I wanted.

## House of Corrections

Eventually, my dad went to college, but in the meantime he worked at unskilled odd jobs, when he worked at the state training school. We lived right across the road from the House of Corrections and a big farm where they raised food for the prisoners. Our house was in the middle of that. I loved talking to the prisoners through a fence when they were farming. My mother forbade me, but I couldn't help it because where was only my baby sister, and I didn't have anybody else to talk to. My mother told me the prisoners were dangerous, but to me they seemed like ordinary people. Once in a while one of them would break out in the night, and we'd hear the sirens. That was sort of scary, and my mother always worried that one of those guys would break in and do something like *In Cold Blood*. Looking back, I bet my mother hated living there, but she never really talked about that.

I feel bad now that I never got to know my mother well. I mean, I loved her and felt close to her, and she knew *me* well— but I didn't know *her.* It's just since I've been a feminist that I realized I didn't know what kind of a person she was. That's partly because in her role as mother she was almost like a "nondirective" therapirst—someone who reflected your feelings and helped you work through problems but never expected anything in return. Her mother, too, was a sounding board, taking on all the responsibility for the physical and mental health of her whole family. In fact, my mother's mother, Beulah Buchanan, was a farm girl from Canada who was an accomplished artist and went to the Art Institute of Chicago. Imagine—that was in 1900 or thereabouts. After she married my grandfather, who also painted, she never painted again. I was told she was a better painter than he, but she didn't want to upstage him. Everyone has his paintings except me. Maybe I said, "Pooh on you. I want my grandma's paintings."

## Saturday Night Baths

Both my mother and grandmother loved to tell stories and had a lot of songs and poems. Like me, they were both the oldest of lots of girls. I'd climb up on my grandmother's lap and say, "Grandma, Grandma, tell me what it was like when you were a little girl!" I can remember her telling me that to iron they put the iron on the stove and could tell by the "ssss" how hot it was. They owned a school dress and a Sunday dress and had a Saturday night bath. They ironed their hair ribbons by wrapping them around tin cans filled with hot coals. Each girl wore two ribbons, one on each braid. Keeping all those ribbons pressed was a big enterprise. She also told me how they made soap—a long, involved process: "Start out by killing one pig..."

When my mother was in sixth grade, she often helped out in the kindergarten room. I always used to ask her to tell me the story about the little boy from England. She said, "Well, there was a little boy who had just come from England. One day he came up to me and said, "Teachah, I have to pie-pie." She couldn't understand him but tried to smoothe it over by saying, "Oh, that's nice, that's nice," and then he went back to his seat. Pretty soon he got up and was back again, saying, "Teachah, I have to pie-pie." Finally—oh, she felt bad about this—the poor kid wet his pants. She told me that when the Charleston became popular, she got so that she could really do it like mad because she'd practice on the way to school and all the way home—two miles a day.

## Giving Up a Music Career

My aunts told me that people would come from all around to hear my mother play the piano. She could play—*anything*. I used to think everybody's mother could do that. When I found out they couldn't—especially when I found out that *I* couldn't—I was shocked. I wish I could ask her all about her musical life because now it turns out our daughter probably inherited my mother's musical talent. I'd like to know who she studied with, how long, how she studied, and how she felt when she gave it up and whether she really missed it. I must have had a big effect on her but she did what was expected of a woman. As a young woman, *I* never sat around and thought, "I could have been a brain surgeon." My mother never talked about having any regrets at all. Never, never.

When I was eleven years old, after my youngest sister was born, my mother got sick. They called me at school to come home. I ran all the way because they had never done that before. Whether it was physical or mental I don't know, buy my mother was lying in her bed shaking. I remember getting her a hot water bottle and covering her up. Soon after that she was in the hospital for maybe two weeks, and I never knew to this day what was wrong. It could have been a breakdown. If she were living now, I'd like to ask her about that. Later on, I did ask her how it felt when she was depressed. I was worried that could happen to me or one of my kids. The only thing she told me was that everything was gray: "I couldn't see any color at all." Now I wonder whether it was a chemical imbalance because she never did say, "I felt sad."

When I was a little kid, I always wanted to be a doctor or lawyer. My mother never discouraged me and always said, "You can be whatever you want to be." Still, I somehow got the message, "Really, a mother is what you'll be." Many girls growing up in those days became feminists; the spirit of the times certainly raised our consciousness. I admired my mother for her kindness and loving support, but I didn't want to be a housewife like her because she didn't have her own life. The life she had seemed boring.

## Sisters

I don't know what my sisters' relationships were with my mother. Maybe her skill was in making each one of us feel special. I'd say, "Oh, Judy is so beautiful and I'm so ugly." My mother would say, "Well, you're smart and Judy is beautiful." Of course, Judy was beautiful *and* smart. My mother couldn't tell me that I was prettier than Judy, but she tried to give each of us a little gift. That was my gift, and it probably fostered in me the desire to be a doctor.

I'm really the lucky one in this group of three women—my mother, myself and my daughter—because I got such wonderful support from my mother, and now my daughter, who's so understanding and is a feminist, has helped me stand up for myself. She's been brought up to be strong and assertive. I wasn't. When she was a little kid, my daughter would say, "Mom, now stand up for your rights. Say what you think!" It wasn't until I was forty years old that I could. That's something that's easier to teach your daughter than to practice yourself.

## The Femininity Thing

I bought the whole traditional femininity thing. At Christmas, my husband and I would give the boys a train and a chemistry set, and we'd give my daughter a toy iron and ironing board. I dressed her in little smocks and told her it was okay for her to cry but not the boys. I'd been a rebel but ended up a housewife. But man! when Betty Friedan's book come out, did that ever help to coalesce all these feelings I had. Everybody else who read it had the same experience. Many years later, I ran as a Shirley Chisholm delegate to the Michigan State Democratic convention—and won.

I did get my degree in education. In those days you had to find a "career" you could lead while your children were in school. What's frustrating is that I really don't know what I would like to have done. Now I teach college students, staff, and faculty how to use the computers for word processing. I don't get much money or prestige, but I love getting up in the morning and going to work. I started working—*for pay*—four years ago when Elena was going to college. I knew that I had to do something because of the "empty nest" syndrome.

I wish I had gotten my Ph.D. because then I could have the kind of life I want right now. But then I probably wouldn't have had my kids; I wouldn't want to have missed out on that. If I could have managed doing both, that would have been ideal. In fact, I did try to do both.

When the kids were little and we were living in Ann Arbor, I tried graduate school, but taking care of the house and kids and finding a babysitter was too hard. In those days if a woman wanted to go to school, it was her "little project." She had to make sure it didn't interfere with her usual duties in any way. The husband only had financial responsibility for his kids, and there was no support from society, either. I was studying library science at the time, and when I went in for some reason to see the head of the department, he said, "*What* are your doing going to *school* when you have *three* children?"

## Miss Congeniality

As a role model, I'm sure I was too nice—Miss Congeniality—except when I was fighting the Navy. I was really involved in opposing "Seafarer," the proposed Navy submarine antenna that would have covered one-third of the Upper Peninsula. That was like a full-time job. I was also working for N.O.W. and the League of Women Voters. I just finished being President of the League in April. That's a tough job, harder than most paid jobs that men do. What's hard about it is being *the* representative of the League in the community. I had to be neutral and squelch all my radical feelings.

I wish I had presented a more assertive model for Elena from the start, instead of when she was nine or ten because, while she is strong and assertive, I think she has some conflict. Maybe she wouldn't have worried quite so much about pleasing everybody. Still, when you live in a small town, you can't afford to be abrasive. That's why I love traveling: I can just be myself.

## A *Mention in* Megatrends

I felt proud when I discovered my name was in *Megatrends*, the bestseller by John Naisbitt and his wife. I discovered the reference to me when I was to give a talk to a group—maybe it was the American Association of University Women—and the president introduced me: "This is probably one of the most famous people that ever addressed our group because her name is in *Megatrends*." She read the quote that I had given the Naisbitts about opposing "Project Seafarer." Here was concrete evidence that I had done something in my life—something important that would make things better for everyone. Feminism has taught us women to be proud of ourselves, which every human being needs to do. Fifteen years ago I might have said I was proudest of my children and, before that, my husband. It's a sign of my own mental health that I thought of something *I've* done.

As far as my mother goes, I haven't emphasized how smart she was. She hid her light under a bushel. She never argued with my father or anybody else, even though a lot of times she probably knew more than they did. She read voluminously.

My mother really didn't enjoy any of the homemaker's tasks, except insofar as it made her family happy and comfortable. Finally, after all of us girls were married and on our own, she decided she just couldn't take sitting around the house anymore and at age forty started working. Imagine, after not having had anything to do with academic life or exams for at least twenty years or more, how she must have felt going into a big auditorium in downtown Chicago to take the Civil Service exam along with all those young hotshots. She said she almost cried every time she read a question. As I recall, she had the third best score of all the hundreds of people who took that test. My dad, who worked at Cook County Hospital where she was applying for a job, said that many of the people taking the test had Ph.D.'s in business administration and so on. It was quite a select group. We were so proud of her, though *she* didn't make too much of it. She was just relieved that she was able to do well enough to get a job.

More than loving her job, she loved being out and being with people. They all liked her because every time we visited her, she'd have pictures lined up on the coffee table to show us, all her friends at work, their children and husbands. Since my dad worked at the same place, they could go to work together, eat lunch together and come home together. They both enjoyed that. Now that she was working, she felt justified in saying, "Well, I'm not going to scrub the floor and do the laundry or shopping by myself." My dad gladly, I admit, pitched in.

## Another Generation

Elena and I are pretty close and know almost everything about each other. There's nothing about my life she doesn't know, except a few maybe really personal things between her father and me. Even then, I still talk to her very freely about sex and things like that. There's not even much of a generation gap at all between us. I would say our relationship is evolving into more of a friendship, although there's some kind of a deeper tie that I wouldn't have with a friend and I still feel protective of her. As soon as I read in a letter from Elena that she got a job at the delicatessen in New York, I wanted to tell her, "Be careful with the knives!"

My mother never got to the point of going out on a limb to tell us the truth of her experience. One thing I remember vividly, though, is when she told us that, if we were ever unhappy or dissatisfied in our marriage, we'd always have a place to come, and that was home. I am grateful for that because I've heard that so many mothers say, "Okay, you've made your bed, and you can lie in it." I hope I've been truthful with my daughters. She does ask me about myself a lot, which gets to the main difference between my relationship with Elena and my relationship with my own mother. I guess I thought of my mother as somebody who was just there, somebody I could turn to, but I never thought about what she herself was thinking and wanting. Elena knows me as a person—my faults, my strengths, my weaknesses. If feminism has done this, I'm really glad. It makes for an altogether happier mother, an altogether happier daughter.

## ELENA RUEHR

I think my mother was born in a Detroit or an Ann Arbor hospital. It must have been in 1935 because... Is she *fifty?* She lived with her grandmother for a while and even remembers being six months old when her grandmother gave her a bath and washed her hair. Her grandfather was a leather tooler who made saddles. She's talked a lot about going to see him.

When I was a little girl, she'd tell me neat stories. One of my favorite ones was about the two horses, Leo and Babe, in her grandfather's stable. When her grandfather told her that Leo was lost, my mom jumped on Babe without a saddle and said, "Find Leo, Babe. Find Leo!" The horse went shooting off into the woods—with her on it. She found Leo and brought him in. I'm not sure how old she was because, as I got older, she got older in the story.

This is one of the saddest stories: Her mother told her not to leave her toys outside after she played. One day she left her favorite dolly out, and it rained. She came back the next morning to find that her dolly was ruined. That kills me.

Another sad story is that one summer she worked at a soda fountain. She saved to buy herself a red bicycle. She ran into the house to tell her parents to come look at it, and when she ran back, she found it had been stolen. God, I felt sorry for her.

She and her sisters all slept in the same bed for a while, and she used to make up stories at night. I like to hear those stories because I wanted a sister. It's fun whenever we get together for family reunions because they're all so close and alike in many ways.

I was in college before I ever asked my father about *his* life because I always used to beg my *mother* for stories. I remember a sad story about her mother. When my mom was ten years old they called her home from school. Her mother had had a nervous breakdown, probably because she had given up a music career.

## The Paper Plate People

I only remember little things about my grandmother—making paper plate people, puppets with mouths that moved. I wasn't very close to her because she always seemed sort of reserved. She scared me, in fact. There's a picture of her in the piano room, the whites of her eyes showing beneath her pupils, and I guess that's an old mystical sign of witch powers or something. Then when I was twelve, she died. After my mother got home,

*Ruthann's mother, Mary Elizabeth Wilson (Richwine). This is the photo Elena takes wherever she goes.*

*Elena and Ruthann.*

*Ruthann and Elena. This is Elena's favorite photo; she says she remembers sitting on her mother's lap.*

she was really depressed all the time. I think it started turning around when she quit smoking.

I guess I must have been eighteen when that picture of my grandmother came on the scene—because I was told that it was taken when she was my age at the time, at graduation. I looked a lot like her, especially when I graduated from high school. When people would see that picture up on the wall, they'd say, "Oh, what a nice picture of Elena," so I got this weird grandmother complex. I felt that she was with me, a kind of Guardian Angel. I still feel her following me.

## A Musical Talent

I don't think I knew that story about my grandmother's plan to go to the University of Michigan until after I had decided to go into music. Later, though, I felt the pressure to succeed because I felt that my grandmother hadn't. Luckily, even though I still feel pressure, it's just part of my own need to be successful. I'm excited about going to Juilliard. For a long time it was sort of a tossup between my work and my family, but I think my work is becoming more important. I'd like to have a family, but I don't think I'd sacrifice my work for that.

When I was taking a women's studies course, I composed a string trio piece in memoriam called "For Grandmothers" because I knew that both my grandmothers had been in the arts, and then when they got married, they both gave it up. My piece is saying, "I'm not going to give up."Actually, I wrote it after I had started carting that picture of my grandmother around. I still take her picture with me whenever I move and put it on my wall wherever I am. My mom doesn't feel the same way I do about the picture. She thinks of her mother as a real person, whereas to me she is a symbol. My mother said she felt her mother was a little tiny person sitting on the ridge of her ear—not saying anything, but just watching.

## "Boys' Legs"

My mother used to tell me about her fourth and fifth grade boyfriend, Johnny Cash. She doesn't know whether it was *the* Johnny Cash, the country singer. Quite the tomboy, she wore a white dress to school one day and played football in it and got grass stains all over it. Her mom got furious and said, "You can't play football anymore." She rode her bike all over, and someone told her she would get "boys' legs." But my mother was the fastest runner in the school.

Sometimes she wanted to be a doctor, sometimes a lawyer. Except for her grandfather or uncle who had faith in her, everyone else discouraged her. People would tell her she should be a nurse instead. When she was a Candy Striper, she discovered she hated nursing—removing bedpans and being a servant. She probably despised the authority of the doctors and having to do whatever they said. I guess teaching was the one other thing left for a woman to do.

## *Stars in Her Eyes*

She also went out with a sweet guy she was really in love with. He got along well with the family but just wasn't ambitious enough for her. Finally, she refused his offer of marriage and right after that married my dad. But she still talks about that old boyfriend with the stars in her eyes.

In high school she dated a lot, and she told me funny stories about her old boyfriends. One was a beatnik motorcycle rider who wrote poetry and played the drums. When they went to the movies together, he'd get so excited tapping out rhythms on the back of the chair that he'd drag her out of the movie theater to go write them down. They'd be making out in the car, and her dad would turn on the lights and get all upset. Her father couldn't stand him because he was a troublemaker. Eventually, he got into a fight with someone and went to jail. He said, "You'll wait for me, won't you?" She said yes but, of course, after a while lost interest in him—fortunately for all of us!

Her rejection of that boy sort of influenced my feelings about boyfriends. In fact, I'm now in the same position with a boyfriend that she was. My mother always tells me, "You should marry someone rich." I get mad because I think, "Look lady, I'm going to make my own money." I don't want to be dependent on anyone because my mom's kind of trapped. She works the same number of hours as my dad—maybe more—yet gets one-thirtieth the money, and although he's getting better, a couple of years ago I'd see my mom going nuts from having to do all the housework. Oh, I just couldn't stand it! I would scream at my dad, and then my dad would scream at my mom that I was such a troublemaker, and then my mom would say, "Now, don't get into our fights."

Finally, she and I had a tear-jerking confrontation, and she said that it was her choice: she was going to stay with him because it was comfortable. If she got divorced, she could never support herself in the way she was used to. She said she was going to deal with it her way, and if I didn't like it, it was too bad. I could just feel my stomach fall to the ground. I finally said, "Okay, I won't bug you anymore." I love my dad a lot, but he doesn't have to treat her the way he does. He'd be happier if they were equal and so would she, but he's stuck in his old habits and doesn't realize it. It's frustrating because, although he's a smart mathematician, he's illogical when it comes to people.

## Marrying Daddy

My parents went to the same high school, and my mom used to wait outside my dad's classes. Because he skipped two grades, she decided he was the one, since she wanted to have smart children. When she asked, "Why did you marry Daddy?" *her* mom would say, "Because he was the handsomest man in the world." When I asked my mom the same question, she'd say, "Well, he was smart, I knew he was going to make good money, and he could play the piano."

He proposed at Miller's Ice Cream Parlour in Ann Arbor. Actually, it was she who said, "Any time you decide to get married, I'll be ready." When they got married, she had to transfer to SUNY (State University of New York), which she regretted because she preferred the University of Michigan. It's really kind of sad.

At SUNY she was able to meet some neat people. She and a girl named Ann became good friends. They both had long hair, played guitar, and went to the class barefoot. I like to romanticize my mother as a bohemian; I guess they were called beatniks. One of the first classes she went to at SUNY was with

Ann. The teacher had put some vocabulary words up on the board, and he asked people to raise their hands and define the words. Mom thought that was such mickey-mouse stuff. Then, grinning when she saw the next word, she raised her hand. "Ruthless," she said. "That's what this class will soon be," and she walked out. The professor looked up and said, "Who was *that?*" Her friend said, "*That* was Ruth!"

Then she started teaching deaf kids. Everyone had signs for nicknames, and hers was the sign for a long braid because she always wore a long braid. She thought the teacher system wasn't very good because they wouldn't allow the students to use sign language. She also taught retarded and emotionally disturbed children. One of her biggest accomplishments was teaching a little boy how to write his name. Those kids calmed down and learned a lot from her.

Oh, she was the best mom in the world! She taught us to be creative. Although we weren't religious, she thought we should be educated and open-minded. She read us the Bible and *The Hobbit* and told us a whole bunch of children's stories that were passed down from mother to mother that some grandmother in our family made up long ago. My favorite was the one about a little girl's "nice woman friend" who lives in a chocolate house. I used to beg my mom every night to tell me a story. *She'd* fall asleep in the middle of the story and *I* would be awake. I'd shake her, and she'd get mad, but I had to know the rest of the story.

Gosh, I had such a great childhood. Because I started grade school, my mom would pull me on a sled to the post office every day. When we'd come to hills, she'd sit down behind me, and we'd go sliding down together. We'd go all over the place skiing, too. I'd stand on the back of her skis and hold onto her. She'd say, "Push, push, push!"

## The Planet Game

With us kids she'd say, "I'm the news commentator, and you're from another planet. Sir, tell me what planet you are from." My brother would say, "My name is Rufelbakti, and I'm from Pluto," and she'd say, "What's it like on Pluto?" Then we'd all tell little stories about our home planets.

My mother says she never regrets having had children. Still, I wish she could be doing something; she's so smart and so talented. She does have a built-in *lack* of need to achieve. It's strange because she does a great deal of volunteer work and is politically involved. When my mother was campaigning on behalf of a local woman for representative, she made deals with my brother and me. For instance, she'd give us doughnuts for going door to door with pamphlets. I must have been five years old when McGovern was running for President, and I'd go around with her and knock on doors and say, "Vote for McGovern!"

My mother has great energy and willpower but not much self-confidence. She works now at Tech as a tutor. She wouldn't take the job at first because she said it was "beneath her dignity" to work for so little money. I said, "Do it; you can always quit." Now she really loves it and has a lot of other opportunities from it. I encourage her to get a Master's degree in technical writing, but she says, "What would I do with a Master's degree?" I say, "Oh, get it anyway. It would make you proud."*

I think my mom wanted to be a college professor like my dad. She could teach almost anything. I know one thing: She doesn't want to take classes with young people. It's "beneath her dignity" again. It's dangerous to think that. You don't want to lose your self-respect, but on the other hand, it shouldn't keep you from doing something that's important to you.

At a young age, it's hard to gauge the influence of the various social factors. I don't remember how I felt during that period when she wasn't a feminist, probably because I was a "normal" little girl. I had dollies and played house all the time, and my mother says she bought me an iron and an "Easy-Bake" oven. She says she feels guilty about that. I remember her getting a telephone call asking if I would agree to be a crown-bearer for Homecoming Queen, and she said to me, "Oh, you wanna do it, don't you?"

But I liked being the adorable little girl. I was the youngest and was my father's baby. At four or five, I knew that looking and acting cute would get me what I wanted. I remember being charming on purpose around my parents' friends.

It was in sixth grade that I became conscious of the National

---

*Ruthann has decided to study for her Master's degree at the University of Michigan in Ann Arbor.

Organization for Women. That is, I knew what N.O.W. was and wanted to be a feminist, but I had a childish view. I remember fighting with my sixth grade teacher about feminism, and as I got older, I became defiantly feminist. I thought that feminism included having nothing to do with men, that having a boyfriend would mean I would have to act like...a girl and lose my independence. I wasn't going to get stuck in all this boy-girl talk. My best fiend Karen and I got along well because she was afraid of boys, and I hated them.

But then I made a conscious decision to become part of the group. I started wearing what people wore, and I made a point of complimenting people: "Oh, your hair looks nice," or, "Oh, did you get a permanent?" Not surprisingly, I had lots of friends in three months, and I started dating. When I got to college, I realized that promiscuity is against women's principles, and I felt I had let myself be used. It took me years to get over that, and women's studies opened up my eyes.

I don't think there's *anything* I haven't talked to my mother about. She's a wonderful "nondirective" counselor. I've told her my deepest, darkest secrets. I probably tell her too much sometimes. Once I was afraid I was pregnant, and she said, "I don't want to know!" She's so accepting of different values and ideas that, as she once told me, the only thing I could do that would make her disown me is become a Mormon.

My mother expressed one fear—of water, since she almost drowned when she was little. She's also afraid of car accidents and gets ridiculously afraid for her children, husband, or any of her family going off and leaving. Their not coming *back* is what she's afraid of, and it's really hard to calm her down. She says she's shy, but I think she's grown out of her shyness. She's not afraid of expressing herself, and she certainly talks in front of groups and has been on TV.

If it hadn't been for my mother, I don't think I'd be a music major or that I would be going to Juílliard. She's the one who gave me piano lessons in the first place and who helped me write music down when I was a little girl. She always assumed that anyone who played an instrument wrote music, just as anyone who can read should write. So many people I've talked to think you need to be Beethoven to write music, and I think that's the biggest problem they have. They think they can't do it, so they don't.

If my mother hadn't been a feminist, I probably would have been married a long time ago. I wouldn't be successful, and I wouldn't be as happy. She is really, really wise, and I feel I've inherited her wisdom. I feel I am she, that parts of me are hers. If it weren't for my mother, I wouldn't be as intellectual. She likes to have intellectual arguments, and that's something that's been important to me, too.

She's changed politics a lot. "Seafarer" might be here today if not for her; certainly, she was a big force in that. The local League of Women Voters maybe wouldn't be as feminist as it is. Many people have done a lot up here, but she herself has made a big impact. She doesn't look or sound it, but she's radical.

Knowing about my women relatives is so important in knowing what's gone before. It gives one such a firm base. In fact, it gives one a sense of immortality. I feel that if I have children, I'll be floating around with them somehow, just as my grandmother is floating around with me. I don't believe in God, so I believe in that. Without it, I'd get lost.

My grandmother's death had a big effect on me because I related my mother's grief to my own in the future. Though maybe it's not the greatest poem in the world, I think "A Prayer to My Mother" expresses, not only how I might feel, but also how I think my mother feels about her mother.

# A Prayer to My Mother

I wondered
    why walk with wanderers
    or travel too long?

My mother said
    "Walk with the wind,
    Step slowly."

I wished
    for futures of effervescence,
    bubbles, that broken
    like crystal, at night
    would glint from moonlight
    and rest in perfect places.

And when I was weary,
    my wishes were muddy cotton balls,
    stuffed tight

I asked
    Why are trees topped
    and reach so high?

She said
    "Wait for winter
    when all things die
    and I, too."
    I too will die.

From tomorrow to tomorrow
    worn welcome mats
    whispers of footsteps.

I'll wait.
>Sunspots and changes
>Moon full and ripe
>or a toenail of light.

Where will I wander? when?
"Tonight."

Behind me
>I look into lullabyes,
>slumbers, soft breezes,
>my cheek in her arms.
>Her heartbeat.
>Rocking, rocking.

What happened, I wonder?

She says,
>"Like mornings, like nights."

And where will I wander?
What will remain?
"I'll follow, a shadow
>I'll be there I'll wait.

And how is this true?

My mother my friend.
I miss you and love you.
Forever.
>Amen.

# Appendix

## INTERVIEW FORM FOR
### *MY MOTHER BEFORE ME*

DAUGHTERS:

During the interview remember to state from whom you obtained your information: Did your mother herself tell you? Did someone else tell you? Or are these your perceptions?

The following questions are just guidelines, and you are encouraged to emphasize other issues, if you wish.

1. When and where was your mother born? in a hospital? Any unusual circumstances of her birth? Anecdotes? Was her father hoping for a son? Was she firstborn, second, third, etc.?
2. What do you know of her early childhood years? Anecdotes? Girlfriends, boyfriends, hobbies, interests, influences, significant adults. Adolescent years. Parents, siblings, school, fears, aspirations, etc.?

What did she hope to become? Do you know about her mother's mother? Was she closer to her mother or to her father? What was her role in the family?

Did she play a musical instrument? sports? Do you know of any talents she had but no longer uses? What were her favorite subjects in school? Favorite toys, games, teachers?

If you don't know very much about your mother's early years, what do you think the reason is? Do you know more about your father's life?

3. Adulthood: Did your mother work? What were her jobs? What was her education? How did she meet your father? When and where did they get married? Was it "love at first sight"? Did she have a 'reason' for getting married? What qualities attracted her to your father? Did she discuss whether her children were planned? How many children did she want? Did she discuss sex and birth control, particularly, in her own case?

Did she express her feelings to you? any regrets? anxieties? Did she discuss what she would rather be doing now? Does she seem to be happy? Does she have friends? Are there things you wish you could tell her and/or ask her but are too afraid or embarrassed? Are there things you wish she would express an interest in? things you wish she would ask you? Do you have any regrets concerning your relationship with your mother? What are one or two things you would ask her right now if she were sitting before you?

4. Was your mother candid about the challenges and realities of being a wife and mother? Did she give you advice about being a wife and mother? Any warnings?

5. How has her influence been felt in your own life? How would your life and your personality be different if you had not had the mother you had?

6. How has your mother's life influenced others, directly or indirectly? What has been her contribution, however small? Was she instrumental in a turning point for you or others?

7. What, in your opinion, would your mother want you to have learned from her example, her experiences?

8. What do you like most about your mother, (a) as a mother and (b) as a person? Do you feel that you do see her as a person?

9. What is/was most important to your mother? What does/did she value most highly? What is/was she proudest of?

10. If your mother is living, give a brief sketch of her present activities and interests.

MOTHERS:

What can you say about yourself as a person, above and beyond your role as a mother? (Since you are also a daughter, please read the beginning of this questionnaire and answer

questions 1 through 10 above; then answer the following questions, as well):

1. Discuss the circumstances of your birth, including date and
place of birth, whether you were born at home or in a hospital;
anything unusual?
2. Discuss your early childhood, including siblings, father,
school, teachers, girlfriends, boyfriends, hobbies, interests,
talents, fears, hopes and dreams, aspirations, significant adult
influences, toys you had and games you played, etc.
3. Discuss your adolescent years, including the areas you
discussed in #2 (early childhood); how did your attitudes, ideas,
aspirations, etc., change and develop since early childhood?
4. Discuss your adult years, including the areas you discussed in
#2 and 3 and tracing your development (how have you
changed?); jobs you've had; current hobbies, interests, activities, etc.

How did you meet your husband? Was it "love at first sight"?
With your daughter have you been candid about the challenges
and realities of marriage and motherhood?

Do you have any unfulfilled dreams? Is there something you
wanted to be when you grew up? If you could imagine yourself
living in a different life than the one you led, what would it be,
where would you be living, what would you be doing? Go way
out with this one, just for fun?

What is/has been most important to you (what do you value
highly)? Of what are you most proud?
5. What is the main thing you hoped your daughter would learn
from your example, your experiences? Have you actually told her
this? Do you feel that you succeeded in passing this on to her?

Is there anything—advice or tips—you might like to give
other women if they asked you?
6. Have you expressed your feelings to your daughter (fears,
regrets, sorrows, joys, opinions, wishes, etc.)? What obstacles are
there in your relationship? Do you have any regrets concerning
your relationship with your daughter? Are there things you would
like to tell her or ask her? If you want to but don't, why don't
you? If she were sitting before you right now, what would you
like to ask her? Do you think your daughter has misconceptions
about you?

# My Mother Who Art in Heaven

Do you, too,
listen for
your mother's voice
in those silent spaces
  between dream & doorbell?

Do you, too,
hear her
unheard wisdom
in those everyday wars
  between will & desire?

Far inside me
an angel sings
a mad, sweet song.

# Afterword

Dear Mother, "who art in heaven" (a.k.a. Muz),

Okay, so I promised I'd write everyday. I'm horrified to realize today in 1991 that it's been eight and a half years since you died, because I meant to keep you up on current events. When I asked you if you were afraid to die, you said, "I just hate to think of what I'm going to miss out on, that I won't know the outcome of things, politics, new inventions and such." I remember wanting to tell you about a new program on TV I thought you'd enjoy called "Cheers."

As you predicted, George Bush did follow Reagan to the White House.

*And* re the fate of the auto industry: 90,000 American workers have been laid off, whereas 3,200 Japanese workers have been hired.

Even though I knew you were usually proven right, still I would secretly pray that your doomsaying would be mitigated by a softer reality.

Love, Jez[1]

P.S. Did you pray you were wrong, too?


Dear Muz,

The remaining hostages have just been released.

Now I feel inspired to peruse the past decade of newspapers so that I might not only get you up to date but also refresh my memory. I've lost track to time. Time has been odd for me, Muz,

*323*

ever since I embarked upon this journey towards the reunification of mothers and daughters, for that is what it became. You never knew how I clung (still do) to your pearls of wisdom. You probably don't even remember that day in Fort Lauderdale when you reminisced about Sunday buggy rides with your father—that scintillating moment for me when destiny shone on that pink condo across the Intercoastal, bounced off the worn stucco and struck me in the eye. Stuck me in the heart, I later discovered.

Love, Jez

Dear Muz,

So I've been on this journey of the heart for the past eight and a half years. The ports have been wondrous, the baggage most often exceedingly cumbersome, and I've been a driven woman. Hence, I don't know exactly what happened when. I guess you missed Granada. Maybe you did see the first episodes of "Cheers." I'll get all of that straight for you at a later date. For now I just want to tell you what happened as a result of our sunset conversation in 1983. (I am aware of the possibility that you may already know everything, even about tomorrow.)

To learn of events leading to publication, you can simply refer to the introduction in my book; and to hear about my "workshops" (I still don't know what to call them) you can read the preface.

The book came out and I promoted it. Would you believe, I had to appear on CNN's "Newsnight" live in Atlanta at 2 a.m. and speak directly into a camera lens for forty-five minutes. You remember me, your third daughter who couldn't speak her name in a small room of people. Thank heavens, I finally took your lifelong advice and enrolled in a public speaking course. Fresh out of that transforming (and humbling) experience, I landed on public radio live in New York. I made it through all that, and— oh, and guess what? I was on Shirley Peters' show in Florida; I know you tuned into her in the '70s.

You were right, as usual, when you said that other daughters (besides me) don't know their mother as a person—her history, esp., childhood and adolescence, little about her life before marriage and motherhood; and you were right, they don't care about all that until she's gone. When being interviewed, I always try to get in the following comment by a teenage daughter: "We don't tend to see mothers as people." I know you'll appreciate that.

Love, Jez

P. S. One day I'll try to express to you the joy and the pain of this journey.

Dear Muz,

You missed out on all the great feedback I got from people who read my book and who attended my workshops. There were so many letters that Aunt Dearie started keeping track; she called herself my "P. R. Lady" and me, as *auteur,* "Victoria" (remember, you said you almost named me "Victoria Juliana" because I was born on VJ Day). Here's a taste of the effect of *My Mother Before Me:*

> I was fortunate enough to have attended your workshop in Illinois with my mother. Because I enjoyed it so much, it has been on my mind ever since. Communication between my mother and me has improved as a direct result of the exercises we practiced there. I learned so much and was never so happy that I'd asked my mother to go somewhere with me. Thank you and your sister for your vision.

Another letter came from a daughter I interviewed. She and her mother had never had a close relationship. She wrote,

> I just wanted you to know I had a heartwarming few days with my mom. It's so true that the petty grievances need to be put aside so that the true feelings of love, connection, and gratitude can be shared and expressed. Mom and I spent several hours going through her old pictures and talking about her life. And it's only the beginning!

That lightbulb goes on in your head—or heart. Becky (see "Radical Changes" in this book) and her mother had been estranged for a couple of years, but then they went over Becky's interview transcript together. Becky wrote me this:

> It was my greatest fantasy. We talked and talked and talked. All sorts of old and boring fights got resolved. It got my parents talking to each other more than they had in years. Your book broke the silence among us.

Your daughter Martha wrote me this after the book came out:

> My pals have all read it and were really moved and have taken action. All have ordered copies for their daughters and mothers. One reader hopes it'll cause her mother to share more stories and be willing to discuss family stuff that hasn't been discussible. Also, reading the book made all of them intent on having their children get to know the real them. One said she realized her son knows NOTHING about her, beyond what a wonderful mother she's been. I guess mothers don't think it's a big deal that their kids don't know them, but then when they read other people's stories, they become aware of what a tragedy it is.

How true, Martha; I've heard that said many times. I have learned that being aware of how you benefited from your mother's life experience can increase your self-esteem and even inspire action. We often overlook our mother's positive influence because it was so subtle. Women I interviewed talked a lot about this "unconscious programming." I found, for instance, after listening again to the tapes and putting it all together, that it was our mothers—of many backgrounds and politics—who subtly programmed us for the women's movement, in general by rewarding us for independent acts. A mother in her seventies who had read *My Mother Before Me* wrote this to me:

> In almost very instance, I noted great admiration for a strong mother whether highly educated or not, yet instilling qualities that would enhance their daughter's life. And usually without the daughter even being aware that now she, too, possessed those very same qualities.

I built a workshop activity around that point, very mindblowing for participants. She goes on to say,

It is comforting to know as a mother like me that in many ways my life continues long after my death.

I have found that for many of us our whole lifestyle and career came from mother. In my case? That's a whole other book. But I thought about how you used to complain about your little office, how your files weren't set up, and you'd say, "Too bad. I know I could write if only I had a system." You had me develop one for you; you never used it, but I do. You were always so generous in letting me learn from your mistakes.

Muz, since you left I'm constantly reminded of all the things you gave me to enrich my life. I'm driven, yes—*in honor of you.*

Love, Jez

Dear Muz,

It's interesting. Take writers, like Virginia Woolf and Gloria Steinem, for instance, who have championed the cause of women as mothers by revealing and analyzing myths and stereotypes. I wonder, how many women would never have written if not for an awareness of their mother's legacy and who she was a woman? Woolf wrote, ".... we think back through our mothers if we are women."[2] As a child, she saw her mother only as "a general presence rather than a particular person";[3] Steinem saw hers as "just a fact of life."[4] It was the eventual heightened awareness of their mother which seems to have inspired their larger interest in women *per se.* Alice Walker (you never got to read *The Color Purple,* which amazingly was made into a movie) says that many of us write our mother's stories: "Only recently did I realize this...I have absorbed something of the urgency that ...[my mother's] stories—like her life—must be recorded."[5]

I know that sense of urgency, and I know that our mother's stories will take us beyond seeing her as a feared god or respected workhorse or beloved martyr. If *your* daughter said, "Mom's hopes and dreams? I just always assumed she never had any," how would *you* feel?

Love, Jez

Dear Muz,

Do you understand my poem to you on page 21? I believe you do, and I suspect you felt the same way when your mother died.

I always wondered whether you might have heard me in the end, when I held your frail hand and whispered, "I love you, Mom. You were a great mother." It then rushed in upon me that you were leaving without having told your stories; they would be lost forever. I said, "And a great person!" Was it too late for you to hear me?

It didn't surprise me that the women who responded to my newspaper ad for interview subjects were mainly those whose mothers had died. They are most painfully aware of the effects of not knowing mother as a person. The intensity of grief and mourning, I think, is in direct proportion to the degree to which you took the now-deceased for granted; and by definition, of course, you cannot be aware you are taking someone for granted; that comes only in retrospect. Death is what brings on that awareness.

I was struck by the fact that so many women whose mothers are still living said with such conviction, "Mom is so healthy, I just know she's going to live forever."

Yet I shouldn't have been surprised. I myself was not prepared to hear that my mother (you) had cancer and that it was inoperable; and even when I was staying overnight in your hospital room the last four nights of your life, I never believed you were about to die—not until your last breaths. That's a big reason so many of us never get around to know, to see, to hear each other before it's too late. I was amused by a daughter whose mother's mortality finally occurred to her—at her mother's deathbed. She decided to take the bull by the horns: "Mother," she demanded, "what will I want to know about you when you're gone?" I know you'll like that one.

Love, Jez

Dear Muz,

You and I and our morbid sense of humor. I fondly remember your turning me on at a rather young age to Charles Addams' work in *The New Yorker.* Martha and I just went to see the movie, "The Addams Family." We chuckled ghoulishly, on your behalf. So proud of your legacy.

Love, Jez

P. S. Morticia is such a fun mother.


Dear Muz,

Speaking of fun mothers, yours comes to mind.

Did your mother ever appear to you as a child in her own life? I presume not, since you made the statement, "I think you'll find that a daughter doesn't really care about who her mother is until she dies." Take a look at the questionnaire in the appendix. It was compiled as I went along interviewing, when women told me the questions they themselves had. Muz, did you know where your mother was born, at a home or in the hospital? Were there any complications with her birth? Did her father maybe want a son? How much do you know about her mother? Do you know who her favorite sister or brother, uncle, aunt, teacher was? Grandma'am didn't have any brothers, did she? Who were her little girlfriends? Did she have any special beaux before she met Grandpa? Do you know what her dreams were? I really wonder. I wish I knew about her, and her mother before her, and her mother before her... as you probably wish, too.

Love, Jez


Dear Muz,

I found an account of the death of a mother in Simone de Beauvoir's autobiographical *A Very Easy Death.* The following passage expresses so well my own experience as well as that of many of the women I interviewed whose mothers have died:

> Her death brings to light her unique quality; she grows as vast as the world that her absence annihilates for her and whose whole existence was caused by her being there; you feel that she should have had more room in your life—all the room, if need be. You snatch yourself away from this wildness: she was only one among many. But since you never do all you might for anyone—not even

within the arguable limits that you have set for yourself—you have plenty of room left for self-reproach. With regard to *Maman* we were above all guilty, these last years, of carelessness, omission and abstention. We felt that we atoned for this by the days that we gave up to her, by the peace that our being there gave her, and by the victories gained over fear and pain... I had grown very fond of this dying woman.[6]

I think that's how you felt about your mother, too.

Love, Jez

Dear Muz,

Now, why is it we don't know our mothers very well? In over four hundred hours of conversation mothers and daughters gave me many 'explanations'. (Okay, I know I'll be writing a whole book on all of this, but just a couple of things.)

Many daughters claim to have a 'sense' of her and don't feel a need to get the details, which they feel are 'rather trivial'. Others think they'll be just plain bored. A seven-year-old said, "I don't know anything about Mommy's childhood." "Well," I said, "after this interview, do you think you'll be more interested in it?" She slid off the couch, actually stood on her head, contemplated my question for a while, and finally replied, "Well, perhaps. But only if her childhood was like mine: action-packed!"

After you were gone, I found photos of you which for some reason I'd never seen before, all from your life before marriage, before I was a gleam in your eye, a whole world I now wish you and I could share. I was utterly transfixed by the blonde little girl with no front teeth, wearing her mother's big galoshes, the child who became my mother with the black hair and crimson lips. It's hard for me to believe I once lacked curiosity about your childhood; now I can dwell forever on anything written in your hand, or stare at your baby picture, your tiny hand's motion caught as a blur by the photographer. (By the way, what do you think of the book's cover photo of you as a baby in your mother's arms? Everyone loves your fuzzy little bonnet.) I stare at your wedding photo, the graceful hand clutching a handkerchief.

Why were you carrying one? Surely you weren't planning to weep. Was it something borrowed or something blue?

Love, Jez

P. S. Did you weep?

Dear Muz,

Interviewers ask me what I wish I could ask you. I always say, "Everything." I want more about your mom and dad and siblings. I want to know what you were doing when Hiroshima was destroyed. What were you feeling? Likewise, the Holocaust; when did you first hear about the concentration camps? What were you thinking about when Dad was overseas? What did you dream about when you were a little girl and then a teenager? What professors inspired you most? When did you decide on Dad as your mate? I see from your scrapbook that you had the lead in at least one school play. Did you imagine becoming a famous actress? You said that Lucille Ball went to your high school. Did you ever talk to her? She reminds me so much of you and Gramdma'am—same voice and diction and zaniness. I'll bet Lucille's mom wore her stockings rolled at the knee, too.

Love, Jez

P. S. Was her hair red back then?

Dear Muz,

You know, if we won't/if we don't ask our mothers for information and to be candid about her life, we lose—oh, so much. Reading the oral histories in *My Mother Before Me* proves how much we miss when our stories aren't told, to name a few:

We lose historical data, especially from a woman's point of view, or from the woman's side of the family, such as, the story of my great-great-great grandmother after the battle of Lexington (see my chapter on you); or what life was like fifty years ago for a girl in a south Texas Chicano family, or a hundred years ago when girls were not permitted to go outside the home to school with their brothers but were tutored at home; or about Eleanor

Roosevelt's Sunday suppers at Hyde Park; or how a Quaker mother set up colonies for war orphans in France during the Spanish civil war; or how life was for a young African American woman from New York State when she moved to Washington to work in the War Department in the forties.

While our mothers are entitled to their privacy (we don't want to be pushy in our interviewing), most daughters are surprised at how forthcoming their mother is. The writer Grace Paley said, "I've told [my kids] everything that was said *to* me or *near* me."[7] Honesty does seem to be the best policy, even though the truth can be painful at times. The main thing is that we must prevent that typical tragedy I heard of so frequently. The mother says, "I don't tell my daughter about myself because she doesn't express an interest"; then her daughter says, "I don't ask my mother about herself because she doesn't invite my interest." The mother says, "I'm afraid of her questions"; her daughter says, "I'm afraid of her answers." There is a great deal of controversy out there over how much and what to tell. One mother I interviewed said, "Better to tell too much than too little."

Another question on everyone's mind is, "Can I be friends with my daughter [or mother]?" Often it seems that counselors tell us it's 'inappropriate', but I see that changing—which is good, since actual mothers and daughters report they are indeed friends, even 'best' friends. A mother I interviewed said, "I would say our relationship is evolving into more of a friendship, although there's some kind of a deeper tie that I don't have with a friend..." I like Judith Arcana's point: "There is a distinction between those mothers who want to be their daughter's friends *as well* as their mothers, and those who do not mother their daughters."[8] Above all, we must not let ourselves be told what we 'should' do about it, and we must not discount what mothers and daughters say about themselves as friends.

Love, Jez


Dear Muz,

I have had eight and half years of practice imagining you as a girl and young woman, Muzzie, but I remember well feeling exactly like the women I interviewed who haven't. One daughter (at age forty) said, "Mom tells me she loved to climb her favorite tree and then sit up there for hours reading. But you know what, Julie?" she said, "I can't picture my mom climbing trees." Why can't we picture our moms climbing trees? doing the jitterbug? madly galloping a horse? madly—anything! We, at any age, don't like good ol' Mom, at any age, dancing on tables with a red rose in her teeth. We don't want to see Mom as a person; we're not taught to (in fact, it looks as though we're taught *not* to). We want her to be—and stay—just "Mom". The mother of three teenage girls described it like this:

> Right now, I'm furniture to these girls, Julie, *furniture*. And for some years to come, they are gonna walk in here when they want to, pull me away from the wall when they need me—like a chair—and then shove me back against the wall when they're through.

Funny, though. On the one hand, we want her to be and stay just "Mom". But on the other hand, we don't like her in that role. Is that a significant conflict, or what? It can be seen in our treatment of her, some of which verges on the downright abusive. I ask people, "Ever catch yourself treating your mom the way your dad does?" Even though she may insist that everyone else—husband, mother, sister, employer—treat her as she wishes (as a person), a mother often allows her children to treat her as they wish (as an object). I couldn't find a word for our particular abuse of mothers, so I made one up: "matrabuse." Most matrabuse arises from idealizing and/or denigrating Mom: at whim we put her either on a pedestal or in the gutter. We know it's hard to look a statue on a pedestal in the eye; it's a convenient way to avoid someone's personhood. We won't look her in the eye, and we won't listen to her, either. The brilliant Simone de Beauvoir wrote, "[My mother's] unpleasant phrases irked me more than if they had come from any other mouth. And I was rigid whenever she would try to move on to an intimate plane."[9] How we reject mother's phrases, pleasant or unpleasant! Over and over during the interviews I heard kind of a song. Any mother could write the tune and lyrics of the all-too-familiar golden oldie, "Ohhh, Mommm!" Muz, you heard four renditions of that one, eh?

Love, Jez

Dear Muz,

There's so much double binding of mothers, right? Do you recognize yourself as a daughter in some of this? We take great pride in our mother's virtues and talents, but *then*...For instance, we tell everyone of our mother's musical talent, but *then* we're embarrassed when she sings. Or we say, "I truly admire my mother's resourcefulness," but *then* we make public jokes about her saving twist ties and tinfoil. (Muz, everyone laughs when I tell about how you would wash Ziploc bags and hang them to dry. I do admire your saving ways.) Your integrity, your honesty! But *then* I felt utterly betrayed when you would refuse to tell someone I wasn't at home when I was.

Did you do this to your mother? We remind her we're all grown up now and need to be left to our own decisions. But *then* we beg her for advice and feedback: "Mom, which dress [car, washing machine] should I get?" In deference to our previous and frequent declarations she says, "It's you who have to wear it [drive it, use it]. It's your decision, dear." We whine, "Oh, Mom, please! I'm just asking for a little feedback here." Reluctantly, cautiously, she says, "Well, okay, dear. I guess that miniskirt doesn't quite flatter you." We groan, "Oh, Mom! Thanks a lot. You really boost my confidence. Remind me not to come to *you* for support."

Does that dialogue remind you of anyone you know?

Love, Jez


Dear Muz,

Ever notice how it's still okay to make good ol' Mom the brunt of sexist jokes?

Love, Jez

P. S. Come to think of it, I just remembered the file you kept on mother-in-law jokes (in the form of cartoons). But you didn't have one on mother jokes. Weren't there any in the papers and magazines, or what? If not, why only mother-in-law jokes? Food for thought, *n'est ce pas?*

Dear Muz,

I've found that when children consider all the influences on them, they can see that their mother is not responsible for many of their negative traits; hence she is not to blame. We must help relieve her of some of that guilt—that "mega-matraguilt," as I call it. How? Stop blaming her. One daughter I interviewed said, "You know what, Julie? Once I grew up, I began to see that the things I'd resented most about my mom are things I'd simply made up, not things she actually expected of me." As a mother herself, she now says about her own two little girls: "No matter what I am or who their mother might have been, my daughters will always have their stuff with Mom to work out."

I say, it's not for Mom to let us go; it's for us to let Mom go.

Love, Jez

P. S. I just now realized that when you wouldn't allow me to work out my "stuff" on you, I'd work it out on Dad, poor thing; he most always let me.


Dear Muz,

Do you remember how you used to talk about feeling guilty that your four girls were kind of chunky? You'd say over and over, "Oh, I feel terrible. It must have been that chocolate milk I fed you kids." Okay, so now I'm in my forties with a cholesterol level higher than someone's bowling score or baseball or whatever; but I want you to know I don't blame you. Instead, may I remind you of other factors? Aunt Henriette's infamous Sunday dinners, for instance. Mmm, good, that goose-gravy, the creamiest soup, creamed carrots, bowls of melted butter containing creamy whipped potatoes, whipped cream on the strawberries and cream. She'd slather the goose in butter so it wouldn't dry out.

Love, Jez

P. S. How many pints of heavy cream was it again that went into Henriette's homemade maple nut ice cream?

Dear Muz,

We need to do less scapegoating and blaming, less idealizing, and more consciousness-raising. We need to walk a mile in Mom's shoes. It's so hard to risk doing that, for as the protagonist in French's *Her Mother's Daughter* says, "...[T]o perceive justly leads to sorrow."[10] It can; but it also leads to knowledge. Judith Arcana asked her mother what kind of animal she'd be if she could; her mother's reply was "...that big yellow cat, you know, the one that runs faster than all the others." Arcana writes, "I was so unprepared for this revelation that I could only cry. My mother, the martyr, the woman who put her husband and children before her from the day of her marriage, would be a cheetah, racing over the African savannah."[11]

Once we have our new knowledge of mother as a person, we are on the road to accept who she is, rather than continuing to resent what she is not—which mostly means, what she doesn't do for us. In my speeches I say:

> There were many times when I felt neglected and rejected because of what my mother wouldn't do. Of course, she did her duty: she told me to cream my elbows and soften my cuticles, chew thirty-two times and floss my teeth. But she wouldn't put up the hem on my prom dress my sophomore year. And before that, when I was in kindergarten, she made me a ballet costume more elegant, maybe, than anyone else's—a dusty blue with pink satin roses—but I wanted layer upon layer of the softest tulle, and she refused! She gave me and my little friends French lessons but wouldn't attend PTA meetings or bake for bake sales. She designed clothes for my paperdolls, but I remember ironing my own clothes when I was five. She let me be the first in my sixth-grade class to wear "Pink & Orange" lipstick, but she threw *Lolita* into the fire when I begged to read it. Once when I woke her up in the morning to get four cents for Brownie dues, she told me to go get it from Mrs. Franz next door!

Three things the audience does not know are (1) those were the hugest traumatic events I can remember involving your mothering of me (I remember screaming, "I hate you, I hate you!"); (2) I now completely understand your choices there (for instance, the hem on that prom dress was only a quarter-inch too long);

and (3) the many things you chose and agreed to do for me you did perfectly—beyond the call of duty, Muzzie—and with little or no recognition, I am sure.

Love, Jez

Dear Muz,

One daughter I interviewed said, "I can't help judging my mom because she was a terrible mother." I said, "Well, what do you think of her as a person?" With no hesitation she said, "Oh, as a person she was fine—no worse than the rest of us." It's clear we judge Mom more harshly than we might a friend.

The protagonist in *Her Mother's Daughter* says, "If you judge others according to what they do or don't do to you or for you, then you can never be better than biased, and personal, and small. Yes, small. Because you can never get the big picture. You have no perspective wider than your personal trivialities."[12]

*Oh, Muz.* May we all finally get beyond the trivial to the universal, put our mothers before us, put ourselves aside long enough to walk in her shoes! That does at least two things: it frees us to consider her positive influence, and it makes for a new kind of mother-daughter relationship—one marked by reciprocity instead of the one-way dependency of a newborn.

Love, Jez

Dear Muz,

It's all so sad. In speeches at hospitals I say that the mother-daughter relationship is "looked upon by some as a syndrome; in fact, one woman called it 'a fatal disease.'" Why is the mother-daughter dyad scrutinized unlike any other? called "the most intense"? called "special"? Much speculation, but nobody seems to know for certain. Some, like Judith Arcana in *Our Mothers' Daughters*, make this point:

> What daughters expect from mothers, even if we are mothers and,

therefore, should know better, is absurdly nonhuman...Often
we have greater expectations as adults than we had as children.[13]

I have found that to be absolutely true. Your daughter Janna's
pal, whom I interviewed in California and who has two daughters, must have put in a lot of time on this. She said (very
articulately), "Your mother is a reflection of your own needs and
desires. She has worth to you only in proportion to her willingness and ability to fulfill them for you." Still, sons are children
of mothers, too; perhaps sons and fathers are somehow exempt
from scrutiny. Yet the preponderance of psychological studies
involve men and boys, not girls and women. Whew! I'm getting
stuffed from all this food for thought. How about you? I wish you
could come back and help me sort out the contradictions I've
encountered. We could do some big studies—a mother-daughter
crusading team.

Love, Jez

Dear Muz,

You were also right in predicting that the backlash against
women would become so much worse. I'm just now reading
*Backlash: The Undeclared War Against American Women* by Susan
Faludi, a Wall Street Journal reporter and Pulitzer Prize winner.
The bad news is the backlash; the good news is that it's such a
relief to see a well-documented report on a trend that seemed so
obvious to me but so few are acknowledging. Being so close on a
daily basis to the subject of mothers and daughters keeps me in
touch with women's general issues, and I believe that in times of
backlash, as now, a strange thing happens. Interest in *mothers*
(i.e., a qualified interest in "The Mother," Mom, and Motherhood) swells, while at the same time interest in *women* ebbs.
Thus, I believe it is even more necessary than ever to promote
the cause of a strong and positive mother-daughter relationship.
There has always been interest in some quarters to disempower
it, or there has been a fear of its power, as Paula Caplan, author of
*Don't Blame Mother,* reminds us.[14] Faludi says that "women [need]
to be armed with more than their privately held grievances and

goals." "Indeed," she continues, "to instruct each woman to struggle alone [is] to set each woman up, yet again for defeat."[15] My study has shown that women in their own mother-daughter relationship can be empowered by seeing that other women, other mother-daughter dyads, share similar grievances and goals; their struggle is not merely personal but societal. When I myself started out on this journey, I thought it was entirely possible that I was particularly remiss and selfish as a daughter, and that's why I didn't know more about my mother (you, dear) as a person. How empowering it was to discover that most other daughters seemed to be in the same boat! Each one of them believed, as I did, that theirs was a unique personal failure. Caplan was quoted in a newspaper article somewhere as saying that there is power in the mother-daughter relationship, if only we would take it. As Faludi says, "[In the '80s] women seemed unaware of the weight and dynamism of their own formidable presence."[16] She quotes Kate Rand Lloyd, editor of *Working Woman:* "What is regrettable to me is we don't yet see...how we really do have tools for changing our own future in our own hands."[17] One of those tools, I clearly see, is the mother-daughter relationship. A big surprise of my study was that daughters of all backgrounds gave their mothers credit for the strength and courage they do have as women. In another significant work, *Strong Mothers, Weak Wives,* Miriam Johnson makes a good case for separating a woman's role as mother from her role as wife when evaluating her strengths as a person. For what we often perceive as our mother's weakness is actually her powerless status as a wife.[18] This explains my finding that women describe their mother as "strong" while at the same time lamenting her instances of "weak" behavior. It seems that women and girls intuit a social or even political basis for their mother's (if not their own) personal limitations, whether they acknowledge or verbalize the insight. I found that most daughters, even while engaged in what has been called "mother-blaming," do not blame their mother for her own lack of power, though many do cite that lack as the basis of limitations, or "weakness."

I wonder how you perceived your mother in this regard—and yourself, too.

Love, Jez

Dear Muz,

A woman who interviewed me on radio in Miami asked why I didn't add commentary. For one thing, it always seemed to put the subjects at ease when they knew I didn't plan to comment on the interviews. Many women are afraid of being scrutinized; they don't like to envision their words, published along with commentary, being compared to what other women might have said. Taken in context, the reluctance of women to speak about themselves as mothers and daughters had much to do, I'm sure, with the publication of *Mommie Dearest*. Everywhere I went women and men both greeted me with, "This won't be another 'Mommie Dearest', will it?" Many consented to speak only when I explained that there would be no mother-blaming on my part, no comparison of one mother's relationship to her daughter with another's.

Muz, in that same connection, I can't tell you how many women said they could not finish reading the '70s book (revised in the '80s), *My Mother/Myself*. I gather it's because of what some have called its "Antifeminism." I've never been able to finish it, either, so I won't comment.

*Anyhow* (as we always say). I have found so much falsehood in the words and books of many of the experts, whereas I have found a lot of truth by listening to women tell their stories, and what I'd hoped is that readers could do the same by reading them. Hmmm, I wonder; would you have wanted me to write a commentary? I am guessing that you would agree with the host of a cable TV women's program in Great Neck. She said that when she read in my introduction that I didn't, she was disappointed; but by the end of the book, she believed I'd made the right choice.

Love, Jez

P. S. I hasten to add that we must always, of course, have dialogue if we are ever to achieve that mother-daughter 're-unification.' It's prerequisite to grounding a mother-daughter relationship in truth, to uncovering the destructive myths perpetuated by some "elements." (I have been having a lot of fun now using Caplan's term "elements."[19] It's more specific than "they," eh? Nifty.)

We cannot and must not proceed in our relationships, socialize our daughters, or treat our mothers according to unexamined myths. This decade we must not advise our daughters, 'Marry early or else you never will because there's a man shortage.' We must not teach our daughters that women in the '70s and '80s who chose a career instead of marriage and motherhood are all miserable, when that is not true. We must make a great effort to study the facts—yes, even statistics. Where did they come from? Who conducted the survey? Are there any opposing studies? We cannot expect to be spoon fed information by those "elements" who may not want us to be powerful and wonder why we have lost our power. It is said some elements have a great deal invested in keeping us passive. They don't want us to vote. They don't want us to dispel myths. They don't want mothers and daughters to be close. They want us to continue to blame our mothers, even for our father's alcoholism, or our brother's gambling debts, or our own 'foolish choices' as 'smart women.' I like what Charles wrote: "I would like to humbly suggest that the real human need of each other is not always 'codependency.'" Right on, my beloved husband!

Like the myth of women's masochism, there is the equally pernicious (and similar or related) myth of women's codependency. I am certain that not every woman—spouse or friend or relative or roommate of a person suffering from an addiction—is 'colluding.' I'm still not even sure that collusion is a valid concept. After all, the definition of *collusion* is 'conspiracy, for the purpose of deceiving or cheating others;' what a terrible and useless term to apply to the unfortunate friends and relatives of a person with an addiction, or to the spouse or siblings of a victim of sexual abuse! I know that many mothers and daughters who have developed a strong bond (or who just dress alike) can get flak; they are in no way "codependent" in the pathological sense, which is the sense that term has acquired.

I chuckle, Muz, when I imagine that if you were living right now, your clippings drawer, marked "Backlash," would include a thick file folder labeled "So-called Codependency." You would have kept better tabs on that whole thing than I have, I'm sure.

Love, Jez

P. S. Which elements, would you say, want to keep us passive and separated? And why is the Recovery/Addictions/Self-Help section (no such thing when you were living) in most bookstores growing larger than the Women's section (among others)?


Dear Muz,

*Backlash* author Faludi observes a "Women Who Love Too Much" group and concludes, "Rather than change their lives, they seem, at best, to have learned how to adjust to intolerable situations."[20] She says, "in the first half of the '80s, the advice experts told women they suffered from bloated egos and a 'fear of intimacy'; in the second half, they informed women that atrophied egos and 'codependency' were now their problems."[21] (You weren't around for most of the first half or any of the second.)

Always so many double binds!

"Natch" (as you would say, Muz), I became very interested in what psychologists and the various 'personal growth' movements are up to as a result of interviewing mothers and daughters. I kept hearing some rather peculiar ideas from women who had been in some kinds of therapy and/or who had attended certain seminars and workshops. The trouble is that then some of them would apply these ideas to other people. A woman (not an interview subject) hoped to convince her mother that her "widow's hump" (a curvature of the spine caused by a decrease in estrogen after menopuase, right?) was caused by a mental state, which I hazily recall the daughter viewed as a bad attitude. She felt sad that her mother "denied" this truth and complained that this was just one instance of several like it (such as wearing polyester instead of cotton) in which she and her mother could not "connect." Perhaps there will come a day when it will be proved there is a connection between polyester and osteoporosis; meanwhile, where is a healthy skepticism amongst some of the Aquarian Age enthusiasts? Several people, when I said you had ovarian cancer, remarked, 'No doubt she brought it on, perhaps by a negative attitude, or *maybe*—Did she suppress a lot of anger or stuff her feelings?' It's funny. The same women who blame their mother for teaching them that their feelings can kill other people ("That will just *kill* your father") also accuse their mother for killing herself with her own feelings (hanged by her hang-ups).

I do not mean to indict psychologists and the Aquarian Age movement. Sometimes they do some good, and the harm they might cause is not always intentional; no doubt they are at times the unwitting tools of backlash engineers. Recently I subscribed to a journal because it advertised an upcoming issue on 'how feminism is being duped by the New Age movement.' So far the article hasn't appeared; in fact, I suspect the journal itself has disappeared. But I have become interested in such topics, having sensed in interviews that mothers and daughters are, in effect, being separated by certain ideas out there. This is an area which could take (me) years to study. Nevertheless, I feel compelled at least to sound a small warning bell. There is a pseudo-feminism, perhaps, out there which speaks of women's "empowerment" but whose solutions and remedies, many involving "creating your own reality," somehow end up instead blaming women, especially mothers, for any reality created. Ironic, eh?

Love, Jez

Dear Muz,

From the interviews I learned that mothers are fearful of being blamed. They have good reason. I heartily refer you to the aforementioned book by Paula Caplan. Mother, I cannot tell you what a thrill it was to turn on the Donahue show one day when I was in a hotel preparing for a speech at a women's club in Toronto. On the screen was Paula Caplan, one of my heroines because of her earlier work, *The Myth of Women's Masochism*. Now she was promoting her new book, *Don't Blame Mother,* and was on with her mother and talking about many of the things I learned from my own study. Muz, she spoke from a certain level of consciousness about mother as a human, a level no doubt higher than my own, since she has more knowledge and experience, but still one with which I can immediately identify. Imagine my excitement: finally, *finally* an expert I'd been searching for everywhere to support my findings, what I'd been saying in speeches, about mother-blaming and not seeing mother as a person, about the double binds, etc. I jumped on the phone right away, not expecting to reach her because I just assumed she was at the show in New York, and I got her on the phone. She was kind enough to agree to see me in her office at the Ontario Institute for Studies in Education (she also teaches at the University of Toronto). As she told me and as mentioned in her books, there have been so few studies of women in general, and she said that what psychologists know and teach about mothers and daughters comes from their own speculation. From Dr. Caplan I learned what I'd suspected and feared: in case studies mothers are still being blamed for all their children's "disorders", such as anorexia, criminal behavior, schizophrenia, low self-esteem, on and on. In the earlier book I mentioned she makes a smashing case against masochism as a reality for women.[22] Today in *Backlash* Faludi says that the American Psychiatric Association recently "decided it was time for masochism to make a come-back, as a new disorder," and she describes the entire process which culminated in the inclusion of this new "female ailment" in the professional manual of mental disorders—despite protests by the APA's own Committee on Women that "the masochistic diagnosis put all the blame on the patients' shoulders, without also taking into account social conditioning and real-life circumstances."[23]

Well, Muzzie, by now you would say that I could write another book. I think you're right, and perhaps I shall. I have found out a lot of good stuff from interviewing, being inter-viewed, doing workshops, and frantically scanning books for support of my own evolving perceptions. In my book there is a chapter entitled "Desarrollo," a beautiful and useful word I learned in the course of that interview. It is the Spanish word for *development*, but as was explained to me, it has the connotation of *evolution*, of unfolding—better yet, *unrolling*. In other words, the whole story has already been written; we must simply unroll the scroll. I like that image, as I feel that my task for the past eight and a half years has been to learn how.

Muz, I didn't mean to reprint the texts of my current readings, but I do want to beg women to read *Backlash, The Myth of Women's Masochism*, and *Don't Blame Mother,* for they will help women know and understand the social context of the mother-daughter relationship. I'm afraid *Backlash* won't get aggressively promoted so no one will read it; and I run into very few women who have heard of the Caplan book on masochism, which is an important exposé, too. Last night I saw that it was checked out of the University of Vermont library only three times in 1986, once in 1988, and not since!

I spoke earlier of my pain on this journey. Much of it—most, really—comes from the fear in knowing how few of us realize that socio-political context of family relationships. There is hope, though. As Paula Caplan says in *Between Women*, "[Many] barriers between women are rooted in the second-class role to which women have been confined. When women begin to examine their relationships with each other, they tend to wonder about their second-class role."[24] It occurred to me that is the reason media interviewers have asked the following question in one form or another, 'Do the women in your book call themselves feminists? It seems they are.' Twenty per cent, perhaps, call themselves feminists, but if I excised from the tapes their declarations, one couldn't tell the feminists from the non-feminists.

Whatever our politics, I truly believe that we—mothers of daughters and teachers of girls and women—must be vigilant; *all* of us citizens must be. Any reader of the painstakingly documented *Backlash* will now know, if she or he did not suspect or know before, not only that 'one can't believe everything one reads' (not even in your beloved *New York Times*, eh, Muz?) but also that it's very dangerous to do so. You tried to teach us that. Mostly I remember your warning me not to read so many comic books or my mind would "turn to mush". It must have been awful for you to watch that happening to your daughter!

Love, Jez


Dear Muz,

Wait till you read in *Backlash* the true story behind the marriage study (involving a "man shortage") by a Yale sociologist and a Harvard economist. It *kills* me that most women haven't heard and may never hear (because it showed up in the back pages of newspapers) the follow up story of a lone crusader at the U. S. Census Bureau, who tried to give us the facts but was stopped. According to Faludi, who checked the latest Census report, "If anyone faced a shortage of potential spouses, it was *men* in the prime marrying years: between the ages of twenty-four and thirty-four, there were 119 single men for every hundred single women."[25] Ha, ha.

Love, Jez

Dear Muz,

Here's what a talk-show guest "expert," a psychologist, had to offer a mother who felt she was helping her daughter find a decent date:

Mother: I don't think it's immoral at all.

Psychologist: It's unethical... inappropriate. You're giving the wrong message.

Mother: What's unethical about it?

Psychologist: Well, ethically, you're a mother. And—

Mother: Right.

Psychologist: According to our culture and the morals and the ethics in our culture, *a mother stays a mother and keeps her life separate from her daughter.* [emphasis mine]

As I struggle to respond to that exchange, I think I'll just say, no comment.

Love, Jez

P. S. Okay, I will comment.

Perhaps this is why at every one of my "playshops" both hosts and participants make a point of telling me they're "glad" or "relieved" or that it's "refreshing" I'm not an "expert." (Isn't that shocking?)

It's all so complex, Muzzie. The one thing I want to share with mothers and daughters from my own study of the literature is that, as they do seem to sense, there is no consensus among the experts out there. In fact, there is great controversy—for instance, a whole movement opposing the traditional theories of 'separation' as a means to 'autonomy'; in fact, the need for autonomy is even being challenged—as a 'male' or 'patriarchal' value not suited to women's natural 'interconnectedness' as a better way to operate in the world. Then other experts warn that ascribing 'relational' needs to women might unwittingly support the backlash—by dragging back in the old Victorian 'female virtues' we've struggled to put behind us.

All I know is that in interview after interview I heard such things as, 'Well, yes. Mothers are no doubt ignored or taken for granted. But, then, of course, it's as a result of the necessary stages towards a daughter's independence'; and, 'If mothers are fulfilling their duty, they will gracefully accept and even promote their daughter's separation.' I kept hearing that this is normal—a natural and inevitable process. But to me something seemed unnatural. I had to ask myself, why all this talk of separation? It seems part of the effort to free women from the constraints of traditional roles. It's being said that daughters need to individuate, that is, find an identity separate from mother. I agree; there is a need to establish 'boundaries', an identity all our own. But then to find ourselves maybe we go into therapy—fine. But then we end up analyzing our *mother* by the way, without knowing her or her life story). We confront her with our 'new knowledge' and 'true feelings', lay on the ultimatums. Or we give up before we start—stop phoning, stop visiting, even move to the opposite coast or another country, or at least to the other side of the Mississippi. Must a society demand this mother-daughter separation? Must we make ourselves ashamed of our similarities in order to become separate people? Must we glorify our differences? I say, no. I found from interviewing mothers and daughters that we don't know our mother because she is expected to stay in character, in her role; she cannot and must not step out of bounds. Mothers and daughters are expected to separate—even though beyond their roles, they were never close—not as people, not as women. How ironic and sad. What we need is a connection—heartfelt, unabashed, and proud—the kind fathers and sons *(and everyone else)* seek.

We cannot be certain of any facts, and my point is that we daughters of mothers can and must take part in finding them; for, Paula Caplan reminds us, "As daughters and mothers we have for generations been trapped in a dark web we did not spin."[26] In *My Mother Before Me* I hoped to provide a forum towards re-spinning at least some of our own true story. Does the part about you meet with your approval?

Love, Jez

P. S. Do you remember when you turned to me once and said firmly, "Stop seeking my approval. I'm a separate person and can't always agree with your decisions, and I feel you're laying a trip on me by constantly asking for my approval." I have found that as women begin to understand their mother as a person, they see it's not required that they agree with each other. In *The Dance of Intimacy* Dr. Harriet Lerner makes an important point: "Having to be different from your mother expresses your real self no better than having to be the same."[27] How true.

Dear Muz,

As you may know I share your love of ancient cultures. Listen to this gem from Marilyn French's *Beyond Power* (remember her book, *The Women's Room?*). She says that the Sumerian word for freedom, *amargi*, means literally, *return to mother.*[28] Isn't that interesting? In our culture it is (stupidly) said that we become more free by *leaving* mother. I always say, if I had a daughter I would name her Amargi, for freedom. Do you feel sorry for me that I don't have a daughter?

Love, Jez

Dear Muz,

In '86, as I listened to the interview tapes for the second time, I took some notes and listed some passages pertaining to 'lack of communication', the overriding and obvious reason given for not knowing more about our mothers. Here's what I noted afterwards:

## IN CONCLUSION

Pride, oversight, abuse of power, miscellaneous fears of the individual, projection, the desperate urge to "separate," are all ways of dealing with lack of communication, the conspiracy of silence. There is reported a sometimes too-subtle indirect communication. In the face of secrecy and taboo people make assumptions (which leads to misconception, misunderstanding, ignorance, superstition, and sometimes, tragedy). They project as truth their own perceptions when there is no self-love; therefore, there is no awareness or appreciation of other people as individuals. Women, taught about the 'need to separate', decide to break away when it is obvious they have encountered a brick wall (the conspiracy of silence to perpetuate the status quo). Oversight, sometimes a tool of the conspiracy of silence, is a convenient way for some to avoid the truth and perpetuate the status quo. Abuse (manipulation) is the attempt to, among other things, wrest information being guarded, often for the sake of self-preservation, or sometimes from a lack of respect for individual privacy. "Protecting" oneself or others from the truth often comes from fear of exposure of that which is unacceptable to the status quo. The enforcer of the status quo is often not the mother but the daughter, who becomes the moralizer, the one who refuses to accept any behavior outside the role.

## IN A NUTSHELL

The number one thing I've learned from this project and want to share is how much we all take everyone and everything for granted. We don't examine pat phrases, we don't consider other people's feelings, we don't put people's feelings above, say, the advice of experts.

I kept hearing, 'Awareness is the key.' It makes sense, indeed. Self-awareness brings awareness of others; through which curiosity is awakened, knowledge is gained, and ignorance and fear are dispelled; from which forgiveness and acceptance are granted; in which receptive and validating climate there is no need for barriers, defenses, or taboos. The authenticity of self and others is assured and the conspiracy of silence is broken, permitting the sharing of knowledge and experience, the ultimate lessening of the abusive tyranny of individual or society, and the reunification of mother and daughter.

*Amen.*

Love, Jez

P. S. When I typed that in '86, I really, *really* knew what it meant.

Dear Muz,

I can see that I might go on and on—and that is not permitted here; guess I will have to write a whole new book, plus produce a workbook and a video, too. I found out a lot of interesting things, little tidbits for a book, e.g., many of our mothers were "tomboys," and hardly any fell in love "at first sight" (it was their men who did and then begged for their hand), and many, of all generations, didn't grow up in a nuclear family unit. More food for thought, but I'm saving room for dessert.

Before I stop, I'd like to grab this opportunity, for which I am grateful, to encourage my readers to check out the following books, which I believe will greatly expand their awareness of mother and/or woman as a person. Though I wish someday to become one, I am yet by no means a scholar of mother-and-daughterhood; but I have read several books in preparation for speeches and presentations. These are some of my favorites so far; I know I'll be adding many more to the list.

Apter, Terri. *Altered Loves: Mothers and Daughters During Adolescence.* New York: St. Martin's Press, 1990.

Arcana, Judith. *Our Mothers' Daughters.* Berkeley: Shameless Hussy Press, 1979.

Beauvoir, Simone de. *A Very Easy Death.* Patrick O'Brian, trans. New York: Pantheon, 1985 (© 1965).

Bernikow, Louise. *Among Women.* New York: Harmony Books, 1980.

Caplan, Paula J., Ph. D. *The Myth of Women's Masochism.* New York: Dutton, 1985.

————. *Between Women: Lowering the Barriers.* Toronto: Personal Library; Edison, NJ: Distributed by Everest House, 1981.

————. *Don't Blame Mother: Mending the Mother-Daughter Relationship.* New York: Harper & Row, 1989.

Carlson, Kathie. *In Her Image: The Unhealed Daughter's Search for the Mother.* Boston: Shambhala Publications, Inc., 1989.

Chernin, Kim. *In My Mother's House: A Daughter's Story.* New Haven: Ticknor & Fields, 1983.

Faludi, Susan. *Backlash: The Undeclared War Against American Women.* New York: Crown Publishers, Inc., 1991.

Fischer, Lucy Rose. *Linked Lives: Adult Daughters and Their Mothers.* New York: Harper & Row, 1986.

French, Marilyn. *Her Mother's Daughter: A Novel.* New York: Ballantine Books, 1988.

————. *Beyond Power: On Women, Men, and Morals.* New York: Summit Books, 1985.

Johnson, Miriam M. *Strong Mothers, Weak Wives: The Search for Gender Equality.* Berkeley: University of California Press, 1988.

Gilligan, Carol, Nona P. Lyons, and Trudy J. Hammer, eds. *Making Connections: The Relational Worlds of Adolescent Girls at Emma Willard School.* Cambridge, Mass.: Harvard University Press, 1990.

Morrison, Toni. *Beloved: A Novel.* New York: Knopf; distributed by Random House, 1987.

Payne, Karen, ed. *Between Ourselves: Letters Between Mothers and Daughters, 1750-1982.* Boston: Houghton Mifflin, 1983.

Rich, Adrienne. *Of Woman Born: Motherhood as Experience and Institution,* Tenth Anniversary Edition. New York: W. W. Norton & Company, 1986.

Tan, Amy. *The Joy Luck Club.* New York: G. P. Putnam's Sons, 1989.

————. *The Kitchen God's Wife.* New York: G. P. Putnam's Sons, 1991.

Walker, Alice. *In Search of Our Mothers' Gardens.* New York: Harcourt, Brace, Jovanovich, Harvest edition, 1984.

Dear Muz,

In the 1986 edition I published your letter written to our friend, Joan, when her mother died. Joan sent it to me when you died. Do you remember writing it?

> Our hearts know we must outlive our parents, but our minds are forever tied, somehow. There are so many regrets, so much anger and love unexpressed; but, finally, only dear memories.

You knew what I, too, have come to know: that all anger, all resentments, all regrets are not what matters. In the end to one who has lost her mother, what matters are those dear memories—*and who that woman was*.

As for so-called "separation," that will come, for all of us, in its time and in its only true and necessary form.

Now I, like my mother before me, am left with only the dear memories.

Good night, dear Muz,
Jezzie

P. S. Muz, wake up! News flash! December 9, 1991, headline in the Burlington [Vermont] *Free Press*:

SOVIET UNION DEAD

Who woulda thunk it? And here is another item I found out today:

*BACKLASH #6 NEW YORK TIMES* BESTSELLER

We've spun another new section of the golden web. Sleep tight, and don't let the bedbugs bite.

# Notes & Sources

## PREFACE:

1. I will be frank (admitting my own limited viewpoint). Many (not all) of the most intellectual, psychologically oriented and/or insightful people—and even some of my feminist friends—seem to have had the hardest time 'getting' it, putting their mother before them for a day or in extreme cases for a moment.
2. Of course, there is also some resistance to it. A few people have asked, 'Why not fathers and daughters?' or 'Why not mothers and sons?' Not always but sometimes I have sensed that the question means, 'I wish you hadn't done mothers and daughters.'
3. Adrienne Rich, *Of Woman Born* (New York: W. W. Norton & Company, 1986) p. xxiv.
4. From the *Inferno*, 1:3, cited in Rich, *Ibid., epigram*.
5. Paula J. Caplan, *Don't Blame Mother* (New York: Harper & Row, Perennial Library edition, 1990), p. 3.

## AFTERWORD:

1. At my birth, my maternal grandmother nicknamed me "Jezebel"; it stuck.
2. Virginia Woolf, *A Room of One's Own* (New York: Harcourt Brace Jovanovich, 1929), p. 132.

3. Cited in Tillie Olsen, *Mother to Daughter, Daughter to Mother: Mothers on Mothering* (New York: The Feminist Press, 1984), p. 71.

4. Cited in Olsen, *Ibid.*, p. 158.

5. Alice Walker, *In Search of Our Mothers' Gardens* (New York: Harcourt, Brace, Jovanovich, Harvest edition, 1984), p. 240.

6. Simone de Beauvoir, *A Very Easy Death* (New York: Pantheon, 1985), p. 94.

7. Cited in Olsen, *op. cit.*, p. 135.

8. Judith Arcana, *Our Mothers' Daughters* (Berkeley: Shameless Hussy Press, 1979), p. 21.

9. de Beauvoir, *op. cit.*, p. 69.

10. Marilyn French, *Her Mother's Daughter* (New York: Summit Books, 1987), p. 250.

11. Arcana, *op. cit.*, p. 34.

12. French, *op. cit.*, p. 250.

13. Arcana, *op. cit.*, pp. 14-15.

14. Paula J. Caplan, *Don't Blame Mother, passim*.

15. Susan Faludi, *Backlash* (New York: Crown Publishers, Inc., 1991), p. 456.

16. *Ibid.*, p. 458.

17. Cited in Faludi, p. 459.

18. Miriam M. Johnson, *Strong Mothers, Weak Wives* (Berkeley: University of California Press, 1988), *passim*.

19. Paula J. Caplan, *Between Women* (Toronto: Personal Library, 1981), p. 18.

20. Faludi, *op. cit.*, p. 353.

21. Faludi, *Ibid.*, p. 337.

22. Paula J. Caplan, *The Myth of Women's Masochism* (New York: Dutton, 1985), *passim*.

23. Faludi, *op. cit.*, p. 360.

24. Caplan, *Between Women*, p. 18.

25. Faludi, *op. cit.*, p. 14.

26. Caplan, *Don't Blame Mother,* p. 3.

27. Harriet Goldhor Lerner, *The Dance of Intimacy: A Woman's Guide to Courageous Acts of Change in Key Relationships* (New York: Harper & Row, Perennial Library edition, 1989), p. 197.

28. Marilyn French, *Beyond Power* (New York: Summit Books, 1985), p. 48.

# About the Author

Julie Kettle Gundlach was born in the "Copper Country" of Michigan's Upper Peninsula. Since childhood, writing has been her main interest. She joined the women's movement along with her mother, who as a master's candidate at the University of Michigan was her roommate in the class of '68.

Julie's mother wanted to make it possible for each of her four daughters to have "a room of her own." In her case, Ms. Gundlach lives with her husband in the Poconos of Pennsylvania in a small earth-sheltered house they designed with two separate studios. In her own room, she took her mother's maiden name, Kettle, as her non de plume.

Julie Kettle Gundlach is available for keynote or panel speaking and for workshop presentations. To inquire or to make arrangements, please call or write/fax her at: RR 3, Box 538, Honesdale, Pennsylvania 18431; (717) 253-5452.